BLACK
ALIVENESS,
OR
A POETICS
OF BEING

BLACK OUTDOORS: Innovations in the Poetics of Study
A series edited by J. Kameron Carter and Sarah Jane Cervenak

BLACK ALIVENESS, OR A POETICS OF BEING

KEVIN QUASHIE

Duke University Press *Durham and London* 2021

Printed in the United States of America on acid-free paper ∞
Designed by Courtney Leigh Richardson
Typeset in Portrait and Avenir by Westchester Publishing Services

Library of Congress Cataloging-in-Publication Data
Names: Quashie, Kevin Everod, author.
Title: Black aliveness, or a poetics of being / Kevin Quashie.
Other titles: Black outdoors.
Description: Durham : Duke University Press, 2021. | Series: Black
outdoors: innovations in the poetics of study | Includes bibliographical
references and index.
Identifiers: LCCN 2020021669 (print)
LCCN 2020021670 (ebook)
ISBN 9781478011873 (hardcover)
ISBN 9781478014010 (paperback)
ISBN 9781478021322 (ebook)
Subjects: LCSH: Aesthetics, Black. | Blacks—Race identity. | Aesthetics in
literature. | Identity (Psychology) in literature.
Classification: LCC BH301.B53 Q37 2021 (print) | LCC BH31. B53 (ebook) |
DDC 809.1/9896—dc23
LC record available at https://lccn.loc.gov/2020021669
LC ebook record available at https://lccn.loc.gov/2020021670

Cover art: *Prayer for Grace*, 2020. © Shinique Smith. Courtesy the artist and
SAS Studio.

CONTENTS

INTRODUCTION

ALIVENESS

What would it mean to consider black aliveness, especially given how readily—and literally—blackness is indexed to death? To behold such aliveness, we have to imagine a black world . . . we have to imagine a black world so as to surpass the everywhere and everyway of black death, of blackness that is understood only through such a vocabulary. This equation of blackness and death is indisputable and enduring, surely, but if we want to try to conceptualize aliveness, we have to begin somewhere else.

This is a story of us, a story of black aliveness as the being of us.

Imagine a black world: The invocation of a black world is the operating assumption of black texts, a world where blackness exists in the tussle of being, in reverie and terribleness, in exception and in ordinariness. This black world is not one where the racial logics and harming predilections of antiblackness are inverted but one where blackness is totality, where every human question and possibility is of people who are black. It is what Toni Morrison, our great thinker, describes as "a sovereignty" of "race-specificity without race prerogative" ("Home" 3, 5). Such a world might not exist in modernity, though it radiates in the will to make a poem, an essay, a song . . . it radiates in the text's imaginary as a philosophical audacity, as an embracing generative quality of indisputable aliveness.

What makes "imagine a black world" so necessary is the exemption of black humanity from our commonsense understanding, the world's lack of imagination for black being that is also its brutal enactments against such being. There is no outright assumption of black humanity in the world (the potency of "Black Lives Matter" as an emblem confirms this), and indeed black humanity has to be argued over and again. And yet we might suppose that every black text rests on a quiet premise of black humanity—that the text and its aesthetics *assume* being.

I am interested, then, in the quality of aliveness notable in the worldmaking aesthetics of poems and essays, in how those poems and essays can be read for what they tell us about our being: about how we are and about how we can be. I am interested both in the ways that the world of black texts constitutes our rightness of being as I am interested in the ethical implications of such a constituting.[1]

The best example I know of aesthetics as aliveness is Lucille Clifton's poem "reply" first published in her 1991 collection *Quilting*:[2]

[from a letter written to Dr. W. E. B. Dubois by Alvin Borgquest
of Clark University in Massachusetts and dated April 3, 1905:

"We are pursuing an investigation here on the subject
of crying as an expression of the emotions, and should
like very much to learn about its peculiarities among
the colored people. We have been referred to you as a
person competent to give us information on the subject.
We desire especially to know about the following salient
aspects: 1. Whether the Negro sheds tears. . . ."]

reply

he do
she do
they live
they love

they try
they tire
they flee
they fight
they bleed
they break
they moan
they mourn
they weep
they die
they do
they do
they do (337)

Notice first the dancing waltz of the anaphora, as if this is a drum- or heartbeat of paired stressed syllables, how this sequence creates a deliberate formation in what might otherwise look like a random gathering of actions, such that "live" precedes and parallels "love," "moan" yields to "mourn." The alliteration guides our recognition of the connection between the poem's verbs, just as the assonance—those rich, deep vowel echoes—threads together another relation of things: the long *e* of "flee," "bleed," and "weep"; the *i* of "try" and "die"; the extended pleasure of the long *u* in "do," "do," "do," especially in closing. These threaded sounds manifest something larger than a simple catalog; they are worldmaking, a cosmological arc of being.[3]

Notice, too, how the poem's speaker directs us where to look and assumes that we can and will know how to look rightly; that is, pay attention to how the poem negotiates the politics of looking via its pronouns, by casting the speaker awry from and as observant of black collectivity. Beautifully, Clifton uses the objectification of the third person to relish in distance and plurality: "he," "she," "they," those people. (Even the singular pronouns, via vernacular phrasing, are sutured to plural action: "he do / she do.") This syntax invites the reader to *behold* the other, and in this way, the poem refuses the specular as a site of black abjection; rather, it instantiates looking as a shared relationality, especially since the looking is something that the reader does in concert with the speaker's prudent guidance: "Look at this," the speaker seems to intone, "and now that—look at that." Clifton's astute use of the third-person plural positions the speaker as observer and chronicler, and reorients the practice of looking beyond its destructive intent to secure racial difference. We know well the peril of such terrible visuality, what philosopher Frantz Fanon codified aptly with the phrase "Look, a Negro!" where the imperative "Look" is one and the same as the name "Negro," where the invitation to look at once invents a category and performs its denigration.[4] Importantly, then, Clifton uses the distance of "they" to encase the scene in its own world; doing such amplifies the potential to behold the humanity of the poem's black ones.

Said another way, the poem's dynamism resides in its elision of the easy alliance between the speaker's roll call and the black us who are exemplified by the calling. The elision is possible because the poem's scene is a black world, full of the blackness of the presenting one and the ones being presented. Masterfully, the speaker stands as an emcee, a host who seems to revel in what it is to look at all this quotidian magnificence rendered via the expansive line of words ambling down the page, staircase or waterfall or slideshow of being after being after being, linked in music and gesturing toward what cannot be said fully since, after all, it is not possible to present every instance of black being in a pantheon or to map it in the sky or track it over all the edge of the earth. Through third-person plurality, Clifton's speaker reorganizes our gaze, an example of what cultural theorist Daphne A. Brooks describes as the critical use of distance to navigate black alienation. Being looked at is a horror for us, and so I love that this poem marshals looking as a constitutive act of black being.[5]

I cannot overstate how crucial it is that the speaker doesn't say "we," as in "we live," "we love," since that pronoun would cement the poem's stance as being against the hateful question—as a black voice speaking to resist the harmful overtures of white volition. Clifton's speaker *witnesses*, such that the reply is not toward white violence but instead recognizes the capaciousness of being; *here the speaker stands not on a side but in the midst of the whole world of black being*. The poem, so gorgeous, unfurls as a text of black world relationality where the difference between the (black) one saying "they" and the (black) ones indicated by "they" reflects the breadth of our humanity. Difference not as a calculus of inferiority but as of our totality.[6]

This is a worldmaking poem: Notice the way its aesthetics negotiate repetition and time, how the verbs ("love," "flee," "weep") are enduringly present, timeless and not anchored by historical sociality. Indeed, the poem's time register moves toward the infinity of the last three lines, which mimic the orthography of ellipses: "they do / they do / they do," eternally and into a future we cannot see. Repetition fuels this infinity, repetition that works according "to *miracle* rather than to law . . . an *eternity* opposed to permanence."[7] "Repetition is holy," poet Nikky Finney tells us, and the repetitious doings in Clifton's "reply" are, exhibit, and make a black world, an inhabiting where blackness is totality, where everything is of people who are black—every capable thing, every small or harming thing, every extraordinary thing or thing of bad feeling . . . all of it is of blackness. This worldness exists in Clifton's beautiful verbs, these quotidian deeds that generate something of a utopia and that render the material excellence of a "they" who spin off the page and outward toward a somewhere, beyond the racist order of the world.[8]

We are supposed to not-see ourselves or to see ourselves through not-seeing; we are, indeed, supposed to fear—and hate—our black selves. But Clifton's poem invites us into a practice of encountering black being as it is, in its be-ingness, in its terribleness and wonder and particularity.[9] Beautifully, Clifton's range of verbs marks a black world as one which hosts pain and love and life, the effects of struggle where struggle is not singularly defined as a condition of oppression. Struggle in being alive. (The sustained inflection of action, "they do" in triplicate, reminds us of this.) A racist happening prefaces the poem, and racist happenings surely linger in every indicative verb in the verse. But in a black world, the racist thing is not the beginning or the end of being, and what matters is not only what is done to the subject but also *how* the subject is. Antiblackness is part of blackness but not all of how or what blackness is. Antiblackness is total in the world, but it is not total in the black world.

In this way, the paratext might be a scene of subjection, but Clifton's poem proper is a scene of aliveness, a world of us told in a reply.[10]

We can think about black worldmaking in regard to the project of black stud-ies. That is, as philosopher Sylvia Wynter argues, black studies' intellectual ambition wants to reject the world of antiblackness and to organize, instead, ideologies of and for a world that could embrace blackness. Such worldmaking manifests also in the declarations of the Black Arts/Aesthetic movement, which emphasizes blackness as an *idea* that could be remade beyond the limits of a racist discourse. This investment in the possibilities of ideation—what literary histo-rian Margo Natalie Crawford smartly describes as a "black post-blackness"—is vital to conceptualizing an overhauled universe realized through aesthetics.[11]

Such dynamics are at stake in Amiri Baraka's 1966 *ars poetica* "Black Art":

> Poems are bullshit unless they are
> teeth or trees or lemons piled
> on a step. Or black ladies dying
> of men leaving nickel hearts
> beating them down. Fuck poems
> and they are useful . . . (219)

The poem seems like a formless ranting catalog, though even in these few lines one can recognize aesthetic formality via the doubling irony where "Fuck poems" is followed by a celebration of poetry's utility or as the expletive works as both an adjective and an imperative. There is formfulness, too, in the deployment of conjunctions to create a propulsive rhythm and in the astute line breaks. As such we can see that "Black Art" is rife with deliberateness as it determines what a poem is and how a poem should work. "We want poems / like fists . . . / Assassin poems, Poems that shoot / guns" (219), the poem declares of its ideal verse and its idealized black subject. Baraka's text becomes animated with combativeness, a ferocious textual explicative that enacts and materializes fury: "Put it on him, poem. Strip him naked / to the world!" (219–220). Its attack names biracial black women, Jewish people, gay men, civil rights leaders, police officers . . . a wide-ranging and rangy pugilism intended, perhaps, to strike every oppressing thing. The intensity of its poetics is so high that one almost misses the breakneck turn three-quarters of the way through:

> Poem scream poison gas on beasts in green berets
> Clean out the world for virtue and love,
> Let there be no love poems written
> until love can exist freely and
> cleanly. Let Black people understand
> that they are the lovers and the sons
> of lovers and warriors and sons
> of warriors Are poems & poets &
> all the loveliness here in the world
>
> We want a black poem. And a
> Black World.
> Let the world be a Black Poem
> And Let All Black People Speak This Poem
> Silently
>
> or LOUD (220)

The casual movement from "Poem scream poison gas" to "Clean out the world for virtue and love" constitutes an astonishing change in tone, syntax, rhythm, sentiment, and ideology, a deviation that gives way to a lyrical invocation that mimics God's call for illumination in Genesis. This is Baraka's speaker at his magical best, summoning restoration after having authorized the decimation of the world that demeans blackness. We should notice especially that this glorious transubstantiation is incited by the repetition of "let," an imperative verb that functions subjunctively to indicate the thing that hasn't yet but still might happen.[12]

If you know "Black Art" in full, you know that I have sidestepped the hefty middle of the poem, which is where its vulgarities lie—it didn't seem necessary to repeat them. One might notice, too, that the world conjured at the end cites "sons" but doesn't articulate the possibility for daughters or even just children, thereby keeping a masculine prerogative intact. My point here is not an indulgence of the poem's ideological limitations but an exploration of one specific aspect of its working: its invocation of a black world. That is, I am struck by its inclining toward capaciousness, yearning, possibility, ideas that recall the case Baraka—as LeRoi Jones—makes about imagination in his essay "The Revolutionary Theater": "What is called the imagination (from image, magi, magic, magician, etc.) is a practical vector from the soul. . . . *The imagination is the projection of ourselves past our sense of ourselves as 'things.' Imagination (Image) is all possibility*, because from the image . . . any use (idea) is possible. . . . Possibility is what moves us" (*Home* 239; emphasis added). This declaration of being transformed by possibility matches the ambition that coalesces in the ending of "Black Art."[13]

Sigh: I am trying to read Baraka's poem through the surrender and magic of its conclusion. In such a reading, the speaker's politics are important to but not determinative of the world to come, since the world is not yet here and the poem breaks open, at its end, into the new thing that is not constrained singularly and ideologically by its beginning. And still, such a reading is complicated by the case that literary scholar Phillip Brian Harper makes about the conundrum of audience in Black Arts poetry, where the goal of speaking against white violence is conflated with the delicate work of trying to call blackness into formation.[14] This conflation fuels the narrowing of the idealized black world and homogenizes which kinds of blackness are presumed to fit in that world habitat.

And yet, the imagining of a world of black aliveness cannot be narrow. Indeed, in trying to reckon with Baraka's invocation at the close of "Black Art," I turn again to the logics of address in Clifton's "reply," the gorgeousness of her use of "they," that sly, embracing, worldmaking syntax that seems to work differently from Baraka's "we." Clifton's capaciousness establishes openness as the ethos of black worldmaking. The worldness of her aesthetic formation is not a contracting imaginary that reiterates normativities or secures boundaries of who we are but instead beholds an expansive relationality where "every form of life that has ever been ever enacted, is a part of us."[15] This is a world of heterogeneity whose only cohering value is the rightness of black being, the possibility of black becoming. If we read Baraka's speaker as a figure immersed in *evolution* rather than as one entrenched against a dominant audience, we can appreciate "Black Art" for its *inclination* toward black totality, its closing call which collates the poem, the world, and the one as a praxis of *becoming*—"Black Art" as an enactment of verse imagining.[16]

The thinking on black being always has to countenance death, as the field of black pessimism makes clear. And perhaps no one has taken up this figuring of being and death more extensively than literary scholar Christina Sharpe, whose *In the Wake: On Blackness and Being* characterizes "wake" as an idiom not only of consciousness but also of life's deathness: "In the midst of so much death and the fact of Black life as proximate to death, how do we attend to physical, social, and figurative death and also to the largeness that is Black life, Black life insisted from death?" (17). This attending to life is what Sharpe theorizes as "wake work," the materialization of being through death such that "even as we experienced, recognized, and lived subjection, we did not *simply* or *only* live *in* subjection and *as* the subjected" (4; emphases in the original). *In the Wake* is Sharpe's pursuit of "the modalities of Black life lived in, as, under, despite Black death" (22). I read Sharpe's study as a definitive articulation of black pessimism as a field, especially its exploration of what cultural theorist Saidiya Hartman describes as the enduring afterlife of slavery and coloniality.[17] Indeed, by placing the terms of death (including "abjection," "negation," "terror," and "nonbeing") at the center of thinking about blackness, black pessimism has reenergized a critique of liberal humanism's uncritical faith in progress and its fallacies of freedom. The meaning of black freedom, these scholars remind us, cannot be indexed to the Enlightenment and cannot be mapped in the syntax of Western norms; there is no end to the condition of coloniality and captivity—no end, but there is life in the midst and aftermath of those interminable conditions. Cohering black pessimism as a field is challenging, especially because some scholars whose ideas are taken up in its name don't identify precisely with its project. And still, I want to highlight here black pessimism's construction of black ontology both as an impossibility in the logic of the antiblack world and as a possibility that requires perceiving differently what the world is or looks like or can be—worldmaking.[18] I believe as black pessimism does that the world of antiblackness excludes black humanity in at least two ways: the antiblack world is built to be against the human, and the idea of the human it permits is built to be against some of us (black people) who are exactly that—human.[19]

And though we might be inclined to emphasize death as a feature of black pessimism, the truth is that terms of life are legible in the field's critical explorations: in the foregoing quotations from Sharpe; in the phrase "the social life of social death," which Jared Sexton uses to frame the field ("Ante-Anti-Blackness"), theorizing that he calls "an ars vita" ("Afro-pessimism"); in the poetic clarity of Hartman's "I, too, am the afterlife of slavery" (*Lose Your Mother* 6); in Nahum Dimitri Chandler's exposition of exorbitance; in the vivacious speaker in Frank B. Wilderson's theoretical memoir *Afropessimism*. We might say, as Terrion L. Williamson has, that black social life is "the register of black experience that is not reducible to the terror that calls it into existence, but is the rich remainder, the multifaceted artifact of black communal resistance and resilience that is expressed in black idioms, cultural forms, traditions and ways of being" (9). An overemphasis on death simplifies the nuanced insights of black pessimism and its related discourses and, in this way, my argument for aliveness is not a sharp detour from this field of contemporary theoretical thought.[20]

My difference from black pessimism might be in my attempt to displace antiblackness from the center of my thinking. That is, though I don't deny the terribleness of the world we live in, nor its antiblack perpetuity, I am interested in conceptualizing an aesthetic imaginary founded on black worldness. Death, nonbeing, the "ontological terror" aptly named by theorist Calvin L. Warren— these are conditions of black being, but they are not total in my appreciation of aliveness. I don't mean to make the distinction sharper than it is, since I acknowledge how diverse the field is and how much terms of life circulate through it. Perhaps the keenest point of contention for me is the specific register of black pessimism's declaration of totality: it is true that every black one of us lives under the legacied terror of modernity and coloniality—that no matter how differently we perceive or respond, terror is a condition of every black life. Or as Wilderson describes it, "violence precedes and exceeds blacks" (*Red, White and Black* 76). My quibble is that the definitive fact of black subjection, true as it is, is not exactly sayable because no statement about every black person can be genuinely sayable. Such a claim might be ideologically or conceptually or theoretically or structurally factual, but its truth is and should remain an opacity.[21]

I am cautious about the declarative assertion of nonbeing and its slippery poetics.

I know that theoretical study produces claims that are as broad and metaphorical as they are generative—they work as provocations; as such, I know that "nonbeing" is a metaphor for the pervasive condition of subjection more than it is a literal description of black being. Simply, every human is of being. I am trying, then, to elide what is elided by hefty terms of subjection, or at least as those terms move beyond the specific nuanced interrogations of their authors. It may be true that subjection prefaces everything in an antiblack world, but in thinking through a *black* world, I am trying to surpass terror as the uninflected language of black being, as well as to suspend the anti/ante position of blackness. In that surpassing and suspending, I am trying to articulate the aesthetics of aliveness. What I want is the freeness of a black world where blackness can be of being, where there is no argument to be made, where there is no speaking to or against an audience because we are all the audience there is . . . and, as such, the text's work can manifest an invitation to study and to becoming for the black one. What I want is the wayward world made through Saidiya Hartman's method in *Wayward Lives, Beautiful Experiments: Intimate Histories of Social Upheaval*, the way that Hartman's close narration deepens the past's historic scope by being as local as possible: by residing in the figure of human life evident via the traces of the one who lived that life. In the prefatory "A Note on Method," Hartman describes this doing: "At the turn of the twentieth century, young black women were in open rebellion. . . . This book recreates the radical imagination and wayward practices of these young women by describing the world through their eyes. . . . To this end, I employ a mode of close narration, a style which places the voice of the narrator and character in inseparable relation, so that the vision, language, and rhythms of the wayward shape and arrange the text" (xiii–xiv). Hartman's use of close narration is genius, because it instantiates a sense of presence and presentness—it instantiates a live and lively *now* to the histories it tells. And in doing so, Hartman eludes the discursive trap of the black historical past as a monolith of terror wrought by the structures of modernity. That is, Hartman offers us a past that, in its aliveness, holds relation to our being now. Hartman is not alone in this praxis of reckoning with the past and the scale of being (of harm, of living) sometimes illegible therein—one could look toward Stephen Michael Best, Sharon P. Holland, Tavia Nyong'o, Robert Reid-Pharr, Jared Sexton, and Michelle M. Wright, just to name a few contemporary thinkers. Sigh: What I want is the ethos of a world like the one Hartman reveals, like those in Lucille Clifton's poems, worlds where black living is compassed by being alive, where aliveness sets the parameters for understanding loss, pain, belonging, for countenancing love, grace, healing. Surely, Clifton's poems can be used to consider antiblackness, but their habitat is not essentially of this.[22]

I am embracing the luxuries of thinking with and through the materiality of texts. That is, in a black world, in whatever manifestations of black worldness texts create, *blackness* (not antiblackness) is totality; in such a world, black being is capacious and right—not more-right-than, just right-as-is. Life-as-is. I believe that the worldness of black texts, if one reads with such a temperament, makes it possible to withstand black being as human being, to behold blackness as one's ethical reckoning with being alive.

An antiblack world expects blackness from black people; in a black world, what we expect and get from black people is beingness.[23]

In a black world, every black being is of *being*, the verb that infers a process of becoming.[24] Near the conclusion of *Red, White and Black: Cinema and the Structure of U.S. Antagonisms*, Wilderson writes, "To say we *must* be free of air, while admitting to knowing no other source of breath, is what I have tried to do here" (338; emphasis in original), an admission that resonates both with the impossibility of imagining a black world and with the sheer urgency of doing just that. I am writing out of that urgency, trying to conceptualize a black world as an aesthetic totality that is free of air and full of ways to breathe. It is why, throughout this work, I hardly use the term "nonbeing"; the human who is black is a being, is of being. The gambit of *Black Aliveness* is that the black one's ontological dilemma is not in regard to not-being or being-against; the ontological dilemma, as such exists, is being.[25]

I will say it once: antiblackness and white supremacy, as they live in and are enacted by any person in implicit or explicit or structural registers, both are sins against the human. I want to be clear that a call to aliveness is not contradictory to this thing I understand to be true.

One further reinforcement: the idiom "a black world" names an aesthetic imaginary that encompasses heterogeneity. I take inspiration, as ever, from the worldmaking conceptualized prominently in black women's feminism. When the Combahee River Collective's "Black Feminist Statement" announces that "our politics initially sprang from a shared belief that Black women are inherently valuable" (15), it signals not only the enduring marginalization of black women in the world but also an imagining determined to locate philosophical and political meaningfulness through the specificity of black femaleness. There is a similar capaciousness in Hortense J. Spillers's argument about black femaleness in the iconic "Mama's Baby, Papa's Maybe: An American Grammar Book," or in Alice Walker's womanism, with its ever-widening pool of human insight cultivated from a black female vernacular idiom. There are other examples too: Anna Julia Cooper's epiphanic "Only the BLACK WOMAN can say 'when and where I enter, in the quiet undisputed dignity of my womanhood, then and there the whole *Negro race enters with me*'" (63; emphasis and capitalization in original); Toni Morrison's telling of the entire story of modernity and coloniality through Sethe and her daughter Beloved, which Saidiya Hartman repeats—revises, elegantly—in *Lose Your Mother: A Journey along the Atlantic Slave Route*; Audre Lorde's belief that a queer black mother's body could be enough to conceptualize what it is to know ("Poetry Is Not a Luxury" or *The Cancer Journals*). Black feminist thinking might be specific in naming black women, but its ambition has always been the breadth of being alive, the principle that the lived experience of one who is black and female is comprehensive enough to manifest totality. Indeed, we might call this work *feminist black studies,* where the commitment to a feminist orientation determines the entirety of what black studies might be.[26]

The world of black aliveness is gendered, binarily and otherwise. It recognizes gender as a site of human beingness but also as a violation. Moreover, the invocation of this world should not be confused with "calling all black people," especially if such hailing intends to exclude or regulate certain habitats of being. In a black world, there is no need—would be no need—to call in or to exclude anyone. The solicitation of a black world is replete with eccentricity and is allergic to the imposition of normativity or authenticity. Blackness here "is . . . broad enough and open enough to encompass, but without enclosing" (Harney and Moten 158), blackness as a commonwealth untroubled by needing to speak *to* or *for.* Such conceptualization liberates us from blackness as difference so as to be able to see—to be—all the black intraracial difference there might be. The black world is an assemblage, an open collective of dynamism, of pull and tug and relationality; this characterization recalls what Hilton Als, in "Ghosts in the House," writes of Toni Morrison: "Situating herself inside the black world, Morrison undermined the myth of black cohesiveness." Exactly.[27]

Since blackness cannot exist fully, humanly, in the world, we will imagine a world where the condition of being alive is of us. In a black world, the case of our lives is aliveness; not death, not even death's vitality, but aliveness. We are alive, we are alive, or, as a poet once put it, "This is the urgency: Live!"[28] Such aliveness is relational and it moves one into other habitats of (one's) being, into and toward more, akin to the stringing together of being in Clifton's "reply."

In *Black Aliveness, or a Poetics of Being,* I am interested in theorizing aliveness through poems of relation and first-person essays, especially in considering the philosophical work of pronouns ("one," "me," "I") and verbs (imperatives, subjunctives). I believe that an aesthetic of aliveness makes possible an encounter with the ethical question "how to be." That is, though an antiblack world would to foreclose ethical possibility for the one who is black, in the totality of a black world, we can conceptualize "how to be" as a reckoning of human capacity, as the right and burden of being.[29]

A note to the reader: In these pages, I am trying to create a clear, readable line. As such, I have privileged the creative works (poems and essays) as well as a particular genealogy of thinkers who are mostly black and female, though the breadth of my scholarly debt is indexed in my endnotes.[30]

(Today I am sad, mad, wild, full of rage in and out. Today is a day in June 2020, summer of racism's recurring pandemic. Today, I am of molecular rage about Ahmaud Arbery, killed by white vigilantes while he was jogging; George Floyd, killed during a police arrest in Minneapolis; Breonna Taylor, a health care worker killed by police fire. And others, many others, including Dominique Fells and Riah Milton, two black transwomen whose murders add to the particular vulnerability of our black transgender folks; like Tony McDade, a black transman killed by police in Florida. And more, including the disregard for black life that manifests as everyday menace: in this season, a black man has been harassed and threatened while birding in a city park, and an eleven-year-old black girl has been assaulted by a white woman while trying to collect her grandmother's mail.[31] Today, when I am thinking about black aliveness, I am exhausted by black death; today I am sad that I am exhausted. Racism is murderous, and its murderousness travels and compounds insidiously and without impunity. By the time this paragraph is published, by the time one reads it, these names and incidents will be old news, replaced by another incalculable catalog of harm. That certainty exhausts me today.

As necessary as "Black Lives Matter" has proven to be, so efficient and beautiful a truth-claim, its necessity disorients me; to hear it said or see it printed as an emblem is existentially disorienting. I want a black world where the matter of mattering matters indisputably, where black mattering is beyond expression. I want to read and study in the orientation of a black world.

Today there is no reconciling the facts of our lives, which seem tethered to death, and the case for black aliveness. Both have to be true at the same time.)

This work begins with a single premise, an instruction, really: imagine a black world. Such a directive acknowledges that the New World plunder of modernity and coloniality enacts a destruction of the world as it was and might have become, that the New World unorders the relationship of the human to place, time, other human. Or we might say there never was a world, that imperialism's destructiveness *is* that it imposed a world logic. Either case describes world-failure that, among other horrors, mobilizes blackness as an antithesis to human life.[32]

In the face of failure that is so unspeakably broad, I use "imagine" as a turn toward the small, an opportunity to understand black worldness as what black texts do . . . as the aesthetics of black art. Reading this way scales the matter of world-and-being to a level I can manage, and though it may not resolve catastrophe, it moves away from summoning black literature to teach about black humanity. (What is there to learn? The human is human.) "Imagine" postpones the logics of address, dominance, and misrecognition—the terms of an antiblack world—that interfere with beholding both black aliveness and a black ethic of relation. This study of aliveness rests on the inclination to imagine that the black text speaks to and in a black world, subjunctive and imaginary as that is, away from the false and damaging expectation that black texts have to speak universally, which means that they speak to the larger racial project or conversation—that is, to people who are not black . . . which indeed they do (a text speaks to any reader who reads it). Simply, I want to elude the imposition of the generic nonblack reader, an imposition that potentially corrupts how we regard the aesthetics of black art, or, at the very least, excludes a black reader from being the "one" who is referenced and imagined as the human person reading, learning, becoming. "Imagine" installs the possibility that a black one might be the reader who could find themself there, beheld in the suspension of literary worldmaking.[33]

"Imagine a black world" is both a way to read texts and a way to understand what is instantiated by the text itself, a choral subjunctive that exemplifies but does not plead. This undertaking is Cliftonian and Morrisonian, since no thinkers or writers have advocated for the textual world of black being like Lucille Clifton and Toni Morrison.

This is a story of us—there are and could be many stories, and this is just one, a story of aliveness rather than of life, since I am determined to avoid the trouble that comes in trying to represent life's unrepresentability. The word here is "aliveness," a quality of being, a term of habitat, a manner and aesthetic, a feeling—or many of them, circuits in an atmosphere. Like breath. We are totality: we *are* and are of the universe; we *are* and are of a black world, this us who are cited by that great poetic riff—"they do / they do / they do."

This is a conversation of us, black us and our aliveness.

1 ALIVENESS

AND RELATION

"Can I say again how alive your being alive makes me feel!?!"

Everything that I might pursue about a concept of aliveness is legible in this sweetness that literary theorist Barbara Christian wrote to poet Audre Lorde after Lorde's presentation at the 1978 MLA convention: "Can I say again how alive your being alive makes me feel!?!"[1] Here, in this declaration, aliveness is constituted in repetition and therefore is unfurling, an experience one encounters rather than possesses—a relational capacity manifested through the speaking one's sensibilities, her feeling, her intelligence. Here, too, is the ordinary quality of aliveness, its inherence (the language is common, but so, too, is the feeling, even as its particularity means that its meaningfulness has never been known before) as well as its exclamation of force and openness (it is framed as a question; the question mark is encased by exclamation). Finally, here is a message about and sent to another that casts attention on the messenger; that is, if we are reading Christian's missive conceptually, we will notice how the messenger is being suspended in a scene of tingling astuteness. This suspended shimmering is her being in the world, which is also an orientation to being.

Again, everything in this and the next chapter leans on what is said finely in Christian's sweetness, which I am invoking as an embedded epigraph: "Can I say again how alive your being alive makes me feel!?!"[2]

"Aliveness" can be an unwieldy notion because it is commonsense but also because it is hard to describe aptly. We might return to Lucille Clifton's poem "reply," especially its fluency of verbs, as a way to start this thinking. Notice there, for example, that the concluding repeated phrase "they do / they do / they do" recasts the poem's other verbs as eternal capacities, doings that have happened, are happening, will happen ever again. These doings are not appraised by quality (how they are done), nor by their object (to whom they are directed), but instead they iterate the idea of *existence*, the manifestness of the "they" who "do." Important, too, is the fact that Clifton's verbs extend beyond a simplistic notion of action or agency. For example, her catalog includes verbs that are neither singular nor discrete acts ("try," "tire," "break," "mourn"), verbs that are exceptionally intransitive through being involuntary ("bleed"), verbs that suggest inhabitance so as to exceed characterization ("live," "love"). Aliveness, then, is not action but something else, perhaps what political theorist Jane Bennett describes as vibrant matter, "a liveliness intrinsic to the materiality of the thing" or the power that constitutes "the force of things."[3]

Aliveness as inherence.

The complexities of this term abound in scholarly discourses, so I want to be clear that I don't mean "aliveness" as an exact synonym of "life," as a distinction between animal forms and inanimate matter. Nor do I mean the condition of exile or belonging conferred by a state, a king, or a community; nor the specificity of blackness as an antithesis or problem to life; nor any discourse that implies hierarchies of worthiness. Moreover, like cultural theorist Alexander Weheliye, I am not interested in taking the human or its categories of life for granted, since I understand black studies to have exposed the human as a heuristic (8), as a category and method of analysis that reveals much about the structures of the modern world. My interest is in an idea of aliveness that eludes quantification and qualification, since one could not be of more or less aliveness nor could one be redeemed by one's aliveness.[4]

Let's assume that aliveness is of every being in a black world—again, inherence. Let's assume aliveness as the force of and in being, akin to the mode of existence that black queer theorist L. H. Stallings defines as "stank matter": "a form of creative energy generated by the self and the self's relationship to sacred forces. . . . Imaginative freedom for a sacred subjectivity that exists before the narratives of gender hierarchy and sexual pathology can coerce it into a social and political subject" (123–124). I am compelled by Stallings's description of stank as a materiality, in regard to embodiment, as I am by her claim of it as a sacred habitat of being. That is, she describes an inhabitance that is material and immaterial, and that exceeds representation, which is not the same as arguing that the inhabitance itself *is* excessive.[5] I read in Stallings's characterization a notion of aliveness as a condition of human *knowing*, which is precisely the territory Audre Lorde travels in her 1977 masterwork "Poetry Is Not a Luxury." This is how the essay begins:

> The quality of light by which we scrutinize our lives has direct bearing upon the product which we live, and upon the changes which we hope to bring about through those lives. It is within this light that we form those ideas by which we pursue our magic and make it realized. This is poetry as illumination, for it is through poetry that we give name to those ideas which are, until the poem, nameless and formless—about to be birthed, but already felt. That distillation of experience from which true poetry springs births thought as dream births concept, as feeling births idea, as knowledge births (precedes) understanding. (*Sister Outsider* 36)

Sigh: Lorde's thinking is so dazzling, it could withstand repetition and transliteration, especially the first sentence: "The quality of light by which we scrutinize our lives has direct bearing upon the product which we live, and upon the changes which we hope to bring about through those lives." Incisively, Lorde declares that the manner and sensation of how we pay attention to our being constitute our being itself, as well as informing what our being is/ becomes in the world. From the outset, in that gorgeous first sentence, Lorde theorizes being as embodied and experiential and reflective and aspirational; she describes feeling and sensation as kin to thought and reason, all in one sentence. Said another way, her claim links reason (the word "scrutinize") to other capacities of knowing, especially habits of the body. And vitally, imagination does not precede experience; instead, the engagement of experience ("distillation") constitutes imaginative potentiality. Lorde's thinking here is an argument about how we understand *being*, especially because she situates knowing (knowledge) as an enterprise ordinated by sensation and embodiment: "For each of us as women, there is a dark place within, where hidden and growing our true spirit rises. . . . Within these deep places, each one of us holds an incredible reserve of creativity and power" (36–37). Lorde advances an idiom where the metaphysical isn't before or separate from the physical, where the physical is not figured only via the body in its contemporary time. To me, this articulation of materiality as the name for one's apparatus of knowing, this explication is a theorization of aliveness.[6]

I am toggling between the terms "embodiment" and "materiality" so as to avoid some of the discursive narrowness of the body as a racialized and gendered notion. That is, because of the pervasiveness of body-mind dualism, Lorde's ideas imply *the body* even as she doesn't specifically deploy that term in "Poetry." This is a crucial observation because it asks us to recognize that Lorde is advancing an argument about the body as the materiality of and metaphor for experience, experience that—as the site of knowing—is material *and* immaterial.

There are two hitches here. One is that claims of the body are often feminized and racialized, as if matter were a distinct and impoverished kind of intelligence. Lorde describes this dynamic well in "Uses of the Erotic: The Erotic as Power," a 1978 essay where she writes that "the erotic is a resource within each of us that lies in a deeply female and spiritual plane, firmly rooted in the power of our un-expressed or unrecognized feeling," and then later, that as "women we have come to distrust that power which rises from our deepest and nonrational knowledge" (*Sister Outsider* 53). This accent on feeling highlights Lorde's investment in the body as a geography of intelligence, her phenomenological argument about how we know. Everyone lives in and through a body, her thinking seems to say, even if only some of us are apprehended via narrow terms of embodiment.[7]

The second hitch relates to the body as singularly material, as the seemingly natural, biologically confirmed textuality of the human. We know this conclusion is false, because ideas about the body have been *invented* to support differing notions of humanity—that is, since the human body becomes known through narrative and rhetoric, there can be no ideological zero-degree claim made about it. (Hortense Spillers and Sylvia Wynter make this point superbly clear.) Importantly, then, Lorde refers to embodiment, but she is not interested in an essential-ized idiom of the-body-is-female-and-has-superlative-integrity. Instead, Lorde's turn to the body articulates a force of being, a capacity of knowing that doesn't accede to binary logic; for Lorde, the body is both immanent and transcendent, a phenomenological sensation of being that incorporates inside and outside. Again, the body is a syntax for describing the aliveness of a human one, or, in Toni Morrison's language, "the body is the vehicle, not the point" (*Jazz* 228).[8]

We might notice, then, that Lorde moves between references that specify femaleness and ones that are more generic. For example, in the foregoing sen-tence from "Uses of the Erotic," she acknowledges the erotic as "a deeply female" plane in "each of us." One way of understanding this fluctuation is to recall that the essay originated as a speech to a convention of women historians; in that regard, there is no distance between "each of us" and the "female plane" of erotic consciousness, since the idealized subject of Lorde's theorizing is gendered female. Literary scholar Lyndon K. Gill reminds us that Lorde's work commits to thinking about human capacity *through* (black) female specificity. As such, her existentialism avoids the ideological trap of binarism and minoritization, and her claims instantiate the (black) female as an appropriate figure for philosophical imagining.[9] Out of this audacity, Lorde, in "Poetry," writes, "For women, then, poetry is not a luxury. It is a vital necessity of our existence. It forms the quality of the light within which we predicate our hopes and dreams toward survival and change, first made into language, then into idea, then into more tangible action. Poetry is the way we help give name to the nameless so it can be thought. The farthest external horizons of our hopes and fears are cobbled by our poems, carved from the rock experiences of our daily lives" (37). This praisesong dissolves the boundary between the magical and the tangible, the sensible and the intelligible, and defines consciousness as a habitat where transcendence and immanence converge. There is a striking parallel between Lorde's language here and that of classic American transcendentalism, especially as articulated in the opening of Ralph Waldo Emerson's *Nature*: "Why should not we also enjoy an original relation to the universe? Why should not we have a poetry and philosophy of insight and not of tradition, and a religion by revelation to us?" (35). A transcendent matter, indeed.[10]

I love the way that Lorde's theorizing is at once epistemological (about the way we know) and ontological (about what being is), a black feminist take on the materiality and immateriality of consciousness. And it is in this regard that I invoke her thinking to characterize what I mean by aliveness in a black world: the becoming of beingness, the sensations that inhabit one's body in its existence and that constitute intelligence, the way that "bodies think as they feel" (Massumi 211). This recourse to feeling situates aliveness as a plenitude that compounds without pattern, aliveness as a poetic, an affective aesthetic beholding of being, an *ars vitalia* as in an instance—or series of instances—of being alive. And here, Lorde's warning that "poetry is not a luxury" becomes clear as a declaration of the inevitability and seriousness of aliveness, of poetic becoming as a necessity for being in the world.[11]

It is hard to express precisely a notion of inevitability without seeming naïve, though perhaps this impasse is a failure of representation, since the terms of aliveness can't be articulated fully or clearly. That is, I don't want to make any possessive claim about aliveness as a counter to the dispossessing dimensions of life in the world. *Aliveness is of and in the one who is alive.* I know that society's structures inflect the concept and experience of a life such that "there is no life without the [social] conditions of life that variably sustain life."[12] And still, what I am trying to do is to write about aliveness in a black world rather than life in the world as we know it—to write about aliveness in the aesthetic imaginary of black thought, which might help us attend to the poetic aliveness inevitable in each black human being. Again, I mean aliveness as instance(s) of being, which is how it is characterized by Celie's statement of ordination and instantiation in Alice Walker's *The Color Purple*: "I'm pore, I'm black, I may be ugly and can't cook, a voice say to everything listening. But I'm here" (176). I love how precisely Celie locates being in the phenomenological claim of the adverb "here," a deixis that points imprecisely to a precise, beautiful state: "I'm here."[13]

Aliveness is quiet, at least in the way that I enunciate the latter term in *The Sovereignty of Quiet: Beyond Resistance in Black Culture*. In that book, I argue for quiet as a metaphor of black interiority, a stay against the social ideas of blackness. But in making the case through interiority—in trying to refuse publicness as the totalizing denominator of how blackness is figured and represented—I might have overemphasized the inner life at the expense of thinking through what it means to be alive in the world or, better still, what it means to be of aliveness in a black world. Consider this another attempt, then, this trying to attend to black aliveness, impossible as it is to characterize it fully, noxious as it is to try to put such aliveness into any service. Aliveness is quiet and interior, yes, but remember that "despite its name, the interior is not unconnected to the world of things (the public or political or social world)."[14] Indeed, by invoking a black world and suspending antiblack logics, I can loosen my investment in the interior as a guiding metaphor. Aliveness, as phenomenological consciousness, collapses the distinction of inside from outside, which collates with Lorde's description, in "Uses of the Erotic," of knowing as an immanence that transcends outward:

> When we live outside ourselves, and by that I mean on external directives only rather than from our internal knowledge and needs, when we live away from those erotic guides from within ourselves, then our lives are limited by external and alien forms, and we conform to the needs of a structure that is not based on human need, let alone an individual's. But *when we begin to live from within outward, in touch with the power of the erotic within ourselves, and allowing that power to inform and illuminate our actions upon the world around us, then we begin to be responsible to ourselves in the deepest sense.* (*Sister Outsider* 58; emphasis added)

Unerringly, Lorde advances a case for the excellence of feeling where being "is not a question only of what we do; it is a question of how acutely and fully we can feel in the doing" (54). She argues for full feeling as a human astuteness, a "self-connection shared [that] is a measure of the joy which I know myself to be capable of feeling" (57). This theorization of feeling-as-knowing coheres "Uses of the Erotic" and "Poetry Is Not a Luxury," and the thinking climaxes when Lorde, in "Poetry," declares "I feel, therefore I can be free" (38). In this maxim, an embodied poetic habitat is not an enclosure but an opening, and feeling is a praxis through which one can meet and be met. What emerges in Lorde's poetic, to borrow Zakiyyah Iman Jackson's language, "is an unruly sense of being/knowing/feeling existence" (2): this is aliveness, this contagious being through openness, this tingling consciousness or habitat of sense that is being in the world, or, as Barbara Christian expressed it, "Can I say again how alive your being alive makes me feel!?!"[15]

I read "aliveness" as a term of relation where the focus is on one's preparedness for encounter rather than on the encounter itself. In this way, to be in relation is to be in the embodied sociality of one's readiness.

My framing of relation as readiness recalls Martin Buber's classic work published in 1923, *I and Thou*, which argues that there are two ways of being in regard to the world, a subject-object orientation that Buber calls I-It and a subject-subject orientation, I-Thou or I-You, which is of superlative excellence.[16] In an I-You orientation, one doesn't understand or know a tree, the weather, another person, but rather one comes into being through an open relation with the tree, weather, person. Such inhabiting upends the self's authority as one relinquishes the preface of knowing anything or anyone; instead, consciousness arrives in the happening of being open. "The relation to the You is unmediated. Nothing conceptual intervenes between I and You, no prior knowledge and no imagination," Buber intones (62), a statement that summarizes his earlier claim: "I can neither experience nor describe the form which meets me, but only body it forth. And yet I behold it, splendid in the radiance of what confronts me, clearer than all the clearness of the world which is experienced" (10).[17] Buber's thinking is a thesis on being and being alive, and his ideas collate to Lorde's arguments for feeling and materiality. Centrally, relation is a principle of intersubjectivity, of riskful surrender to being in shared otherness: "The You encounters me by grace—it cannot be found by seeking," and then later, a vital repetition: "The You encounters me" (Buber 62). And even this language is inept, since Buber's arguments warn against abstracting the other or the self, a warning that undermines the sentence "The You encounters me." (If neither the You nor the I is

knowable, neither can be spoken of.) Relational inhabitance is aspirational—
that is, one never achieves it, nor can one determine to live in it fully. Buber
declares this much in the closing of his argument's first section: "And in all the
seriousness of truth, listen: without It a human cannot live. But whoever lives
only with that is not human" (85). This contradiction is a necessary acknowledgment of the impossibility of living in a preconscious state; and still, Buber is
sure to remind us that the yearning for and through relation is our salvation.[18]

In our common consideration of relation as a theory of twoness, we emphasize
the meeting (with the other) and idealize the other as the site of encounter. But
I want to privilege the matter of *orientation*, that quality of presence or habitat
of readiness formed not by the expectation of the other but by the shedding of
expectation. Readiness here allies with dance scholar Danielle Goldman's *I Want
to Be Ready: Improvised Dance as a Practice of Freedom*, which describes improvisation
as a collusion of preparedness, intention, and surrender that ignites "practices of
freedom" (4). Goldman's framing accentuates my emphasis on the thresholding
aliveness of relation as the *capacity* to meet and be met rather than the actual
meeting.[19]

We might think of relation as a poetic of alive-being, as exemplified in
Édouard Glissant's own classic work, 1990's *Poetics of Relation*. I am compelled,
especially, by Glissant's combination of the two terms—"poetics," "relation"—
into a schema for theorizing New World blackness. Specifically, Glissant conceptualizes the abyss of Atlantic slave history as an aesthetic, political, and
spiritual state of undoing, a terrifying opening that potentially surpasses "the
ontological obsession with knowledge" (19). For Glissant, being in the world
is an opacity, an inhabitance that is indescribable and, as for Buber, that does
not yet exist: a "totality in evolution, whose order is continually in flux and
whose disorder one can *imagine forever*" (133; emphasis added). Such totality of
aesthetic possibility resonates with Lorde's notion of embodied intelligence;
indeed, in a moment of flourish, Glissant offers an explication of totality that
seems eerily resonant with Lorde:

> The world's poetic force (its energy), kept alive within us, fastens itself by
> fleeting, delicate shivers, onto the rambling prescience of poetry in the
> depths of our being. *The active violence in reality distracts us from knowing it.*
> Our obligation to "grasp" violence, and often fight it, estranges us from
> such live intensity, as it also freezes the shiver and disrupts prescience.
> But this force never runs dry because it is its own turbulence. Poetry—
> thus, nonetheless, totality gathering strength—is driven by another poetic
> dimension that we all divine or babble within ourselves. It could well be

that poetry is basically and mainly defined in this relationship of itself to nothing other than itself, of density to volatility, or the whole to the individual. (159; emphasis added)

Glissant doesn't ignore the sustained destructive reality of violence—his opacity is an anticolonial argument against the racist construction of black Atlantic being—but he also remains invested in an energy, an errant force that corresponds to the depths of a human being. And poetry, he argues, is a frame for explicating and enacting this totality, this aliveness that is everywhere and everything.[20]

Aliveness is inevitable because it is *totality*, a black world rendering that implies neither universality nor prescription (the word is not "totalitarian"), but instead refers to the everything of being in a black world. As such, there is no *being* other than being-in-relation, no *being* other than being-of-aliveness. And despite my attempts at summary, Glissant is right that "the idea of totality alone is an obstacle to totality" (192), which means that totality cannot be understood or corralled. Suffice it to say that totality idiomizes being as a "circulation [that] goes in all directions at once, in all the directions . . . opened by presence to presence: all things, all beings, all entities, everything past and future, alive, dead, inanimate, stones, plants, nails, gods." This "totality of all being" is the aliveness of a black world (Nancy 3).[21]

What does black world relationality look like in a poem? For an answer, we could think with another example from Lucille Clifton, her untitled verse known widely by its iconic first line:

won't you celebrate with me
what i have shaped into
a kind of life? i had no model.
born in babylon
both nonwhite and woman
what did i see to be except myself?
i made it up
here on this bridge between
starshine and clay,
my one hand holding tight
my other hand; come celebrate
with me that everyday
something has tried to kill me
and has failed. (427)

This poem generates into full bloom from the invitation of its initial question, which sets forth not a relation between the speaker and the addressed but a call to the speaker's instantiation.[22] We can appreciate this formation better by reading the poem literally and linearly, and by paying attention to its vacillation between question and answer. Notice, for example, how the opening question bleeds into the brief declaration, "i had no model," the shortest, simplest, most direct statement in the entire verse, one that is emphasized by a period and a line break. The definitiveness of this statement shifts the opening query ("won't you") from being a plea to an imagined reader into being a platform for the speaking one. In fact, "i had no model" is so assured that it nearly forecloses continuance since there might not be anything else to be said after such a conclusion. Of course, to stop here would be to exist as the foreclosed; Clifton's speaker is too alive, too keenly of pursuit for that. She, the speaker, expands from the declaration of modellessness, asking, "what did i see to be except myself?" Notice that this second question, especially in its irony, is aimed by the speaker toward herself, and in keeping with the poem's dialogic pattern, the answer is another four-word declarative statement, "i made it up." The line break here isolates this claim and emphasizes "i made it up" as the poem's fulcrum, its center. And yet in a poem of such volatility, the center cannot hold.

Clifton's "won't you celebrate with me" is a slim and simple poem, but its dynamics are exceptional. Indeed, I am trying to highlight Clifton's exquisite use of invitation as a volatile form of the speaker's aliveness, the speaker who is the one who both poses the questions and offers the replies. This interchange exemplifies the speaker's relationality, her being called by/toward a practice of knowing. Clifton aestheticizes the speaker's pursuit through the use of line breaks that amplify the compounding meaning within and between phrases. That is, the enjambment tethers each insight to the next, asserts a definitive thing only to undo it. Notice the striking example of "my one hand holding tight / my other hand," where the line break seems to imply the image of a fist, though what is being regarded is not only a tautness and a posture of strain but a haptic relation, the world made in the small space between one hand and another. (For example, the image is either of one hand holding the other or of one hand that is tight while the other is accounted for as "my other hand"—in both cases, the image multiplies.) Enjambment propels and animates "won't you celebrate with me" as a poem of swerve, surprise, and discovery. And to behold its praxis of relation, we have to read with and as the speaker, to be capable of the poem's unfolding not as a lesson to the "you" but as an *instance* of the black female speaker, her becoming-oriented in these verse moves.[23]

What a fantastic excellent thing, this poem of relation that chronicles a sequence of becoming—"won't you celebrate with me / . . . / . . . i had no model / . . . / i made it up"—and that, in conclusion, morphs the opening question into a gentle command, "come celebrate / with me." To whom is this offer made, this scene of regard that is astute to threat and that is still tender? To the speaker herself, the one whose capacity for becoming is being signaled through the poem's unfurling. Notice, for example, the image of "starshine and clay," where starlight is not adequate heat to *set* clay, where a star's quality of light and clay's quality of materiality indicate potential . . . all of which is reflective of the idiom of becoming. (Even the words "bridge" and "between" cohere with this notion as further evidence of Clifton's verse prowess.) Notice, finally, the present perfect tense—"has tried," "has failed"—which infers that tomorrow, the relating begins again, this sustained work of being alive. I love the philosophical intelligence of Clifton's ode for celebration, how its speaker encounters herself as a site of knowing, how her inhabitance radiates through a lyric approximation of voice such that the speaker *surrenders* to feeling so as to be *transformed* by feeling.[24]

I am trying to untangle this poem from its common interpretation as an anthem of opposition. Surely the speaker reckons with the harm of an antiblack, antiwoman world. And still, if we read "won't you celebrate with me" through its aliveness, we can behold its rendering of the speaker's knowing as happening through unknowing—an idiom of knowing as commencement, not conclusion. In a conceit of aliveness, we can appreciate Clifton's speaker as speaking in and to the world of herself, as a figure figuring (again, reckoning with harm, among other conditions), as a black female voice in thought. The poem renders this black female knowing as a wellspring capacity, an ontological case that moves not against but toward. I love the world and worldmaking of this poem, its self-oriented relationality where the speaker is also the addressee, such that when she says, "come celebrate," she is invoking herself as one who can withstand the invitation, whatever it may yield.

I love discerning and thinking with the work that Clifton's speaker does through the poem, work that is akin to the miracle of surviving every daily killing threat. "Come look at us," the speaker seems to whisper to *herself* as a being of multiplicity, a call that echoes the moment in Zora Neale Hurston's *Their Eyes Were Watching God* when Janie has finished telling her story to Pheoby and she, Janie, sits alone in her bedroom, remembering the telling and its wonder: "Here was peace. She pulled in her horizon like a great fish-net. Pulled it from around the waist of the world and draped it over her shoulder. So much of life in its meshes! She called in her soul to come and see" (184). Clifton's poem is a discourse on this call to study what one has endured, what one has become and is becoming through the enduring. In her slim, spare poem, we can glimpse the speaker's force of being, the surprise of her breadth as she is "sent" by herself to herself in the way Fred Moten means that term: "To be sent, to be transported out of yourself, it's an ecstatic experience, it's not an experience of interiority, it's an experience of exteriority, it's an exteriorization. And so we're sent. We're sent to one another. We are sent by one another to one another. . . . We're sent by one another to one another until one and another don't signify anymore" ("Interview"). I might take mild exception with Moten's characterization of interiority, since I understand this invocation as a principle of Lordean knowing, which means it is interior *and* beyond. And still, I am compelled by his "being sent" as an apt notion for thinking about "the fugitive being of 'infinite humanity'" (Moten, "The Case of Blackness" 214), as a synonym of aliveness: in a black world, we can be sent to one another and this being-sent characterizes not only how we are oriented to another but how we are oriented in our breadth of being.

I am being-sent in myself, which is the aliveness of a poem that permits a speaker to say "come celebrate."

The consideration of black aliveness is a consideration of knowing, about how we navigate knowing through terms other than reason or the binaried conditions of interior-exterior—aliveness as a fuller habitat for being in regard to one's being. Aliveness is an argument for blackness oriented toward towardness, and its case can only be made through a discourse of relation and in the terms of material habitat enacted within the poetic. "The highest point of knowledge is always a poetics," a leaning toward and an opening, Glissant tells us (*Poetics of Relation* 140).[25] Such poetics is a scene of relation, as it is for Lorde, Clifton, and here again in June Jordan's "These Poems," an *ars poetica* from her 1977 collection *Things That I Do in the Dark*:

These poems
they are things that I do
in the dark
reaching for you
whoever you are
and
are you ready?

These words
they are stones in the water
running away

These skeletal lines
they are desperate arms for my longing and love.

I am a stranger
learning to worship the strangers
around me

whoever you are
whoever I may become. (2)

I am interested especially in Jordan's characterization of the poetic as
materiality—as "skeletal lines" and yearning arms, as "stones in the water /
running away," where the awry movement could describe the water, the stones,
or both together as one propels the other. We might notice materiality also in
the opening metaphor, poems as "things that I do," particularly the speaker's
use of that enduring verb of human enactment and aliveness, "do." This description enlivens the poetic not as a thing written or made but as a thing one *does*.
Furthermore, Jordan's first three lines collate together synonyms of poetry such
that "These poems" is enjambed with the superfluous pronoun "they," which
is followed by a metaphorical referent for poems. It is as if the speaker were
saying poems ("These poems") poems ("they") are poems ("things I do")—and
if we read darkness as an oblique idiom of the poetic, then the speaker's manifesto commences with a four-part chant: poems poems are poems are poetic.

This tumbling opening sets up the deployment of relation as an invitation
to surrender. In Jordan's poem, the second person materializes as a corpus
of abundance for the speaker, who beckons toward an other who is not yet
known or met. The yearning is *toward* the intensity of being and of preparedness, an orientation marked by the query, "and / are you ready?" This question
might seem undirected, but it belongs expressly to the speaker, especially in
light of the first-person exposure in the poem's fourth stanza: "I am a stranger,"
the speaker asserts, privileging her own vulnerability, "I am a stranger / learning to worship the strangers / around me." I have repeated the stanza's first declarative line to emphasize the speaker's admission of transience, that rather
than marking the other as a stranger, Jordan's speaker situates otherness as
her relationality and announces herself as a subject of hesitant becoming. "I
am a stranger," says the poet, since what else is poetic inhabitance but a summons to yield to the sentiment of being alien? Appropriately, then, in the
beautiful closing couplet, it is the speaker whose capacity is capacious, a disposition most notable via the subjunctive verb in the last line: "whoever you
are / whoever I *may* become" (emphasis added). The poet-speaker here is left

alive in the poem, the one who will be made and unmade, the one oriented by becoming through a relational habitat. In Jordan's poem, the speaker occupies the subject position of both I and you, and the poetic is a "form-of-life," a genre for black being.[26]

Jordan's use of the stranger as an idiom of aliveness calls to mind Toni Morrison's "Strangers," her first-person narration of an encounter with an unknown fisherwoman. The essay is a relational marvel for its meditation on the borders of being—and the necessary, terrifying trespass of those borders—but also for the way that Morrison's prose unveils the speaker, Morrison herself, as the object of study; that is, the stranger here is not the fisherwoman who appears at the edge of the backyard and disappears after a single promising meeting, but is Morrison and the affective register revealed in her longing to embrace this strange woman's otherness. Morrison uses the encounter to figure through the upheaval of relationality: "To understand that I was longing for and missing some aspect of myself, and there are no strangers. There are only versions of ourselves, many of which we have not embraced, most of which we wish to protect ourselves from. For the stranger is not foreign, she is random, not alien but remembered; and it is the randomness of the encounter with our already known—although unacknowledged—selves that summons a ripple of alarm" (70).[27] This distilled clarity reprises the relational materiality in Jordan's "These Poems," the lurching toward the reckoning lurking within a poetic inhabitance. I read it as an articulation of the knowing to be had in a black world invitation to "come celebrate."

At stake in my study of Clifton and Jordan and Morrison is a claim about the second person not as an encasement of the other where the authority resides with the speaker, but as an occasion to consider the tender becoming of the speaking one, the one who calls the scene into being, the one who yields to the risk and possibility of venturing to say "you."[28] Again, relation's movement, its directionality, is an opening toward: "Relation is a direction which is not the direction toward unity but which remains a direction in any case" (Glissant, *Poetics of Relation* 10).[29] This towardness describes the aliveness I am conceptualizing through black poetics, the pulse of being and happening, the characterization of becoming that exists all over the world of black texts. In the relation of a black world, one can say "you" and can be undone by the saying.

This is aliveness, poetry as a knowing, as epistemology, "a revelatory distillation of experience" (Lorde, "Poetry Is Not a Luxury" 37): the poetic, which invites us to live in subjunctivity, which casts subjunctivity as an essential condition of being alive; the poetic, which as an ontology asks "what if." Indeed, what I am naming as a poetic might properly be characterized by the ancient Greek term *poiesis*, "the activity in which a person brings something into being that did not exist before."[30] In a black world, such ontological making constitutes the intelligence to be had in being through relationality, an aliveness that is of us and of the textual worlds we make.

2 ALIVENESS

AND ONENESS

In a black world imaginary, there is aliveness, blackness that gushes with existence, the *knowing* that Audre Lorde theorizes as embodied consciousness. Such aliveness carries the relational name of "oneness."

"One" is the pronoun case in which a human conceptualizes being through the capaciousness of herself, through the act of rendering herself as the figure of the impersonal. It is the syntax of philosophical self-projection where the speaker throws herself into question and possibility, imagining the instance that she is and is not (yet). As such, "one" is a fictional case and a habitat of apprehension; the person speaking through "one" makes herself into an object of specificity and breadth—she multiplies through this imaginary praxis. This is oneness, which is not synonymous with terms of individuality: oneness where the subject is always relational. The language here may be slippery, but I mean simply to advance oneness as the name for the praxis of beholding one's self, of engaging one's being as the basis for existing *in* and existing *with* one's questions of being.[1]

Oneness as a grammar of the materiality and immateriality of consciousness.

To be clear, oneness is not akin to individuality. The individual, as such circulates in the Western imaginary, is an incompatible and bankrupt idea for my study of black aliveness. For one, the notion of individuality is not possible for a black subject in an antiblack world, since blackness is always not only a collective designation but a collective indictment. There is no conceptual individuality possible for one who is black in an antiblack world. And indeed, the idea of individualism is too entangled with racial capitalism to infer the relational—the spiritually philosophical—register I mean by oneness.[2]

Oneness belongs, or should belong, to one who is black. And yet, the idea of oneness as an essential, even sacred, quality of being is antithetical to our common discourse of blackness. There is no one *for* blackness, no one *of* blackness—"What is missing in African-American cultural analysis is a concept of the 'one'" (394), Hortense Spillers asserted in 1996. Following Spillers, we can understand this conceptual absence—though it is only conceptual because each human is, in fact, a one—partly as a feature of New World slavery, particularly the gendering of the enslaved subject as both ideologically ungendered and ideologically feminine. This gender calculation produces the idea of blackness as nonbeing, as failed being in the terms of modernity. Said another way, the black exemption from oneness travels through black femaleness.[3]

I want, then, to consider oneness through black female figuring, via occasions where black female speakers inhabit the philosophical assumption of first-person expressiveness, where their "I am" constitutes instances of beholding the immanence and transcendence of being. I am interested in the ways that a black speaker's articulation of "I am" enunciates a state of worldness as well as an instantiation of her possibility. I know that these terms—"oneness," "immanence," "transcendence"—might give pause if we think of them as being conversant with individuality, transparency, overcoming. But all I mean here is the rightness of being that brings about one's becoming—the being that obliterates being. We might be anxious about oneness as a betrayal of community, though we should remember that the essentializing of community is a function of an antiblack reality. In a black world, one can be of relational oneness, relation as a world of one's becoming that includes being more than one.

I am in search of a oneness articulated through black femaleness, in particular statements of black female audaciousness—as in Lucille Clifton's speaker in "won't you celebrate with me," who announces, "i had no model." In Clifton's poem, this modellessness conspires with the invitation "come celebrate / with me," unfurls as a case of possibility realized through the audacity of being. And embedded in the claim "i had no model" is the speaker's contestation with her difference, her exemption from the scene of mattering:

> . . . i had no model.
> born in babylon
> both nonwhite and woman
> what did i see to be except myself? (427)

The poem's reference to difference and exception recalls the title of Gloria (now Akasha) T. Hull, Patricia Bell Scott, and Barbara Smith's 1982 anthology—*All the Women Are White, All the Blacks Are Men, but Some of Us Are Brave*.[4] In both examples, the troubling calculus of difference is used to generate righteous self-regard. That is, a pernicious idea of difference, where black femaleness marks degrees of the (non)human, confirms black exclusion from the open idea of being. And yet difference, as a concept, cannot be discarded easily, especially since nonhierarchical differentiation is a feature of relation and relation is essential to conceptualizing oneness.[5]

This entanglement means that the notion of difference has to be refigured in light of black female regard, which is precisely what happens in *The Cancer Journals*, Audre Lorde's reflections on her experience of cancer. The collection opens with a speaker poised in existential awareness: "Each woman responds to the crisis that breast cancer brings to her life out of a whole pattern, which is the design of who she is and how her life has been lived" (7). Here, the speaker explains that the particularity of one's life is the basis on which one has experience, that one's living is a theoretical model ("a whole pattern") for beholding each happening. I know this is a commonsense idea, but its straightforward conceptual clarity resonates with Lorde's earlier arguments about consciousness and extends the philosophical inflection of the notion of self-regard. Interesting, too, is how Lorde's pronoun case moves from the impersonal idioms "each woman" (as in the foregoing quotation) and "some women" (later in the paragraph) to the first person: "I am a post-mastectomy woman who believes our feelings need voice in order to be recognized, respected, and of use" (7). This movement reflects the capaciousness of the speaker, who expresses herself through a mix of personal and impersonal, through the plural ("our feelings") and the singular.

Later, in the third journal entry, this world of self-centeredness becomes explicit: "*I feel so unequal to what I always handled before, the abominations outside that echo the pain within. And yes I am completely self-referenced right now because it is the only translation I can trust, and I do believe not until every woman traces her weave* back strand by bloody self-referenced strand, will we begin to alter the whole pattern" (9; italics in original, emphasis added). Lorde's speaker might well have said "alter the whole world," since her stance is against patriarchal disregard for women's experience and intelligence. And yet the repetition of "whole pattern" works to collapse the world of one's being—what is implied earlier—with the social world. In making this claim, Lorde constructs first-personness as a subjectivity of exception and exemption, *a human case that orients through one's singular differences*. This is the theoretical apparatus of her encounter with cancer, a philosophical first-person subjection that she designates as "sister outsider" and explicates in an October 1979 entry: "*I am defined as other in every group I'm a part of. The outsider, both strength and weakness*" (11; italics in original).[6]

Exemption and exception: in *The Cancer Journals*, autobiographical study, even something as episodically casual as journal entries, swells with conceptual insight.[7] The intellectual character of Lorde's first-person thinking is evident in an entry dated just after her mastectomy:

March 25, 1978

The idea of knowing, rather than believing, trusting, or even understanding has always been considered heretical. But I would willingly pay whatever price in pain was needed, to savor the weight of completion; to be utterly filled, not with conviction nor with faith, but with experience—knowledge, direct and different from all other certainties. (23; italics in original)

Lorde advocates for the supremacy of knowing that comes through experience ("*knowledge, direct and different from all other certainties*"), seeming to echo Michel de Montaigne, who, in "Of Experience," acknowledges that in the pursuit of knowledge, "when reason fails us, we use experience" (407).[8] Moreover, she aligns her speaker with the biblical Eve, whose yearning to know exceeded faith and initiated a fall into ungrace. Again, as Lorde does in "Poetry Is Not a Luxury" and "The Uses of the Erotic," she collates true knowing with embodiment. And throughout *Journals*, Lorde's intellection appeals to her exquisite practice of self-reflection:

Once I accept the existence of dying, as a life process, who can ever have power over me again? (25; italics in original)

Where are the models for what I'm supposed to be in this situation? But there are none. That is it, Audre. You're on your own. (28)

The enunciation of singularity, another instance of modellessness, is not literal as much as it is intended to incite and express the speaker's understanding, to authorize a different conceptualization of her capacity. These ideological investments are realized beautifully in the speaker's comments upon leaving the hospital:

> In that critical period, the family women enhanced that answer [to the question of death]. They were macro members in the life dance, seeking an answering rhythm within my sinews, my synapses, my very bones. In the ghost of my right breast, these were the micro members from within. There was an answering rhythm in the ghost of those dreams which would have to go in favor of those which I had some chance of effecting. . . .
>
> For instance, I will never be a doctor. I will never be a deep-sea diver. I may possibly take a doctorate in etymology, but I will never bear any more children. I will never learn ballet, nor become a great actress, although I might learn to ride a bike and travel to the moon. But I will never be a millionaire nor increase my life insurance. *I am who the world and I have never seen before.* (47–48; emphasis added)

This passage leaves me breathless, how it travels toward that striking crescendo of instantiation: Notice how the speaker begins with "the family women," a cohort of her friends, her lovers, and her daughter that is fused to her body and metabolized as her removed breast. And after a random catalog of dreaming and loss described in the future conditional tense ("I will never . . . I will never"), the speaker declares herself—singular but also composed of many women—as totality and impossibility: "I am who the world and I have never seen before." Her accounting of possibility marks the limits of capitalist reality for her black female self ("I will never be a millionaire") and then surpasses such valuation with a surrender to her becoming. Has there ever been a statement that articulates the risk and surety of aliveness as clearly as this one; that conceptualizes a poetic calculus of being human as finely as this declaration of being-as-poiesis? Maybe not.

"I am who the world and I have never seen before." What compels me are three ways that this definitive expression of exceptionalism functions: For one, Lorde means the statement *literally* as a characterization of the representational invisibility of black queer women, as in "Where were the dykes who had had mastectomies?" (50). Second, this statement is *epistemological* since it theorizes how knowing happens—that one knows through surprise, ignorance, the upending of clarity. And third, most vitally, Lorde's exceptionalism is *ontological*, an enunciation of being through a revision of God's statement of immanence to Moses ("I am that I am"). Not even the speaker herself has encountered herself in this manner, this capacity, so new and alive she is, so rife with knowing "direct and different from all other certainties" (23).

"I am who the world and I have never seen before," this idea of a black-female one, an idiom of certainty that dissolves into terrifying uncertainty, an audacious subjectivity that is at once of immanence and of transcendence.

In Lorde's writing, black femaleness is the position of thought—this is its oneness, where oneness is relationality, the "being singular plural," "the moment when one consents not to be a single being."[9] My pursuit of an idea of oneness co-opts the first person as a philosophical grammar of being. Philosophy, after all, can be described as "life itself—the life of an individual," or more precisely the *questions* about being alive considered through the life of a one.[10] As such, philosophical inhabitance is less the particular case of "I" and more the audacious habitat of one, an engagement of righteous query: to bear the weight of being that includes beholding oneself as an object of and for one's study. We can recognize such audacity in the long arc of black women's thinking across various genres:

— Sojourner Truth's 1851 Akron, Ohio, convention address testifies through her first-person singularity, summarized by the misattributed refrain "arn't I a woman."

— Anna Julia Cooper announces in 1886 that "only the BLACK WOMAN can say 'when and where I enter . . . then and there the whole Negro race enters with me'" (63).

— Hortense Spillers's 1987 speaker proclaims indispensability at the beginning of "Mama's Baby, Papa's Maybe": "Let's face it. I am a marked woman, but not everybody knows my name. . . . My country needs me, and if I were not here, I would have to be invented" (203).

— Trudier Harris begins *From Mammies to Militants: Domestics in Black American Literature* (1982) with this brilliance: "Called Matriarch, Emasculator and Hot Momma. Sometimes Sister, Pretty Baby, Auntie, Mammy and Girl. Called Unwed Mother, Welfare Recipient and Inner City Consumer. The Black American Woman has had to admit that while nobody knew the troubles she saw, everybody, his brother and his dog, felt qualified to explain her, even to herself" (4).

— Patricia J. Williams's *The Alchemy of Race and Rights: Diary of a Law Professor*, a 1991 book of American legal theory, opens thus: "Since subject position is everything in my analysis of law, you deserve to know that it's a bad morning. I am very depressed. . . . So you should know that this is one those mornings when I refuse to compose myself properly; you should know you are dealing with someone who is writing this in an old terry bathrobe with a little fringe of blue and white tassels [*sic*] dangling from the hem, trying to decide if she is stupid or crazy" (4). This finely rendered theorizing operates on the premise that black female being is being.

— Barbara Christian's enduring essay "The Race for Theory" (1987) states, "I can only speak for myself. But what I write and how I write is done in order to save my own life. And I mean that literally. For me literature is a way of knowing that I am not hallucinating, that whatever I feel/ know *is*. It is an affirmation that sensuality is intelligence, that sensual language is language that makes sense" (61; emphasis in original).

I am struck, always, by the repetition of self-regard as an essential component of black female relationality, self-regard as an inauguration of philosophical endeavoring: from Clifton's "no model" to June Jordan's "we are the ones we have been waiting for" to Ntozake Shange's choral "i found god in myself / & i loved her/ i loved her fiercely" to Alice Walker's womanist who "Loves herself. *Regardless*" to Maya Angelou's "phenomenal woman" and Nikki Giovanni's abiding "I am so perfect so divine so ethereal so surreal / I cannot be comprehended / except by my permission"—this from a poem that begins with a speaker full of capaciousness who proclaims, "I was born in the congo / I walked the fertile crescent and built the sphinx," and concludes her self-invocation with "I am bad."[11] These citations are a small sample of a canon of intellection that dares to imagine a black female subject as *first person*, where that term doesn't imply indigeneity (as in the case to be made for First Nations peoples), Enlightenment rationality, or integrity of voice; first person here is the syntax of relational inhabitance, the possibility that the surprise and incommensurability of being could belong to one who is black and female, the "monumental first person" of the one who dares to say, I am and I am becoming.[12]

The particularity of this conceptual move requires that I be repeatedly explicit about the quality of surrender—of openness and fluency—in black female first-person instantiation. Specifically, I am thinking of the argument Stephen Michael Best makes in *None like Us*, especially his critique of the historical conflation of *voice* and community as a black studies imperative. Voice, he suggests rightly, becomes something of a cult, a rigid compulsion that disregards other aesthetic dimensions at work in black art, especially a recognition of an "aesthetics of the intransmissible" that strives not to represent or assert blackness but rather "to either close itself off or use itself up" (22). Contemporary visual artists are "in the process of enacting a kind of thought that literary critics are not yet willing to entertain, that they [artists] may be enacting a 'style' of freedom:

freedom from constraining conceptions of blackness as authenticity, tradition, and legitimacy; or history as inheritance, memory, and social reproduction; of diaspora as kinship, belonging, and dissemination" (22–23). Best wants us to explore the possibility of one's "beautiful elimination," the capacity to encounter erasure and obliteration (29). His provocation delineates the limits of voice—the first person—as a trope of recuperative black aesthetics, a limit that is inflected by collectivism as a response to pervasive antiblackness. Inspired by Best, I want to insist on reading the vocative in a *black world imaginary* and as a term of *relation*, relation that encompasses risk, surrender, obliteration, relation that operates not on the security of being but on the openness of becoming. I am trying to recognize the fluency and nuance in black first-person vocative instances. Take, for example, Giovanni's ego trip mentioned earlier, which closes,

> I am so perfect so divine so ethereal so surreal
> I cannot be comprehended
>   except by my permission
>
> I mean . . . I . . . can fly
> like a bird in the sky . . . (126; ellipses in the original)

If we look critically, we can appreciate Giovanni's speaker's voice searching for its right to know so that it might surrender into what it doesn't yet behold, especially there in the ellipses, which break open the speaker's unrepresentable being, a chasm to which the egoed one has surrendered. I am reading this example of the first person, and the others cataloged earlier, as lyric inflections. That is, the lyric idiomizes voice as subjectivity *and* subjection; in the lyric, the speaker speaks fully—declaratively—without betraying the vulnerable hesitancy of their knowing. The vitality of the lyric voice is toward the speaker's surrender to the *energy*, the rambunction, of voice. We often misread the lyric via "the assumed solidity of the speaking, universal 'I,'" and, as literary scholar Anthony Reed argues, in doing so, we miss the ways in which the form has evolved, especially in regard to black poetics (99).[13]

Poetic being is experimental being (or being experimental), and what I intend to recognize via the first person is an idiom of our oneness *through relationality*, to use relation to license a black (female) philosophy of self-regard. I intend to remember that "one" is a fictional case, a projection for being in the world, an "Afro-fabulation" thought experiment, in the phrasing of performance studies theorist Tavia Nyong'o.[14] Oneness doesn't belong to the reparative work of black community instantiated by antiblack terror. No, oneness resides with the one and the world of the one's becoming. Moreover, no one, truly, can be excluded from the capacities of oneness, just as no one can presume to possess or be in possession of it.

One, the proper impersonal pronoun that casts its speaker not as an individual secured against other individuals but as a figure of being, a projection for conceptualizing being. As such, my consideration here is of the lyric "one" rather than the lyric "I."[15]

Of course, if we are talking about oneness as a dialectic of being, then we must revisit Toni Morrison's abidingly important 1973 novel *Sula*, especially its title character, whose audacity is totality, whose orientation beholds oneness as an ordinary feature of her consciousness. We could consider being and relationality through the novel's many couplings, including a girlhood friendship between Sula and Nel that lasts beyond death; romantic partnerings that seem to break under stress (including between Nel and Jude, Eva and Boy-Boy, Hannah and various men, and Helene and Wiley Wright); and platonic alliances that, in their intensities, prompt some kind of reckoning (for example, Plum and Eva; Sula and Hannah; the grouping of boys named the Deweys; Eva and Sula; Eva and Hannah; Sula and Ajax; Sula's dalliances with random men; and Sula and Shadrack). In this landscape of relations, the common wisdom is that "Sula never competed; she simply helped others define themselves" (95), though such an assessment invites us to overlook Sula's own intersubjective vitality. Indeed, Sula is not merely the figure who animates the novel's dynamics, but instead her being is in-process . . . Sula is one of relational becoming: "She *had been looking* all along for a friend, and it took her a while to *discover* that a lover was not a comrade and could never be—for a woman. And that no one would ever be that version of herself which she sought to reach out to and touch with an ungloved hand. There was only her own mood and whim, and if that was all there was, she decided to turn the naked hand toward it, discover it and let others become as intimate with their own selves as she was" (121; emphases added). This exposition comes soon after the townspeople render judgment of Sula's selfish doings, especially her affair with Nel's husband and her decision to put Eva, her grandmother, in a nursing home. Notice, then, how the verbs ("had been looking," "discover") focus our attention on Sula's subjectivity-information; that is, against any easy dismissal of Sula's motivations, the passage privies us to her process of discernment. Notable also is the way the voice here nearly slips from narrator to character, especially via the em dash, which delays and highlights the phrase "for a woman." In this syntax, the tag comment collates Sula's and the narrator's ironic emphasis on the difference between a generic conception of being where relationality might be possible, and the restricted subjectivity that is imagined for women. It is a shared verbal exclamation, "for a woman," nearly as exasperated as it is definite. As such, the narrator is allied with Sula, and the narrative positions us to appreciate the thinking that underpins her resolve toward self-regard. A close reader of the novel will likely remember a similar realization of exemption-and-exception that coheres Sula's friendship with Nel: "So when they met . . . they felt the ease and comfort of old friends. Because each had discovered years before that they were neither white nor male, and that all freedom and triumph was forbidden to them, they had set about creating something else to be" (52). The novel brims with discernments like this one that portray a black female subject philosophizing life through *her* life, a one engaged in being and becoming.[16]

Since Morrison's novel is an *ars erotica*, it presents Sula's relationality through encounters with the erotic:

> Although she did not regard sex as ugly (ugliness was boring also), she liked to think of it as wicked. But *as her experiences multiplied, she realized* that not only was it not wicked, it was not necessary for her to conjure up the idea of wickedness in order to participate fully. During the lovemaking she found and needed to find the cutting edge. *When she left off cooperating with her body and began to assert herself in the act, particles of strength gathered in her like steel shavings drawn to a spacious magnetic center, forming a tight cluster that nothing, it seemed, could break.* And there was utmost irony and outrage lying under someone, in a position of surrender, *feeling her own abiding strength and limitless power*[,] . . . the postcoital privateness in which *she met herself, welcomed herself, and joined herself in matchless harmony.* (123; emphases added)

At the end of this passage, notice especially the verbs—"met," "welcomed," "joined"—which usually indicate connection between one and another one but which are attached, each time, to the reflexive pronoun "herself." This syntax reinforces the "matchless harmony" of Sula's experience, an electric habitat of contemplativeness as a conflation of embodiment and intellection. Said another way, Sula's inhabitance of being navigates through a lyric conceptualization of materiality (a "cluster") that doesn't last (it dissipates) but that nonetheless informs her understanding of herself as a one of relationality. We are watching Sula conceptualize and enact capaciousness through the imperative for beholding herself.[17]

What follows this determination is Sula's coupling with Ajax, perhaps a culmination of interest piqued twenty years earlier when Sula was an adolescent girl. As adults, Ajax and Sula have sex that is so sublime, it initiates in Sula a postcoital desire to rub or scrape off his skin layer by layer so as to study the body's materiality. "*If I take a chamois and rub real hard on the bone, right on the ledge of your cheek bone, some of the black will disappear*" (130; italics in original), the passage subjunctively begins, before extending for nearly a full page of italicized meditation. It is in this relationship with Ajax that "Sula began to discover what possession was. Not love, perhaps, but possession or at least the desire for it. She was astounded by *so new and alien a feeling*" (131; emphasis added). Morrison's language parallels Lorde's statement of exception, "I am what the world and I have never seen before." Sula is inquisitive and of discovery, so of course she would surrender to this foreign, thrilling feeling. And yet, what complicates this moment is that Sula's surrender includes performing acts of domesticity that seem contrary to her earlier self-belief: she anticipates and prepares for Ajax's arrival by putting her hair in a ribbon, cleaning the house, setting the table with a rose; she indulges his whininess about life's difficulty by telling him, "Come on. Lean on me" (133). If we forget that Sula is in process, then we might read this happening as a lapse or a confusing self-betrayal. But Sula is relational, and being with Ajax offers her a chance to refine what being is. She is free to risk inquisitiveness about this new feeling, rather than only to conserve or protect herself in keeping with a notion of female frailty. Indeed, since it is true that "during the lovemaking she *found and needed to find* the cutting edge" (123; emphasis added), Sula is almost compelled to pursue the risk. What matters more than Ajax's presence and his eventual absence is the inquiry ignited by her doings. As such, her display of domesticity is a scene of play, a fantasy akin to her daydream of dissecting Ajax's body, another opportunity for Sula to deepen her study of her life. Sula *feels* herself, feels in and through herself, and becomes other-than-she-is through this encounter.[18]

To be "astounded by so new and alien a feeling"—this is black female audacity, a relational inhabitance of being oriented toward one's becoming new. Such a disposition is reinforced in the chapter's conclusion, after Ajax is gone, when Sula wakes up with

> a melody in her head she could not identify or recall ever hearing before. "Perhaps I made it up," she thought. Then it came to her—the name of the song and all its lyrics just as she had heard it many times before. She sat on the edge of the bed thinking, "There aren't any more new songs and I have sung all the ones there are. I have sung them all. I have sung all the songs there are." She lay down again on the bed and sang a little wandering tune made up of the words *I have sung all the songs all the songs I have sung all the songs there are* until, touched by her own lullaby, she grew drowsy, and in the hollow of near-sleep she tasted the acridness of gold, left the chill of alabaster and smelled the dark, sweet stench of loam. (137; emphasis in original)

I love how this passage describes Sula's totality, she who countenances small-ness and obliteration with inventiveness—with a self-made song of songs, sung without audience; she whose orientation is of oneness—supreme and wide open, full and emptying, a being the world and herself has never seen before, "a new dimension of being," as Spillers termed it in an early reading of the book (93).[19] We should note that Sula's totality is inflected by the subjunctive, by possibility and risk and becoming; for Sula, "[a] conditional subjunctive replaces an indicative certainty" (Spillers 95). Moreover, this deathbed oneness resonates with my claim for an expansive understanding of the black female vocative; consider the case Spillers makes about the black female singer:

> To find another and truer sexual self-image the black woman must turn to the domain of music and America's black female vocalists, who suggest a composite figure of ironical grace. The singer is likely closer to the poetry of black female sexual experience than we might think, not so much, interestingly enough, in the words of her music, but in the *sense of dramatic confrontation between ego and world that the vocalist herself embodies.* . . . In this instance of *being-for-self*, it does not matter that the vocalist is "entertaining" under American skies because *the woman, in her particular and vivid thereness, is an unalterable and discrete moment of self-knowledge.* (165; emphases added)

Yes, yes, yes: black female oneness is this vivid "thereness," "unalterable and discrete," a wonder of consciousness materialized through the metaphysics of being in one's voice.

Morrison's *Sula* is a superb philosophical meditation, especially in regard to Sula's audacious conceptualization of herself as a one through whom life can be understood. This imagining of oneness turns on Sula's appreciation of her distinction (black and female), as well as on her willingness to give up the distinction in favor of being and becoming totality. That is, oneness, as an imaginary—as a fictional case and a projection—sustains Sula in her embrace of the everything and nothing of existence. We see this existential breadth in an exchange with Nel when Sula is near death: after Nel cautions her against the arrogance of her thinking—"You *can't* do it all. You a woman and a colored woman at that. You can't act like a man"—Sula responds, "You repeating yourself. . . . You say I'm a woman and colored. Ain't that the same as being a man?" (142; emphasis in original). Sula's statement of difference refuses Nel's construct of black femaleness as a diminishing mark of otherness. Instead, in Sula's worldview, a person who is black and female is *also* a human being and therefore is capable of figuring being through the specificity of her difference, which is, after all, no difference at all. Akin to Audre Lorde's relationality, Sula's difference exists *within* the subject rather than as an ideological discourse outside and against the subject.

Sula, this mighty rendering of black female being through which we can study black existence, *Sula*, where freedom already is in and of the one.

I have leaned on Morrison's character to explore what is essentially a matter of ethics—how to be—even as literary scholars like Alex Nissen have argued that Sula, in her self-centeredness, "is not fully a moral agent and cannot be a model for emulation" (276). Such a conclusion fails to appreciate Sula's *relational* orientation; indeed, the full regard Sula tries to have for herself is the full regard she wants to have for other people—to engage others as if they are of full regard. Her worldview depends on the mutuality of encountering others as ones of their own unfurling totality. (Remember that she is described as having "no ego and no greed" and that she wants to "let others become as intimate with their own selves as she was" [119, 121]). Embedded in relationality is an invitation for open being where fullness inclines toward and inspires fullness.[20]

The reluctance to acknowledge Sula's deep ethicality might derive partly from the specificity of her being black and female—it is unusual to encounter the question of existence articulated so clearly through a black female subject for whom pure existence, the rightness of her existence, is never really in question (in process, yes, but not in question). As such, Morrison's novel rests on the gambit that a black woman could proceed in life as if she were the idiomatic human. For Sula, being alive and being of a righteous human inhabitance doesn't depend on commonsense ideas about possessive individualism, nor is it hampered by disproving nonbeing. No, Sula's oneness is a relational totality, a black world instance where "How do I live free in this black [female] body?" becomes a question of oneness.[21] Again, oneness authorizes one to be more and more human, to seek more and more capacity for good(ness) and right(ness), an ever-widening pool of being that surpasses narcissism. Our challenge, then, is to imagine oneness as the plurality possible through the *specificity* of one's open inhabiting of the world.

And Sula's example makes me want to be clear about abstraction and transcendence as features of relational oneness. That is, the very notion of becoming infers projection, idealization, transformation. I know that classic relational theory argues against abstraction, an argument expressed well by Édouard Glissant's claim that the universal "is a sublimation, an abstraction that enables us to forget small differences; we drift upon the universal and forget these small differences, and Relation is wonderful because it doesn't allow us to do that" ("One World in Relation" 9). But this insight conflicts slightly with the *transcendence* inherent in relation, the fact that in relation, one is called to surpass and trespass—transcend—the *imagined* boundaries of one's being. Relation, as cultural philosopher Lewis R. Gordon argues in *Bad Faith and Antiblack Racism*, is at once immanence and transcendence, where transcendence is a deepening of the surprise of one's being, rather than a transcendence that moves the self into a metaphysical that has no connection to embodiment or experience. In refining this point, it might help to emphasize that Sula's oneness is established via the erotic; as such, her transcendent postcoital meditation isn't an instance of overcoming as much as it is a surrender into being everything and nothing, an occasion of breadth. Transcendence here commingles with immanence, immanence with transcendence.[22]

Describing oneness is complicated. Better, perhaps, to say that aliveness is of a black world orientation where oneness is "inglorious," as theologian J. Kameron Carter means the term to describe "God's being as a unified difference of persons [that] already contains every possible difference, including the difference of a created, 'exterior' world" (78). Such an idiom of godliness helps us to appreciate Sula's oneness, an ethos that surges from the wildness of feeling, a worldliness of inhabitance that cannot properly be called a model—a prescription or rubric—since it is an invocation into dynamic being. Indeed, when Clifton's speaker says, "i had no model," we might well understand this confession for its ideological astuteness—that there is no model, there is just the knowing in living and the living through.

Oneness is a practice of knowing that could be described as I-am-knowing-as-I-am-knowing. In this compounded phrase, the first clause establishes certainty and the second revels in dissolution. The ethos here is a fidelity to what one knows so as to deepen and then surpass that knowing.

I am knowing as I am knowing.

There is no better study of this notion than *Sula*, which asks us to consider that the world of being lives also in people who are female and black.[23] Sula, who encounters and is remade, who encounters and becomes; she who reminds us that relation is not a dissolving into the other but a capacity to become more and more through the relation. Relational being is like being a poem, a textuality that is itself and that also unfurls as more every moment.[24]

Ah: in relation, you are a poem, are poiesis—being brought and bringing one's self into being. This is oneness, is subjunctive inhabitance.

"One" is a fictional case, it is imaginary; it works properly, perhaps entirely, via abstraction: the self abstracting itself. I am enthralled by "one" as a pronoun for an aliveness that constitutes specificity, materiality, *and* breadth; consider this example from Gwendolyn Brooks's *Maud Martha*: the scene happens in chapter 30, titled "At the Burns-Coopers'," and narrates the brief time Maud Martha spends as a domestic worker for Mrs. Burns-Cooper, a character described as "a little red and white and black woman" (158). Like the novel as a whole, this chapter is brief and episodic, refracted through the interior consciousness of Maud Martha, who doesn't say much in exchanges with other characters but whose voice, habitat, and urgency radiate through Brooks's poetic language and through free, indirect narration that allies narrator and protagonist. *Maud Martha*'s is a relational world, and none of its thirty-four vignettes could be said to be more or less vital than any other; it is, really, a gathering of happenings that elides sequentiality or causation, privileging instead the intensity of its title character's experiences. At the close of this scene, Maud Martha decides to quit the job:

> I'll never come back, Maud Martha assured herself, when she hung up her apron at eight in the evening. She knew Mrs. Burns-Cooper would be puzzled. The wages were very good. Indeed, what could be said in explanation? Perhaps that the hours were long. I couldn't explain *my* explanation, she thought.
>
> One walked out from that almost perfect wall, spitting at the firing squad. What difference did it make whether the firing squad understood or did not understand the manner of one's retaliation or why one had to retaliate?
>
> Why, one was a human being. One wore clean nightgowns. One loved one's baby. One drank cocoa by the fire—or the gas range—come the evening, in the wintertime. (163; emphasis in original)

The abstraction here is fantastic, even radical, as the speaker forgoes explanation—transparency—and lapses into a meditative tableau where her decision emerges as a dramatic scene of death, judgment, and the clarity of being before a firing squad. And though I love the last sentence's insistence that cocoa can be made by gas range, it is the philosophical shift from first-person singular to third-person impersonal that takes my breath away—the ideological procession from "I" to "one." In this move, Brooks's characterization bypasses the presumed authority of the first-person voice so as to imagine her black female speaker—of interior voice—as the case of a "one," the address of the human engaged in exemplary study. Maud Martha throws her voice, an astute deployment of distance and self-abstraction toward discerning more clearly the depth of her feeling and knowing. The abstraction is not a deferral of feeling or particularity, but a deepening of precisely that: "One was a human being. One wore. . . . One loved. . . . One drank. . . ."

In Brooks's idiom, the referent for Maud Martha's speaking moves from "I," the authoritative singular first-person pronoun, to "one," the impersonal pronoun. And yet, what is achieved in the movement to "one" is the force of *personal* reckoning, the speaker's encounter with her ontological condition. As such, one is not individual but is personal, an instance of aliveness. What a beautiful rendering of a beautiful instance of a human being being of and in her oneness.[25]

In "Interstices: A Small Drama of Words," Hortense J. Spillers argues that "the fact of domination is alterable only to the extent that the dominated subject recognizes the potential power of its own 'double-consciousness.' The subject is certainly seen, but she also sees. It is this return of the gaze that negotiates at every point a space for living" (163). Here, Spillers advocates for one's act of *seeing* as a profound agency, and I want to extend seeing not only as a "return of the gaze" but as a calculus of self-orienting: of seeing one's self, of being engaged in the act of beholding one's self as a one. Or, to be the object and subject of study, to be the theorist of one's being as well as to be the thing made in the theorizing of being: again poiesis, where ideation constitutes the breadth of aliveness rather than inaugurating the denigration of breath. This characterization resonates with the lyric poem, a domain of being where a speaker can render themself as object for the sake of beholding experience and feeling. In this way, the lyric is a "textural and textual" world (to borrow from Anthony Reed), not "the assumed solidity of the speaking, universal 'I,'" but the subjective consciousness of one multiplying, dissolving, even extinguishing, one free to withstand their intimacy intimately. (Remember that the lyric's condition of objectification operates on ecstasy, which, in the Greek, means standing outside oneself.)[26]

I know that the matter of objectification is endemic in antiblackness, though in black critical studies, there is an inspiring engagement of being-object—DuBois's "How does it feel to be a problem?," Fred Moten's resistance of the object, Spillers's black femaleness that awaits a proper verb, Frantz Fanon's "Then I found I was an object in the midst of other objects," Margo Natalie Crawford's exploration of the "strategic abstraction" in the Black Arts movement. This engagement extends to contemporary black poetics: Lucille Clifton's "homage to my hips," Tracy K. Smith's "Flores Woman" (as well as much of *Duende*), Dionne Brand's "Blues Spiritual for Mammy Prater," nearly all of Robin Coste Lewis's *Voyage of the Sable Venus*, Jericho Brown's "Colosseum," Nikky Finney's "Aureole" and "Head Off & Split," Danez Smith's *[insert] boy*, Rita Dove's "Oriental Ballerina," Harryette Mullen's *Muse and Drudge*, Lyrae Van Clief-Stefanon's *Open Interval*, Marlene Nourbese Philip's idiom of the tongue in *She Tries Her Tongue, Her Silence Softly Breaks*. My prejudice here is the poetic, and I could stretch this random list for pages. Or I could limit my scope to poems that attend to examples of exceptional objectification, poems about Saartjie Baartman, the black woman misnamed as the Venus Hottentot (for example, Finney's "Greatest Show on Earth," Elizabeth Alexander's *Venus Hottentot*). Or all of Bettina Judd's *Patient.*, that exquisite rendering of black women's harming "ordeal" with the science and economies of display, women like Anarcha Wescott, Betsey Harris, Lucy Zimmerman, Joice Heth, Henrietta Lacks, and Bettina Judd herself.[27]

Sigh.

Here's the point, at least the place where I want to focus for now: as with Audre Lorde's *The Cancer Journals*, I want to consider how texts exploit the electric vagary of materiality, how they explicate knowing through the language of being-object. I am interested, especially, in seizing these lyric renderings as instances of the personal-impersonal inherent in first-personness. In this pursuit, I am following Elizabeth Alexander's insistent question from *The Black Interior*: "Where is our abstract space, our space of the real/not-real, our own unconscious?" (7). Or, more expansively, the argument Phillip Brian Harper undertakes in *Abstractionist Aesthetics*: "Abstractionism . . . entails the resolute awareness that even the most realistic representation is precisely a *representation*, and that as such it necessarily exists at a distance from the social reality it is conventionally understood to reflect. In other words, . . . any artwork whatsoever is definitionally *abstract* in relation to the world in which it emerges" (2; emphases in original). This declaration of abstraction articulates a framework for locating oneness in the aesthetics of objectness, a doing that is (more?) possible in a black world imaginary. And though neither of the two examples that follow uses the pronoun "one," in each case, the projection of the speaker as subject, object, god—the inglorious of Carter's characterization earlier—manifests a compelling abstraction that is consonant with the language of oneness.

First, Evie Shockley's "my life as china" (5) from her 2011 collection *The New Black*:

> i was imported : : i was soft in the hills where they found me : : shining
>   in a private dark
> : : i absorbed fire and became fact : : i was fragile : : i incorporated burnt
>   cattle bones'
> powdered remains : : ashes to ashes : : i was baptized in heat : : fed on
>   destruction : :
> i was not destroyer : : was not destroyed : : i vitrified : : none of me was
>   the same : :

i was many : : how can i say this : : i was domesticated : : trusted : :
    treasured : : i was
translucent but not clear : : put me to your lips : : i will not give : : i will
    give you what
you have given me

I love the double colons here, how they punctuate the poem's prose lines with a syntax of analogy, making explicit the one-to-one correlation between the subjected black female and the enamel material object.[28] But the punctuation also implies the relationality of the speaking one, each colon appearing as a visual approximation of the self meeting herself. I want to start, then, with the idea that the poem's doubleness multiplies the speaker's capacity, she who is figured as a porcelain object and violated human, and who narrates the scenes of her being. Notice, for example, how the speaker's voice becomes atmospheric in the sequence, "i was soft in the hills where they found me : : shining in a private dark." The second clause abandons the first-person referent so even as we understand it to mean "[i was] shining in a private dark," the absence of noun and auxiliary verb disconnects the act from a specific subject. As an elliptical phrase, "shining in a private dark" emanates broadly as if it were a description of something spiritual. A similar expansiveness and unmooring happen with "fed on destruction" and especially "was not destroyed," where the speaker's referent again eludes and surpasses the specificity of "i." We are to understand, via the rules of grammar, that the first-person refrain, and even the auxiliary verb, applies sylleptically (syllepsis: a phrasing in which one word inflects two others differently). But the poetic moves in "my life as china" ask us to attend to the vagary of voice.

In this regard, the poem's center is the dramatic clause "i vitrified," where the lack of an auxiliary verb intensifies the action as a statement of immanence and transcendence. The speaker wasn't *made into* glass by something external but *became* glassy substance. I don't mean to preclude the harmful impact of external forces but more to displace the sequence of impact as operating from external to internal, as if the world of happening changed the speaker. The subject-verb pairing here instantiates the speaker's willfulness, a god-minded force who incorporates force (against) into more force (of being): "i vitrified." And as if to reinforce our sense of her multiplicity, the speaker says "i was many" as a prelude to articulating her right to opacity: "i was translucent but not clear."

Such willfulness exists in tension with the fact that things happened to—were imposed on—the speaker, as in "i was domesticated : : trusted : : treasured." But even here we have to read through the syllepsis to appreciate the relationship between "trusted" and "treasured" and the phrase "i was." That is, domestication stands firmly as a term of harm ("i was domesticated"), which inflects how we understand "trusted" and "treasured" but not entirely, because those words float untethered from the syntax. In this short sequence of five words, the speaker agitates between being subject and being object of the three happenings (the three verbs) described.

Shockley's doubled aesthetics amplifies the oneness of the poem's speaker, the vast terrain of her harsh and vibrant encounter with being. Indeed, the poem's doubling (in its logic and its language) encourages us to recognize the speaker's speaking as an encounter, as her facing herself. It is in the context of oneness, then, that I read the poem's shift to the imperative and to the second person: "put me to your lips : : i will not give : : i will give you / what you have given me." We have seen already the capaciousness of the speaker engaged in the act of narrating her living, and this closing directive reinforces that capacity. Again, the verbs do superlative work in these last three lines, moving from a demand or a dare ("put me") to a refusal (where "give" means either "provide" or "yield") and finally to a remarkable threat of relational openness. The final declaration ripples as the habitat of the speaking one, her compounding claim that is directed to the cosmos that she is and has become.[29]

The instances of doubling in Shockley's "my life as china" unfurl a world of the speaker's becoming through the paired colons and the sylleptic syntax, the work of being-object. The speaker's oneness intensifies through all this object work that is neither loss nor exchange (not one thing for another) but an accumulation. As such, Shockley's speaker doesn't possess herself, her china-made life, as much as she is possessed by the force of being in relation with herself.[30]

In "my life as china," the question is about being of the force of one's life as object, or, said another way, "The / question is: once made into an object-for- / the other, how can the thing-for-itself survive?" (16). This is the way that Cameron Awkward-Rich announces the relationality of black being in a poem from *Sympathetic Little Monster*, a collection that studies object relations via a transgendered subject caught in the perils of identification. In the face of (un)ordinary gendered encounters, Awkward-Rich's speaker suspends in transit, a being flung and in flight through the social prerogative of identity. But the travel here—and *Transit* was the title of his first verse collection—is not necessarily *between* two places but *through* states or genres of being. That is, rather than constructing a black trans speaker as a symbol of binaried gender, Awkward-Rich's poems instead characterize the speaker's being as a state of traveling *through*. In this way, he instantiates a black transgendered figure of oneness, a speaker who encounters their own difficult self and who is object and subject of their study. It is a centering of the speaker as a one of relational becoming, a black world where the matter of gendering is of the one.[31]

This undertaking is supported by the book's explicit structure, including poems that are called essays (as in "Essay on the Awkward / Black / Object"); poems that sometimes exile each stanza to a single page such that one poem takes up eight or ten pages, as if each stanza is a metaobject or an image in a stop-motion film or an island in a string of islands of being; poems that cite James Baldwin and Frantz Fanon, film and photography theory—poems that name themselves as theory (there are five pieces here differently titled "Theory of Motion"); poems that use the slash, double and single, as both an excessive separation of line or phrase or stanza and a conceptual rendering of the book's thinking about identity and subjection. And these dynamic formal qualities are balanced by clear-line prose language—nearly half the poems are prose poems where the break of line is an accident of the order of the page. What is hard to summarize here is how much *Sympathetic Little Monster*'s form resonates with its exploration of states of being object, how much its play with poetic genre questions the category—the genre—of being itself.

Take, for example, the book's fourth poem:

The Little Girl Dreams of Dying

& wakes up in a world where she does not
exist. At school she read about a man with
two faces. Everything in life is somehow
twinned. The man looks back & forth back &
forth back & forth at the exact same time. I
wake up floating out to sea. The sun is falling
into the ocean staining the water red. The first
sentence is a lie. The little girl flies to all the
wrong conclusions. Let her try again. The little
girl dreams of dying & wakes up an image. She
reads about a god & sprints into his shadow.
The little girl splits the terms of the world.
Splits the world. Splits. (5)

The poem begins in motion—and on the ampersand, a graphic rather than a word—as the bridge title bleeds into the verse's first line. Such bridging is a metaphor for the practice of wrestling with image, body, and being. ("Bridge" is also the title of a poem that comes two pages after this one.) Indeed, the speaker bridges his observation of the dreaming little girl spoken of in the third person, who is an iteration of the speaker himself. That is, in this poem, as happens throughout the collection, the speaker multiplies as a subject and also multiplies the subject. (For example, in *Sympathetic*'s first poem, the speaker is referenced via "I," "she," and "you.") This compounding sustains the speaker's gendered subjectivity—he—even as he encounters scenes of having been seen and known as a girl. In "The Little Girl Dreams of Dying," the speaker is either recalling a moment from his young life or dreaming the moment himself. As such, when the poem proclaims, "Let her try again," the call is being authorized by the speaker in regard to a version of the speaker. "Let her try again" becomes, then, an exceptional articulation of oneness, the speaker refracted into his multitude.[32]

This refractivity is centered in gendering, and in lieu of being able to study the entire collection, I want to highlight the speaker's declaration of flux as the habit of his embodied consciousness. In "Essay on the Theory of Motion," which follows "The Little Girl Dreams of Dying," the speaker repeats the insight of a queer theorist who feels "most at home in airports, / because there everyone is *in transition*" (7; emphasis in original). The gendered specificity of this claim is reprised in the very next stanza, embedded in parentheses for emphasis and modulation:

(Let's get the obvious out of the
way—you were a girl & then you
weren't. You moved into a boy & the
girl moved into misplaced language,
into photographs.)

Such clarity about unsettled inhabitance organizes the poetics of *Sympathetic Little Monster*. And to appreciate fully the refraction in "The Little Girl Dreams of Dying," we might read the imperative, "Let her try again," as a turn—a volta of sorts—where the speaker starts over or shifts voice, as a moment of reorientation that enunciates and incites the speaker's ethos of revision. The poem's language is cosmic, worldmaking in its small tenderness toward the girl-being, and it exposes an investment in the instability of image: not only the horizonal trick of a sun "falling into the ocean" but the fantastic doubleness of "The little / girl dreams of dying & wakes up an image," where the word "wake" could mean "becomes" but could also mean "revives." With such fluency, Awkward-Rich is putting pressure on ideation, ideal, image, attending to a black gendered subject facing the obliterative condition that is being-made-object. I don't only mean objectification as a harming antiblack and gender-oppressive condition but also obliteration as the inevitable everyday being alien to one's self, where selfhood exists as a practice of gathering and appraising and discarding or, more precisely, selfhood as being possessed by and dispossessed of being. Or, as gender theorist Gayle Salamon describes it, "The body as it exists *for me* ... only comes to be once the 'literal body' assumes meaning through image, posture, and touch" (25; emphasis in original). I am compelled by the way Awkward-Rich's verse makes gendered subjection a site of object-thinking, including the ampersand that is the official first word and that points attention to the impossible act of looking "back & forth at the exact same time." I am compelled, even more, by the ecstatic and excessive disintegration of the final sequence: "The little girl splits the terms of the world. / Splits the world. Splits," as if the sentence devolves to its most vital word, "splits," which seems singular but could mean either to leave or to cleave. In this sylleptic moment, the final single word has no subject, such that the one who splits could only properly be beheld as a one. One splits, becomes a self-in-motion looking at the self-in-motion, animated both by the logics of harm and by the terms of a human becoming, a human shattering into his manyedness.[33]

In "The Little Girl Dreams of Dying," the black transgender male speaker who once was and was never that little girl becomes both subject and object to himself, a world of being in himself, a one. That concluding declining sequence eludes completeness as would be apt for oneness that is not after authority—authority is not enough; what oneness promises and alerts is the freedom to be and to become. Not authority but surrender: "The little girl splits the terms of the world. / Splits the world. Splits."[34]

The right to be of one's knowing, however incomplete knowing is, this right is the thing being for itself, a relationality of self—relation, which differs from identity and its suturing to "the terms of the world." Again, to be the object and subject of study, to be the maker and theorist of one's being, as well as to be the thing made in the acts of being: you being, you becoming. Awkward-Rich offers up a poem of self-study, and "isn't that what / a poem does—studies a thing with two hundred faces, then severs all / but one?" (48). I love the way that these poems, in their lyric domain, operate through the subject who renders himself/themself as object, for the sake of conceptualizing experience, feeling, states of becoming. And how fantastic it is to watch this unfurl with a black transgender male subject who is of a "sometimes plural and always volatile self-center."[35]

These poetics of objectification fulfill the idea of being-as-force (will? soul?), an aliveness that doesn't capitulate to terms of bodily integrity but that reimagines materiality—feeling—as an inauguration of one's immanence and transcendence. It is for this reason that the lyric idealization of voice, ragged and rangy and hungering—pursuant in its diffusion, diffuse in its pursuance—is useful throughout my conceptualization of black poetic inhabitance. In studying aliveness, I am interested in a thinking-speaking subject whose thinking and speaking are not in opposition to feeling, a thinking-speaking subject whose doing is the intelligence of being and becoming.

To be clear, again: oneness is not akin to individualism, not even close. Think of Sula, she of oneness, on her deathbed, finding relation through her reencounter with the catalog of songs she has heard and has sung. Such reencounter constitutes connections with the songs and their singers and writers, with people who were present when she first heard the song. (In the novel, Sula's life and death are a connective thread through the community.) Or think of Maud Martha, whose shift in pronoun from "I" to "one" not only allows her to imagine the broad case of her being but also projects toward the case of other people who might crave the comfort of cocoa made by fire or gas range. Oneness is relational, and the aliveness made possible through being figured as a one is relational—it enables more and more relation. The poverty of a racial capitalist logic wants to dominate how we understand oneness as if it were synonymous with individuality, but antiblack thought cannot withstand blackness or oneness. Oneness belongs to the human, and in antiblackness, the black one is neither a human nor a one. In studying aliveness, I am thinking in a black world imaginary, where oneness is relational, where oneness is a right of and lives in the one who is black.

In "Poetry Is Not a Luxury," Audre Lorde writes, "The quality of light by which we scrutinize our lives has direct bearing upon the product which we live, and upon the changes which we hope to bring about through those lives. It is within this light that we form those ideas by which we pursue our magic and make it realized" (*Sister Outsider* 36). I have used this declaration to theorize aliveness in the previous chapter, and it works also to explicate oneness, since Lorde's claim about "the quality of light" is an invitation that depends on the one doing the perceiving. Oneness is the case of subjectivity for one in self-study (studying will become relevant later in regard to ethics), as if a black one could say unquestioningly, "I study myself more than any other subject. That is my metaphysic, that is my physics" (Montaigne 413). In that quotation, Montaigne celebrates experience as embodiment and as a philosophical matter, the knowing to be had through the personal impersonal of the case "one." All of this is holy work—remember Lorde's references to immanence and transcendence, or Sula's inglorious godliness—all of this is figuring the one as the beginning of the making of the world. Such audacious inhabiting of being is poeticized in Lucille Clifton's "testament":

in the beginning
was the word.

the year of our lord,
amen. i
lucille clifton
hereby testify
that in that room
there was a light
and in that light
there was a voice
and in that voice
there was a sigh
and in that sigh
there was a world.
a world a sigh a voice a light and
i
alone
in a room. (243)

Here, in this poem, voice is set into relief as an apparatus of worldly being, voice as an idiom of relational becoming—notice, for example, the resonant repetition of "room," "light," "voice," "sigh," "world," "i," repetition that sets these terms as equivalences of each other. The aloneness is multiple, for even the line break cannot separate "i" from the compounded sequence of "a world a sigh a voice a light." Notice, too, that the conjunction "and," like Awkward-Rich's ampersand, bridges to the more that one is and is becoming. Clifton's "i" is a relational grammar, a pronoun of oneness whose cosmology is to be found in the world of a room.

"All the women are white, all the blacks are men, but some of us are brave"—this aphorism that serves as the title of an iconic book of black women's studies is really a poem and a statement of immaculate theorizing. Notice, for example, how the declaration sidesteps identity and instead signifies black femaleness as a human characteristic, "brave." In this assessment, black femaleness is a manner of being alive that eclipses the social logics of identity. And though difference and exclusion reside in the calculation, this conceit of black femaleness is not marginal but instead is righteous, a rightness of being akin to the Combahee River Collective's determination that "Black women are inherently valuable" (15).

". . . but some of us are brave"—appended next to the signifying "some of us," they said "brave," that adjective marked by racial and gendered and national specificity, a term that is at once poetic and political, describing character and consciousness and will. Brave, as in audacious and ordinary and alive, frail and full of need. Ready and of surrender. Adjective, yes, but also a name, even more radical than that—a statement ontological and imperative: Brave. Undeniably here. Not woman, not black, not authenticity, but something else: human, a maker of things, a god of ideas, a one in and beyond the world—a knowing that being doesn't reside in identity but instead arrives in relation.

Again and finally, if we attend to it, we might notice how some writers use black femaleness as a philosophy of aliveness. And, if we attend to it, we might use these models of black female intellection for thinking about blackness in a black world, blackness that belongs to the black one and that demands of the one their regard for their oneness.[36]

3 ALIVENESS

AND AESTHETICS

In a black world's rightness of being, one can be—can yearn to be—moved, devastated, broken. Such an orientation of worldness is realized in the made-text, in attending to the aesthetics of the created thing: its shape and form, its poetics, its effects and affects rendered via language.

The terms of aesthetics sometimes seem antagonistic to racial matters, as if blackness itself were formless, as if aesthetic discourse were contrary to the political contexts of black arts. These disavowals are flawed since, as philosopher Monique Roelofs argues, "racial formations are aesthetic phenomena and aesthetic practices are racialized structures" (83). Simply, as performance studies has shown us, attempts to segregate aesthetics from politics misunderstand the mutual conditions between lived life and art; such attempts also misappreciate the philosophical bearing of representational practices.[1]

This is aesthetics as a form-of-life, aesthetics as a schema for considering the aliveness of phenomena and the phenomena of aliveness, the "quality of light by which we scrutinize our lives," in Audre Lorde's language (*Sister Outsider* 36). Or, to cite Toni Morrison's Nobel lecture, "We die. That may be the meaning of life. But we do language. That may be the measure of our lives" (203).[2]

In linking aesthetics and aliveness, I am trying to turn toward the animating capacities evident in the art object, following media studies scholar Amit S. Rai, who calls for antiracist politics that "move beyond reactive dialectics and representational strategies [and toward] something else, experimenting with duration, *sensation*, resonance, and *affect*" (64–65; emphases added).[3] This commitment to sensibility echoes the case that LeRoi Jones (Amiri Baraka) makes in his 1967 essay "The World You're Talking About": "The Black Poetry is a sensitivity to the world total, to the American total. It is *about*, or *is* feeling(s). Even governmental structures are made the way people *feel* they should be made. The animating intelligence is a total of all existence. . . . Ways of making sense, of sensing. . . . Worlds. Spectrums. Galaxies. What the god knows" (n.p. [first page]; emphases in original). Jones's title and argument advance precisely an understanding of black feeling as an instantiation of textual sociality, "a *world* of humans and their paths and forms" (n.p. [first page]; emphasis added). And in collating animacy, intelligence, and existence, Jones articulates aesthetics as the aliveness of worldmaking.[4]

In my engagement with poetics, I am interested in aesthetics as a means to explore the specificity of aliveness. And though I have emphasized the syntax of pronouns and point of view, we can also consider aliveness through the quality of verbs. Think again of Lucille Clifton's "reply," where being is particularized through the poem's sustained present tense:

> he do
> she do
> . . .
> they try
> they tire
> . . .
> they moan
> they mourn
> . . .
> they do
> they do
> they do

Notice the work these verbs do to enunciate blackness as phenomena, this sequence of being that is at once definitive and untrackable, present and of presence. The poem's simple and marvelous sequencing reinforces why it matters to read aesthetically, since without attention to the sensible, Clifton's catalog of doings might appear only as antiracist counternarrative. Which would be a loss, really, since her exceptional music ("moan"/"mourn," "try"/"tire") and her rendering of quotidian excellence deserve to be appreciated more wholly.

We could explore how the temporalities of verbs constitute worldness, especially in the instance of the subjunctive, the syntax of imagining. We know subjunctivity as an expression of desired or conditional action. As such, subjunctive utterances, through their wishfulness, seem to create or manifest a scene for happening, as if the subjunctive is a spell that casts its subject into the suspension of an imaginary. This claim recalls the consideration of being-object in the previous chapter, where a habitat of *introspection* yields a moment of *prospection*, though now I want to highlight time as a feature of prospection, how subjunctivity conceptualizes experience as a toggling between then (past), now (present), and what may come. That is, even though the subjunctive is more properly a mood rather than a verb, it inflects a condition of dynamic time via the one speaking through its syntax.[5] There are plentiful examples in Terrance Hayes's *American Sonnets for My Past and Future Assassin*, a collection that signals its temporality in the title and that throws its speaker(s) into suspension via the rubric of the-slaughter-to-come. Throughout the seventy sonnets, Hayes puts forth a black male speaker who is a poet or singer or songmaker, a speaker whose bid to sing is animated by the assassin trained on his life. That killer, in one sense, is antiblackness, and repeatedly the speaker encounters the ideation of blackness that renders him both as a feared force and as a shadow of/to himself, an immaculate agent who is also powerless. We might think of *American Sonnets* as a study of poetic ontology, an aesthetic materialization of the speaker's feeling asunder in existence.[6] And as Hayes's poetic invites the speaker to behold who he might be in regard to the rapture of killing possibility, the temporality remains superlatively in the present: the speaker recalls past happenings and projects into the future, but the existential tremor of voice, sustained from poem to poem, is of a one figuring *now*. Here is an example from sonnet 55, titled as are all of them "American Sonnet for My Past and Future Assassin":

My mother says I am beautiful inside
And out. But my lover never believed it.
My lover never believed I held her name
In my mouth. My mother calls me her silver

Bullet. Her mercy pill, the metal along her spine.
I am my mother's bewildered shadow.
My lover's bewildering shadow is mine.
I have wept listening to a terrible bewildering
Music break over & through & break down
A black woman's voice. I talk to myself
Like her sister. Assassin, you are a mystery
To me, I say to my reflection sometimes.
You are beautiful because of your sadness, but
You would be more beautiful without your fear. (65)

The meditative formality of the sonnet, its inclination to exaggerate or resolve a question, resides in the repetition we see early in the poem, as the speaker toggles between the mother's and the lover's (dis)belief. That repetition gains intensity through three successive iterations of the word "bewilder," as in "bewildered" (line 6) and "bewildering" (lines 7 and 8), iterations that are the first volta in the poem:

I am my mother's bewildered shadow.
My lover's bewildering shadow is mine.
I have wept listening to a terrible bewildering
Music break over & through & break down
A black woman's voice. . . .

Let me pause to unpack what I think happens here, since its occurrence will animate how to apprehend time and subjunctivity in the poem's conclusion. First, as is the case throughout *American Sonnets*, the speaker often reckons with his being through femaleness. (Hayes uses the idiom "a black male hysteria" to open five poems, revising the common designation of hysteria as a dismissed female condition of somatic trauma.) Notice, for example, the speaker's negotiation of his being vis-à-vis the female shadow; notice, also, that the speaker moves from intense abstractions about mother and lover toward a specific encounter with breaking—his being brought to tender terror through identification with a black female singer: "I have wept listening to a terrible bewildering / Music break over & through & break down / A black woman's voice." I am struck here by the compounding terms of undoing articulated via prepositions of movement ("break *over* & *through* & break *down*") and by the intensification in the rhyme (the r's, b's, l's and d's in "terrible bewildering"), as I am by the subtlety of the speaker's relationality with the singer. That is, rather than being moved by the singer's *singing*, what Farah Jasmine Griffin describes as the facile idiom of black woman singer-as-muse, the speaker is transformed in recognizing the singer's own affective vitality—he is moved because he beholds that the terrible beauty in her song is also a terrible beauty in her experience of rendering the song.[7] This relationality, enunciated via the present perfect tense ("I have wept"), propels the speaker to a more acute sensibility in the present, a further identification through femaleness: "I talk to myself / Like her sister." We might call this, as Hayes does, being *bewildered*, where the word means not confusion but being taken out of one's sense of commonsense—being made wild or being lured into the wild.

"I talk to myself / Like her sister": The speaker is *thrown* by the singer's *thrownness*. And here is where the poem registers subjunctive time, via the direct address of line 11 as the speaker projects himself through looking at his reflection:

. . . Assassin, you are a mystery
To me, I say to my reflection sometimes.
You are beautiful because of your sadness, but
You would be more beautiful without your fear.

The lines of address multiply as the speaker announces himself as sister and then as the killing one he has internalized. Moreover, the sweet closing recognition couples the temporality of the speaker beholding his (now) beautiful sadness with the possibility that he or his sadness might be something more in another (future) instance. This is subjunctivity, the doubt and vitality of leaning into one's relationality, the animating of being through the expressiveness of might-be.

Consider again the temporality in the closing couplet, not just the gap between the speaker's now-beauty and that which may come but the temporal sensibility of the implied if-then phrasing in the final line: *if* you were of less fear, *then* you could be of more beauty. Reading through the syntax of if-then heightens the prayer quality here as the declarative statement hesitates because it is not yet achieved.

The matter of subjunctivity and poetic time relates to my consideration of aliveness, especially because the phrase "imagine a black world" is a subjunctive clause—an imperative one too. Notably, the keenness of temporal suspension is different in examples where the subjunctive coheres with the imperative, where there is no disjuncture between the wish, the command, and the achievement.[8] Indeed, the subjunctive-imperative of "imagine" yearns and instantiates at the same time; the one who says "imagine" expresses a still-to-come authority in the present. This attribute constitutes another aestheticization of aliveness, as is the case with Nikky Finney's "The Making of Paper" (*The World Is Round* 100–102):

for Toni Cade Bambara, 1939-1995

In the early 1980s I spent two years in a writing workshop that the writer Toni Cade Bambara held in her house in Atlanta every first Sunday. Anybody in the community who was writing was welcome: students, bus drivers, carpenters. I adored the opportunity to sit at this great writer's feet. She knew so much about so much. She later moved to Philadelphia. She was later diagnosed with cancer. We talked on the long-distance line when we could. I would always ask was there anything she needed that I could send. She usually answered no. But in out last conversation, which took place one week before she crossed over, she held the phone a little longer. "Maybe . . ." she said, ". . . maybe you could send some paper, and what about one of those fat juicy pens?"

Imagine that,
you asking me for paper.

For the record let me state:
I would hunt a tree down for you,
stalk it until it fell
all loud and out of breath
in the forest.
Much as I love a tree;
fat, tall, and free.
As antiviolent and provegetarian
as I am.

Never much
for strapping a gun
to any of my many hips,
for any reason whatsoever,
but on the copper penny eyes
of my grandmother, I tell you
this: I would hunt a tree down for you.

And when found
I would pull it all the way down the road
through congested city streets all by myself
and deliver it straightway
to your hospital bed,
one single extra-large floral arrangement,
something loud and free,
with red and purple bow.

Or better yet,
this tree-loving
gun-hating Geechee girl
would strap a Wild West
gun belt-machete
around her hips
enter the worst part of the woods alone
and go trunk to trunk
until the right one appeared
growing peaceful in its thousand-year-old
natal pot.

Look it
right in its
round rough ancient eyes
and confess away,
tell it straight to its woody face
my about-to-do deed.

I'd even touch it
on its limbs,
fingers begging forgiveness,
give as much comfort to it
as I could, while trying to
explain the necessaryness
of its impending death;
me standing there,
my *Gorilla, My Love* eyes
spilling all over everything,
sending up papyrus prayers
that all begin with,
"I'm so sorry but Toni Cade needs paper."

Only then would I slash its lovely body
into one million thin black cotton rag sheets,
just your uncompromising size.

Send you some paper?
Oh yes,
paper is coming Toni Cade
wagonloads

in the name
of your sweet Black writing life,
from Black writers everywhere
refusing to leave
the arena
to the fools.

Paper is on the way.

Though an elegy, the poem's proper subject is not Toni Cade Bambara but the speaker, the speaker's twitching toward being through the poem's length. The subjunctive-imperative first line, "Imagine that, / you asking me for paper," initiates the speaker's voice, since the expression is performative, a thought of surprise that is said out loud. Here, the praxis of make-believe animates the speaker's voice immediately with force and doing, closing the gap between here and the wherever of Toni Cade. We see this animation in the way "Much as I love a tree" and "Never been much" approximate the urgency of everyday speech. Yet even in haste, the speaker lingers on the tree of her imagination, as in "Look it / right in its / round rough ancient eyes"—the briskness is there in the clipped syntax that replaces the full subject-verb clause (as in, "I would look it"), as well as in the double use of "it" . . . both are features of spoken excitability. But notice, too, how the speaker materializes the tree and materializes the moment of contending with its shape, particularly via the alliterative compounding of adjectives that attend deliberately to the tree's eyes: "round rough ancient." In Finney's poem, we are in the midst of a conjecture that has the heft of presence as the speaker imagines and exists in suspension with this tree. The poem teems with dynamism, the tingling of the speaker's instance of *being in becoming*, her wish that arrives as an achievement. "Imagine that."[9]

"The Making of Paper" showcases the speaker's capacity to make something happen, to be and become the happening of relationality. Importantly, the speaker doesn't try to idealize or conjure Toni Cade, who is addressed directly and who is referred to in regard to her art ("your sweet Black writing life"). Instead, the poem figures the *speaker*, her expressiveness and energy and ferocity, her being a one in devotion. I love the way that the time of relationality in this poem is radical, as much now as it is also timeless. I am reluctant to use that term, "radical," though I can't think of another word that characterizes how the habitat of "Imagine that" animates the speaker's becoming not as an occurrence in the future but as a scene in the present. Said another way, this relationality achieves a sublime expression of wish through an idiom that brings the wish into being.[10] If "The Making of Paper" enacts devotion, it is the speaker who is revealed as the subject of its devotioning, the speaker whose vocal vitality tingles on, off, and beyond the verse page. In regard to these poetics, we might recognize three closing things: One, that Finney merges the speaker's voice with Bambara's, since the injunction "refusing to leave / the arena / to the fools" is one that Bambara wrote on a postcard to Finney. This merger maps one voice on the other through shared speech that surpasses time and space. Two, we might read the poem's last line as a temporal reiteration of its title—not "the making of paper" but the promise, "Paper is on the way." Both the dramatic widowing of this final line and its declarative spoken quality imbue the phrase with the force of imperative, the forever capacity of one saying a thing that hasn't occurred but that will happen shortly and surely—the will of the one to breech the gap between now and tomorrow. That final line enhances the timelessness announced in the title and stands as a perfect accomplishment of the aesthetics of worldmaking. And finally, as an extension of my insistence that the poem is not, precisely, about Bambara, we might appreciate how much the speaker's rambunctious poetic materiality (the voice, the imagining, the fidelity to accomplish) amounts to an activism that is roused by and partner to Bambara's legacy—the poem is the materialization of the speaker speaking out in honor of Bambara and against legacies of violence and exclusion, as if the speaker comes into her voice through speaking about and speaking to her elegiac subject. Said another way, the speaker's verse urgency makes literal the relationality of aliveness conceptualized in one black woman saying to another, "Can I say again how alive your being alive makes me feel!?!"[11]

I love the way Finney's "The Making of Paper" uses the subjunctive-imperative to reorder time and to execute a heightened expressiveness that such warped time permits. I love the poem's animacy of performative language achieved through a wish that is also a command. The poem's instantiations are of timelessness, since the work to be done (make paper) is being done (in the poem by the speaker) and what remains is the sweet devotional promise one must steadily bear: "Paper is on the way."[12]

Subjunctivity in this way, entwined with the imperative and animating of being, comprises an aesthetics of aliveness. Indeed, I am reminded of the call in the opening passage of Audre Lorde's "Poetry Is Not a Luxury"; again:

The quality of light by which we scrutinize our lives has direct bearing upon the product which we live, and upon the changes which we hope to bring about through those lives. It is within this light that we form those ideas by which we pursue our magic and make it realized. This is poetry as illumination, for it is through poetry that we give name to those ideas which are, until the poem, nameless and formless—about to be birthed, but already felt. That distillation of *experience* from which true poetry springs births thought as dream births concept, as *feeling* births idea, as knowledge births (precedes) understanding. (*Sister Outsider* 36; emphases added)

It is nearly counterintuitive to consider experience as a praxis that houses possibility, but in Lorde's thinking, *experience is subjunctive* because it merges what is deeply felt with what has not yet occurred. *Experience, then, is a state of suspension in the intensity of presence and possibility, a state of readiness and surrender.*

This framing of subjunctivity—as relational surrender, in regard to the thrall of experience—reaffirms aliveness as a call toward dispossession. That is, following the work of Fred Moten and others, I think of aliveness as an inhabitance that runs counter to possessive investments of subjecthood. The alive one does not possess herself, even as her aliveness animates her being in the world. (Think again of Sula.) In a black world orientation, we could countenance risk and threat as if one were free to be suspended in human happening.[13]

Such a study of particularized dispossession exists in Ruth Ellen Kocher's *domina Un/blued*, a book-length collection on domination and submission as terms of erotic sexual desire as much as they are terms of empire and coloniality. The subjunctive is all over *domina Un/blued* and its investigation of subjection. We know, following Patricia J. Williams, that enslaved people "were either owned or unowned, never the owner" (156). It is this fault line that Kocher brings alive on her pages abundant with white space, pages where language is sometimes subsumed below the footer's bar:

Exercise 3.

Possessive case for the word 'slave' does not exist in Italian.

The slave owned not own nor owns
Nor evolves. Nor provision any make consonant belonging. (4)

This insight, appropriately named an exercise since it has to be practiced into becoming, is from "D/domina: Issues Involving Translation," and it exemplifies the wild and wide-open materialities in Kocher's book, the way that words float unexpectedly in columns and at the bottom of pages and unpredictably across horizontal planes. Kocher's poeticization of ownership continues in "Exercise 4," which asserts that "black is only a thing the slave owns that is nothing" and then later,

the writing done by the slave in a notebook belongs to no one
no one belongs to the slave (9)

In this sequence, Kocher's use of "done" as a verb keeps the black one in a syntax of subjection, object even to one's own writing. Her book's early poems acknowledge the complex racialized landscape of domination, and yet Kocher does not shy away from thinking through dominion as a feature of human-to-human erotic exchange. Indeed, throughout Kocher's poems, small scenes of complicated hunger for another, of sexual rapaciousness, become moments of meditating on being. For example, consider how she takes up possession—through the subjunctive and the imperative—in the poem "Domina":

What boy in leather pants
to gaze but   O   the long hallway that wields you finally

wild breasted thing.

Imagine he cries   He stiffens   The carcass of a derailed train that
sits
at an angle to its track

so together you make an arrow pointing away.

Imagine he walks into the club & the purple lasers him into two so
one eye

belongs to the him coming toward you and one
stays just a step behind   measures the pace   stalks the beat
         him coming

towards you   his reflection pooled across every mirrored wall
Mercury's quick desire but   O   only him wantless to look at others

as they look at him but   O   if he could see—and to see to see
to see them see him see

Sweet brute

drop

to your knees. (28–29; emphases in the original)

Though small, this poem is dense—even difficult—so let's focus on the first five lines: For one, notice that the poem's politics of dominion depend on the complicated locality of voice, such that the speaker, the one who beholds the "boy in leather pants" and who exclaims via apostrophe, is and is not necessarily the same as the dominant/dominating subject. That is, the intimacy of the apostrophe and the switch to the second person ("the long hallway that wields you") suggest that the positionality between speaker and dominant could shift. This volatility exemplifies Kocher's nuanced exploration of dominion— of power as a generic term as well as power as a term of colonial and racialized harm. The poem's flux heightens via the phrase "Imagine he cries," which is followed immediately by the direct present tense, "He stiffens": in one sense, the point of reference seems to move from a voice that is outside the scene to one that is enmeshed in the materiality of his stiffening. Or, in another reading, the subjunctive-imperative "imagine" slips so as to modify both the crying and the stiffening. Whatever the case, in five quick lines, Kocher enacts a scene of charge and intensity where status is not static.

Even more compelling is the dynamism in the exclaimed word "O," which is an expressive sign that marks both a speaker's articulation of feeling (surprise, pain, joy) and a direct address to an elevated someone or something. This latter use is the vocative quality of "O," its elegiac and romantic speech capacity. In "Domina," the direction of the address is not defined—the speaker doesn't say "O boy," for example—so the exclamation dangles as an expression of feeling (experience) as well as a call toward something or someone beyond the time of the scene. As such, the apostrophe seems to indicate the making-present of the possible, and everything hangs in exquisite subjunctivity.[14]

This aliveness that decomposes easy subjectivity occurs also in the poem's repetition, especially "if he could see—and to see to see / to see them see him see," where the reiterated word ("see") unsettles the authority of looking and codifies a funhouse of desire and being. Who is seeing, we are left to wonder, and the answer becomes no more clear in the poem's closing lines: *Sweet brute / drop / to your knees.* Who speaks this tender call, and who is the tender one? It is as likely that the submissive boy makes this command as it is that the speaker—who inhabits the dominant role as narrator of the happening—has succumbed to the tension and entered the plane of things. I love, too, how the tenderness of *"Sweet brute"* recalls the honored attention of the opening phrase, "What boy," since in both instances the adjectives ("sweet," "what") indicate a kind of affection, a specialness. This is subjection as holiness, what Darieck Scott names as "extravagant abjection," that trail of Os down the page, where begging and demanding and experiencing become indistinguishable. All of this intense feeling and suspension that yields prayer is subjunctivity, the aesthetics that render blackness as small, tingling inflections.

Kocher's bewildered poem thrives on its scene of smallness. Indeed, the capacity-in-smallness is the reason why, throughout *Black Aliveness*, I have emphasized short poems (with the exception of Finney's "The Making of Paper") rather than ones of epic scale; I want poems that are portable, poems that dare to try to carry the world of worldmaking in scant space, poems that conjure aesthetics to materialize cosmologically. By focusing thus, I am interested in the text's aliveness, the text as an object of animacy that invites encounter. The truth is that every made text, every song or poem or story, is alive; it has a voice or a speaker who is alive, and it beholds the world of aliveness. Said another way, the made-text is evidence of aliveness in at least two ways: in its own materiality as a thing made by an alive one, and in the world of being it imagines.[15]

"Every story is a travel story—a spatial practice," which means that every telling holds traversal and, as such, can incite relationality and worldmaking.[16] There is no genre more capable of this doing than the first-person or personal essay, that superlative form of relation and self-study.

As a genre, the essay installs both a scene of happening and a one immersed in the happening. Commonly, we know the essay as a brief composition "from a limited and often personal point of view,"[17] though more formally, in "The Essay as Form," philosopher Theodor Adorno historicizes the essay as a hybrid between science and art: "Instead of achieving something scientifically, or creating something artistically, the effort of the essay reflects a childlike freedom that catches fire, without scruple, on what others have already done. The essay mirrors what is loved and hated instead of presenting the intellect, on the model of a boundless work ethic, as *creatio ex nihilo*" (152). For Adorno, the essay arrives as if made out of nothing (*creatio ex nihilo*) other than the being (the experience) of the self. In this way, the essay constitutes matter, materiality, in three ways: as a form of being, as a form of being-in-the-world, and as a form that makes a world out of being. And yet, as dynamic a habitat as the essay might be, we should remember that the essay's capacity resides in what is small, even piecemeal.

We might think of the first-person essay, then, as a genre that generates from the declaration, "Let me tell you something that happened to me."

This inclination to tell of an experience is deceptive because it seems to initiate a listener, an audience or reader to whom the essay's working is directed. But the full energy of the essay ordinates toward self-study. Simply, *the essay aestheticizes the speaker*, privileging the will and wandering and affective intensity of the one who is of the happening. The author is the essay's hero, writer Carl H. Klaus argues in a fantastic survey of the genre and its classical figures, though I might modify this claim to suggest that what is found in the essay's terrain is the writer's proxy, the speaker, since we can't properly access the writer themself.[18] Indeed, focusing on the writer might ignite biographical expectations of representation and authenticity that cohere too readily to blackness. I will come back to this question of audience later, but for now I want to be clear that my investment lies in highlighting the speaker persona as an iteration of the essay's aesthetic and material abundance, the speaker as a figure through which telling and encounter happen.[19]

Let me extend this point a bit: with the essay, what we get on the page is the speaker's voice, a mess of feeling and aching and raging and thinking, a sliver of the capaciousness of being; the essay, properly, is the speaker's dwelling, a pursuit of discovery that marries ignorance and arrogance. Again, one turns to Adorno, who writes, "The essay becomes true in its progress, which drives it beyond itself, and not in a hoarding obsession with fundamentals. Its concepts receive their light from a *terminus ad quem* hidden to the essay itself, and not from an obvious *terminus a quo*" (161). Adorno reminds us that the essay is motivated by something beyond its own completeness, and that its dynamism rests in its capacity to inspire a point of mysterious ending rather than its serving as a clear beginning. More important, the time quality of the essay is *after* (*terminus ad quem*), not before, and the speaker suspends in the aesthetic habitat; that is, the speaker is not in control of the essay's working (the essay is not about transparent conclusions) but rather the speaker *arrives* through the telling. I know that this claim might seem contradictory to common understandings of authority over one's story, though in advocating for the essay as a relational praxis, I want to emphasize that the drive to narrate, which might imply control and mastery, exists in negotiation with the surprise that narration exposes.[20]

The essay is a genre of black oneness, a relational textuality of the speaker's preparedness to surrender to their becoming, site of the speaker as a rhetorical revelation. If every first-person essay conceptually begins, "Let me tell you something that happened to me," the act of telling is not *about* the happening, but the act of telling *becomes* a happening in itself. In this regard, the subject of the invitation is the speaker—the speaker is the essay's *you*. The keenest word in this characterization might be one I used earlier, "aestheticization," which anchors the notion that the essay enacts an aestheticization of the black one in and as aliveness, the essay as a case for rendering the pleasure and intelligence of the words for the saying.

The essay is neither argument nor conclusion but a genre for encounter, a form for "an everyday abstraction of blackness," in film scholar Michael Gillespie's language (9).[21] As such, it asks, "What is experience?" as writer John D'Agata notes. I love D'Agata's clarity here, since he reminds us that the essay is a schema of discovery that questions rather than confirms the definitiveness of experience.[22] In accord with its etymology, the essay stages a display of the speaker's trial, their encounter with being, even though this performativity can be hard to recognize given the genre's use of conversational language that mimics common speech. Indeed we should not interpret this performativity as an antithesis to the essay's oneness, since we've seen already the value of projection as a feature of alive being.[23]

This is the essay as poetic subjunctivity.[24]

Though D'Agata does not make specific reference to black aesthetics, his claim that the essay uses experience to explore the nature of experience is especially relevant in a world of blackness. As theorist Stuart Hall observes, "We tend to privilege experience itself, as if black life is lived experience outside of representation. We have only, as it were, to express what we already know we are. Instead, it is only through the way in which we represent and imagine ourselves that we come to know how we are constituted and who we are" (30). Like Hall, my investment is against an easy conflation of blackness with a simplistic notion of experience. In reading the essay as a genre of black aliveness, I am emphasizing the aesthetic dynamism that Patricia J. Williams describes as the always "rhetorical event" of rendering experience (11)—the dramatization of the speaker, the exhibition of flourishes of syntax, diction, repetition . . . all of the techniques of making and unfurling, techniques of rendering one's being in experience that are also how experience comes to be and comes to mean. (Again, Lorde's "the quality of light. . . .")[25]

There is an instructive example early in Dionne Brand's *A Map to the Door of No Return*, where, in a meditation on the heft of history, the speaker descends into feeling as knowing: "One enters a room and history follows; one enters a room and history precedes. History is already seated in the chair in the empty room when one arrives. Where one stands in a society seems always related to this historical experience. Where one can be observed is relative to that history. All human effort seems to emanate from this door. How do I know this? Only by self-observation, only by looking. Only by feeling. Only by being a part, sitting in the room with history" (24–25). In the syntax, the speaker moves between "one" and herself in the first person and, as such, the location of authority about one, history, diaspora is sutured to the clean specificity of a room, a chair, a black female subject's feeling. Even the question, "How do I know this?" could be read as a moment of self-interrogation, as if it is whispered by the one to the one about the one, as if manifesting a figuring of experience.

"How do I know this?" she asks, that enduring question of aliveness. I love the first-person essay as a prompt for imagining that a black one could sit in wonder and ask, "What is experience?" in the full iterative complexity of such a query.

Before turning to an example, let me assert again:

— The idiom of the essay is of autonomous passage for the one. That is, if the essay's vibrant rhetorics can correlate to authenticity, it is in regard to the ethos of authentic movement as choreographer Romain Bigé has explained it: "to sit with the (in)authenticity of one's self." Bigé's terms remind me that dance as a practice is of relation (again, Danielle Goldman's *I Want to Be Ready*), each dance as an occasion of embodied consciousness where the dancer is a one enacting movement as a locus of intelligence. In dance, the dancer is (being) and is (becoming), so perhaps the essay, as a habitat, is like dance.[26]

— The essay's relationality lies in performativity, in its functioning as a site of disidentification for the speaker who is both the one who is telling and the one who is the subject of the telling.[27]

— "Distance," "disidentification," and "orientation"—these are terms of phenomenology and are vital to how we understand the dynamics of the essay. Indeed, in this way, my suggestion that every first-person essay conceptually begins, "Let me tell you something that happened to me," is apt for not using the word "about" (that is, the phrase is not "Let me tell you *about* something that happened to me"). As it is, the statement emphasizes a narrative that is embodied and imminent and in process: the telling is not *about* the happening; the telling *is* the constitution of the thing itself.[28]

— The essay invokes and appropriates the scene as a moment of being object and subject, staging "the act of being seen and being seen in the process of being seen" (Thompson 10).

— As a materialization of being, the essay is a volatile embodiment; an instantiation and incantation, a magic thing where words are substance and are capable of making substance; a corpus of transformation or crossing, like the rhetorical trope of chiasmus that enacts becoming, exemplified well via the narrator's yearning at the end of Toni Morrison's *Jazz*: "Make me, remake. You are free to do it and I am free to let you" (229). The essay offers an "aesthetics of existence."[29]

— The essay is a call to and of the one, an aliveness in aesthetics that surpasses representation. Not evidence or authority but the being alive, a collation of experience and existence that confirms its phenomenology since "from a phenomenological perspective, every act of description is at the same time an act of constitution; that is, whenever we describe the world, we are, in a very real sense, remaking it" (Fryer 228).[30]

— Finally, the essay levitates as a nuanced privacy, akin to what Elizabeth Alexander—in reading Michael Harper's Black Arts poetry—describes as a "pride [that generates] from an angle of profoundest intimacy, as though nothing is worth saying loudly unless it is felt from a place" of depth (80–81). Yes, yes, yes, as though nothing but one's black intimacy is worth saying loudly.

In "Of Practice," Michel de Montaigne makes the essay's ethic clear: "My trade and art is living," he writes, and then later, "I expose myself entire. . . . It is not my deeds that I write down; it is myself, it is my essence" (189, 191). Or Patricia J. Williams, in *The Alchemy of Race and Rights*, who enacts the black self as a "floating signifier" in a first-person speech act, and who confesses, "I deliberately sacrifice myself in my writing" (7, 92). This is the essay, which, like Lucille Clifton's speaker, says "come celebrate" and mobilizes subjunctivity on behalf of a one of black aliveness.

To further the case for a poetics of the first-person essay, which could also be called the lyric essay,[31] I want to consider an exquisite example, Jamaica Kincaid's exploration of colonialism, tourism, and Caribbean modernity in *A Small Place*. We don't often think of this book through the aesthetics of the personal essay. Indeed, since its publication in 1988, *A Small Place* has been read either as a searing condemnation of white (American and European) tourism or as a misguided critique of Antiguans. These critical assessments privilege the text's arguments and also tend to lean heavily on psychological interpretation of Kincaid's biography; as such, these readings collapse the writer with the author function, her narrative persona, and overlook the book's aesthetic doings. Given this, I want to attend both to the speaker who materializes (in) the telling and to *A Small Place* as a scene of the speaker's undoing, of her being both subject and object of the essaying. I want to read as if the speaker's becoming on the page constitutes the book's revelatory dynamics.[32]

Central in *A Small Place*'s aesthetics is the presentation of unsettledness, first in the way the speaker seems to disorient the reader and then in the speaker's own tumble into ambivalence that reflects a depth of black feeling about and within the colonial condition. "If you go to Antigua as a tourist, this is what you will see" (3) is the book's first sentence, a dare of a phrase that ensnares the reader and establishes an antagonism that will energize the arc of what follows. Immediately, the speaker asserts herself obliquely and aggressively by overdetermining the reader, who is co-opted into a discursive world via the command "you." Notice, too, that the second-person invocation consists of both a subjunctive ("if you go") and an imperative (direct address)—that the essay begins in the aesthetic of "imagine." We know, then, that we have to read this provocation thoughtfully so as to keep the textuality of the speaker in view. That is, we can't infer only that the address is directed to a (white) reader, especially since the speaker herself is also revisiting the island after a long absence. If we engage the book as a relational inhabiting, then the opening's invocation via the subjunctive *includes* the speaker in its command, a call of worldmaking that arrests the speaker in her conjured scene of small island-ness. In this claim, I read "if you go" as a disorienting rhetorical function, one that cues us to notice the speaker's unsettled subjectivity. What we gain from such a reading is the capacity to attend to the speaker's anger and regret and confusion and ambivalence, her exasperation and her embarrassment for having such conflicted feelings; what we gain is a sense of the essay as a home of the speaker's grappling with experience and an appreciation for Kincaid's deployment of the force of the genre.[33]

I am interested in *A Small Place* as a textual landscape of the black speaker's relationality.

Kincaid's essay is composed of four untitled sections, each a meditation on being in Antigua. While the first section, just referenced, uses the second person almost to the exclusion of explicit reference to the speaking "I," parts 2 and 3 rely principally on first-person disclosure. The last section, which is a brief poetic reprisal of Antigua's colonial history, deploys an omniscient third-person voice to reinforce the speaker's intimacy.[34] But I am getting ahead of myself in summarizing the essay's narrative kinetics: we can recognize relation as a praxis in *A Small Place* by paying attention to the pronouns in the essay, how the direct address ensures the first-person speaker's authority of voice without having to say "I." It is an act of control, or delay, maybe even a gambit to orient the scene of colonial happenings appropriately. Throughout the initial pages, the speaker assails the imagined reader through second-person conjecture:

> You are a tourist. . . . You disembark from your plane. You go through customs. Since you are a tourist, a North American or European—to be frank, white—and not an Antiguan black returning to Antigua from Europe or North America with cardboard boxes of much needed cheap clothes and food for relatives, you move through customs swiftly, you move through customs with ease. Your bags are not searched. You emerge from customs into the hot, clean air: immediately you feel cleansed, immediately you feel blessed (which is to say special); you feel free. (3–5)

The speaker's assumptions about the reader multiply, even to the level of projecting what the you feels: "You are feeling wonderful" (5). Later, the speaker summarizes the power of the colonizer with another astute accusing projection, "You see yourself, you see yourself" (13), the repetition emphasizing the insight and the authority of its saying. Not only do these summations codify the reader, the white you, but they secure the speaker as part of a black collective ("we Antiguans, for I am one . . ." [8]), at least momentarily. Moreover, this second-person encasement establishes a clear distance between the one speaking and the ones held captive in her lure. And still, even in this torrent of clear address, the speaker seems distanced from herself—as if she were a voice offstage that is describing a scene of ridiculous actors in ferocious syntax.

The rhetorical intensity of the direct address is so total in the first section that the use of "I" at the start of part 2 is startling: "The Antigua that I knew, the Antigua in which I grew up, is not the Antigua you, a tourist, would see now" (23). This is a statement of exposedness, of the speaker entering the stage explicitly as opposed to being shrouded in the authority of the second-person capture; in this doing, the speaker inhabits a tone that is more vulnerable and hesitant (notice how the repetition and commas create that pause: "The Antigua that I knew, the Antigua in which I grew up, is not the Antigua you, a tourist, would see now"). We can recognize an affective shift in the relationality of the speaker's speaking, as in "Let me show you the Antigua that I used to know" (24), which is how she prefaces this section's telling of small incidents that track a history of colonial wrongdoing. Such an offer opens up a narrative intimacy that is not quite mutuality since the speaker is cajoling the reader into accountability and maybe even remorse. We see this affective dynamic in the speaker's interrogations:

> Do you ever wonder why some people blow things up? I can imagine that if my life had taken a certain turn, there would be the Barclays Bank, and there I would be, both of us in ashes. Do you ever try to understand why people like me cannot get over the past, cannot forgive and cannot forget? (26)

> Have I given you the impression that the Antigua I grew up in revolved almost completely around England? . . . Are you saying to yourself, "Can't she get beyond all that, everything that happened so long ago . . . ?" (33–34)

> Have you ever wondered to yourself why it is that all people like me seem to have learned from you is how to imprison and murder each other, how to govern badly, and how to take the wealth of our country and place it

in Swiss bank accounts? Have you ever wondered why it is that all we seem to have learned from you is how to corrupt our societies and how to be tyrants? You will have to accept that this is mostly your fault. (34–35)

Reading through this sequence of indictment, it is clear that the speaker seeks from the reader neither answer nor reparative gesture; instead, the persona seems to revel in the chance to *feel* the wild, hot anger of being harmed by colonial plunder, of having to do that reveling in a language that is unyielding. ("For isn't it odd that the only language I have in which to speak of this crime is the language of the criminal who committed the crime?" she concedes in a parenthetical notation [31].) The case I am pressing is to notice the speaker, the intensity of her difficult feelings, the impossibility that the discursive would to make of her being. The speaker's voice here is almost oxymoronic (deictic?) conceptually, *speaking imprecisely from a precise location of feeling*, addressing impossibility with crisp insight. It is not the claims against history that seem aesthetically compelling as much as the emotional ache articulated as she, the speaker, moves through telling this thing that happened—and is happening—to her, this terrible unsettling happening . . . and doing so in a dialogue that is and will always be of one, since the addressed cannot possibly respond or engage. As such, rather than try to assess the speaker's politics, we might instead ask, "Who is this speaker, and who is she *becoming* in this narrative?" That is, I am trying to implore us to read this essay as an essay, as home for/of its speaker. This orientation, of beholding the speaker as a one who is being figured through the narrative, is essential to discerning the laced comments in this section, including this intense claim: "Even if I really came from people who were living like monkeys in trees, it was better to be that than what happened to me, what I became after I met you" (37). This sentence registers as a sigh, as if the speaker is momentarily exhausted in struggling through the whole world of her feeling and thinking. We might want to read this sentence for its declaration against colonial terror or for Kincaid's complicity in not dismissing the racist claim (the "even if" clause), though such interpretations miss the affective textuality here, the tumbling suspension of the speaker's inhabited sensibility. Or, as Audre Lorde told us, "I feel, therefore I can be free" (*Sister Outsider* 38).

"I feel, therefore I can be free": Again, I don't mean to suggest that there are no ideological dimensions to *A Small Place*; I mean, instead, to focus on the essay as a habitat of a black one's navigation through being subject and object of the essaying, what literary theorist Phillip Brian Harper might call "the abstractionist aesthetics" of pronouns.[35] As a genre, the essay is not of argument or proof or even evidence; it is instead of the *experience* of black being, the flight into one's variousness. In this regard, Kincaid's speaker is the hero of the essay, she who makes the scene for her own encounter and feeling.

Such appreciation allows us to acknowledge a vital moment that begins the book's third section:

> And so you can imagine how I felt when, one day, in Antigua, standing on Market Street, looking up one way and down the other, I asked myself: Is the Antigua I see before me, self-ruled, a worse place than what it was when it was dominated by the bad-minded English and all the bad-minded things they brought with them? How did Antigua get to such a state that I would have to ask myself this? For the answer on every Antiguan's lips to the question "What is going on here now?" is "The government is corrupt. Them are thief, them are big thief." Imagine, then, the bitterness and the shame in me as I tell you this. (41)

This in medias res instance of the first person is particular because it is so wrought with tender confession. Here, the speaker turns the performativity of "imagine" upon her own affective constellation, inventing a scene capable of her ambivalence. This is not just a citation of shame, but something else—the meeting of an intractable terribleness in an attempt to travel the small place of her black life with some modicum of fearlessness. It is an astonishing intimacy, the habitat for which the speaker has made through the praxis of her telling. Scholars readily note that Kincaid's writings exhibit "a very personal politics" (Bouson 89), though this display surpasses and dispenses with politics by its ordinary name. No, this sublime invocation, "And so you can imagine," ascends to a level of being beheld in deep feeling.

More than all this, however, is the fact that this moment is the proper anecdote of *A Small Place*. Conceptually, the anecdote works as an essay's most specific materiality, the unremarkable incident animated via telling. In this regard, the anecdote constitutes the "something" of the phrase "Let me tell you something that happened to me," the something that might be humorous or trivial, that is unreliable because it is casual and is uncorroborated by sociality: the anecdote is the materiality around which a speaker can flutter since it is small, unremarkable, compelling. Intimately unreliable.

I come to thinking of the anecdote through the genre of the personal essay but also through David Wills's writing about literature and public function. Wills defines the anecdote as "the explicit but secret other side to narrative . . . and conversely, as *the becoming literary of any text*" (22; emphasis added). Wills is right to designate the anecdote as a surfeit, an intimate but casual textuality that can support a dynamic relation. And the potential or energy of the anecdote is not truth or precision; indeed "the anecdote is most often . . . consigned to a discursive structure in which truth and certainty are not at issue; where disbelief is willingly suspended to enable the gratuitous, the frivolous, the autobiographical, the fictional to be given free rein" (Wills 24). One could say that the anecdote is virtual, in Deleuzean terms—that which is real but not fully actualized. Not pure or raw, but a buzzing, nearly there thing that exists on the edge of the limits of representation or capture.[36]

At the heart of every essay, there is an anecdote, the narrative of a specific happening that is flush with feeling though it remains ordinary until scrutinized (and remains ordinary afterward). The anecdote is a site of transformation, in that it is a materiality that the speaker manipulates but, ultimately, doesn't control. Something happened, and now there is the telling, and in the telling there is becoming. The anecdote doesn't supplant the happening—it could not possibly do that—but it is perhaps a viable site for the speaker's being in regard to the world of her being. Said another way, the speaker and the anecdote exist in relational encounter.

Again: "And so you can imagine how I felt when, one day, in Antigua, standing on Market Street, looking up one way and down the other, I asked myself: Is the Antigua I see before me, self-ruled, a worse place than what it was when it was dominated by the bad-minded English and all the bad-minded things they brought with them?" And then, "Imagine, then, the bitterness and the shame in me as I tell you this" (41). Not only am I thoroughly moved by the way the speaker's anecdote begins in full stream of a sustained self-conversation, but I am taken by the way in which this anecdote is rendered as an unspecific specificity. We can imagine it, a moment on a random day when, caught in a certain sunlight, the speaker comes upon a thought that she might have had before but without conscious notice: How did it come to this, and do I belong here? Such questions might have been related to an incident—or not, since whatever spurred the questions has been lost to memory. (It is almost too ordinary to remember.) The point is that this textual moment triggers deep feeling and crystallizes as the speaker's reckoning. We should notice, too, that this anecdote is prefaced by two sections (nearly forty pages) of deliberate rage-work. To me, this deferral enhances the drama of the anecdotal moment that is not presented specifically but that is *felt* specifically—intensely—by the speaker.

The thrilling diffuseness of the small happening: I love that Kincaid's anecdote is encased in a call to imagine, since this call gestures to how impossible the happening is to describe and share, how difficult it is for the speaker to be of regard to the happening for herself (never mind to try to relay it to a reader), as if it can only be instantiated by a world other than this one. "Imagine . . . the bitterness and the shame in me," the speaker says as she conjures up a capacity to be of bitterness and shame. I love that the speaker, in thrall of the essay's aesthetic, sets a scene not to criticize white wrongdoing but for her own engagedness with the difficult. This is the capacity of the personal essay, where the black one can invoke a habitat for being and then can surrender into that habitat toward her becoming.

The essay lets the speaker do the work that is hers to do in the best way she can imagine.

It is not a surprise, then, that this section and its intimate anecdote feature prominently when scholars question Kincaid's racial politics. For one, the speaker's reencounter with Antigua does not shy away from addressing her dissonance with her kin. And the acknowledgment of embarrassment seems directed to the book's generic reader, who has been signaled as white (the "you" of the opening), which means that A Small Place appears to denigrate blackness while pleading to the virtues of whiteness. Literary theorist Greg Thomas summarizes a common sentiment in arguing that "when attention is drawn less to what Kincaid says explicitly to white tourists, and more to what she says about black Antiguans, her political outlook is exposed for its crude conservatism" (118). Thomas's claim is about the book's content, though he minimizes that A Small Place begins with a critique of whiteness and of the destructions made by colonialism, at least as such destructions are experienced by a speaker who herself is something of a tourist. Moreover, in my reading, Kincaid's political undertaking exists not only in the essay's content but especially in its aesthetics, her deployment of the genre's form toward instantiating a black diasporic speaker in the midst of a complicated affective subjectivity. Kincaid the writer—and her persona, the speaker—is trying to reckon with her feelings, their messy and necessary rightness; she is trying to make a world for being where she can think-feel her rightness.

Sigh: I am uneasy about trying to defend A Small Place in regard to its ideas about antiblackness and its overtures toward a dominant (white) reader, not only because I understand those overtures as an aesthetic apparatus of the speaker's relational doing but also because in a black world, the book and its speaker (never mind its writer) do not need defense. In mounting this defense, I am enacting an anxiety of audience that works awry of the aliveness of the essay form.[37] Simply, if the essay is the terrain of the speaker, then what is being assayed by A Small Place is the speaker's exploration of the ambivalence of home in the enduring harmful legacy of colonization. She, the speaker in this book, feels the dissonance and disorientation of Antigua, and the essay constitutes a space for her trial, as in to try to encounter the world of her affective being in regard to this small place. "Let me tell you something that happened to me," the speaker says, which means that we must acquiesce to her right to understand—to experience—the ravages of colonialism on her own terms. And through the telling, the speaker establishes and traverses a scene of mattering, an erotics of feeling and of becoming.

Surely *A Small Place* is not only a private conversation, but what if we read its speaker as having a relational encounter with herself, including the ambivalence of return to a place that she cannot now bear? What if we permit that the world made by the speaker's act of telling is one where, rather than only articulating pride or self-assuredness, the speaker gets to countenance shame as a part of black being? In a black world, we could countenance shame.

The first-person essay is a display of a speaker's inhabitance of disorientation in regard to the thing that happened—disorientation that, as Sara Ahmed argues, is a relational condition. As such, the pronoun of Kincaid's first-person essay might not be "I," at least not conceptually, since "I" indicates more control than resides in the essay's worldness. No, the subjectivity of the first-person essay here might be "me," the singular object case, or at least the oneness invoked in asking, "How am I me?" as a question of being subject and object at the same time. I find this conclusion useful in tracking the arc of the speaker in *A Small Place*, where the heft of direct address gives way to the subjectivity of beholding shame's oneness.[38] Indeed, in the book's final brief section (it is five pages), Kincaid's speaker mobilizes her me-positionality into a sense of oneness and offers a stunning call of relationality:

> Again, Antigua is a small place, a small island. It is nine miles wide by twelve miles long. It was discovered by Christopher Columbus in 1493. Not too long after, it was settled by human rubbish from Europe, who used enslaved but noble and exalted human beings from Africa (all masters of every stripe are rubbish, and all slaves of every stripe are noble and exalted; there can be no question about this) to satisfy their desire for wealth and power, to feel better about their own miserable existence, so that they could be less lonely and empty—a European disease. Eventually, the masters left, in a kind of way; eventually, the slaves were freed, in a kind of way. The people in Antigua now, the people who really think of themselves as Antiguans (and the people who would immediately come to your mind when you think about what Antiguans might be like; I mean, supposing you were to think about it), are the descendants of those noble and exalted people, the slaves. Of course, the whole thing is, once you cease to be a master, once you throw off your master's yoke, you are no longer human

rubbish, you are just a human being, and all the things that adds up to. So, too, with the slaves. Once they are no longer slaves, once they are free, they are no longer noble and exalted; they are just human beings. (80–81)

This passage exhibits *A Small Place*'s characteristic syntax, especially its long conversational sentences full of the speaker's lively and casual—nearly flippant—ease ("Eventually, the masters left, in a kind of way," "I mean, supposing you were to think about it") and its deployment of parenthetical asides. The voice here resolves the philosophical question of master-slave relation with the looseness of the phrase "of course." Such flourish reminds us that the essay's grappling works through the specificity of the speaker, her me-ness, that the historical matters at hand are indexed to the particularity of their relation to her everyday experience and her ordinary language for that experience. Indeed, it is this ordinariness, this intimacy, that contextualizes the passage's turn toward universality, a turn that is not a naïve notion but that carries the weight of the speaker's rugged essay-work.[39]

A Small Place is of a black one who is navigating the intimacy of happening, a subject who can speak broadly through the specificity of her encounter with herself. And in the doings of Kincaid's mighty book, we remember that to be able to say one, to be of or as "one," is not to be deferent or imperial; it is to be rendered as a being via cosmological terms, of being open(ed) to textures of one's inestimable totality that is and is of a world.

Kincaid's speaker isn't organizing a *communal* affective encounter—this might be what some critics read as a failing. But perhaps the orientation of the black essay is toward what literary theorist Darieck Scott calls a politics without defense: "a politics that does not organize itself around a stance of defense or aggression, a politics that assimilates to itself racial identities and histories but choosing not to battle against them but rather to let them, as it were, flow through the self—even overwhelm the self—and yet become transformed" (245). Scott argues for a capacity to exist within the political undefensively, akin to what I have explored in the aesthetics and affect of Kincaid's speaker, she who is not responsible for a politic against whiteness nor a politic in sustenance of black people (Antiguans or otherwise). *A Small Place* is hers, her world of feeling, and its force of being might well inspire other encounters that will have their own force of black being. (Such might be its sustaining work.)[40]

The essay is of the one of blackness, the voice speaking out toward its own (imagined) self, which is an act of worldmaking.[41]

The personal essay is superlatively of affect (emotions are "a form of . . . world making" Ahmed argues),[42] of the being of experience that is possible through aesthetics. We should read this form *as* a black world; otherwise we'd be inclined to look for its argument about antiblackness rather than honor its embodiment of blackness.

Again, the black world of the black essay constitutes and inspires a heterogeneity of us, not respectability or fidelity to community but a world of black particularity—the heterogeneity of blackness. In the essay, then, we encounter not a text of evidence but an aesthetic of experience, "the work of art [as] a being of sensation and nothing else: it exists in itself."[43]

The essay, this poetic of subjunctivity that beholds blackness as a capacity of wandering and wondering, free, as in the way one is in knowing that "God is a question, not an answer."[44]

4 ALIVENESS

IN TWO ESSAYS

Black aliveness is of the heterogeneity of us, and the praxis of the essay locates heterogeneity through one voice at a time in the worldliness of its being. The essay displays and approximates the experience of being, but it does not corroborate or confirm or argue—it aestheticizes and beholds the thrill of inhabiting aliveness. The essay is a black ecstatic as literary theorist Aliyyah I. Abdur-Rahman defines such: "The black ecstatic is an aesthetic performance of embrace, the sanctuary of the unuttered and unutterable, and a mode of pleasurable reckoning with everyday ruin in contemporary black lives under the strain of perpetual chaos and continued diminishment" (345). Yes, and in its black worldness, the essay's attention to ruin and strain is part of rather than the totality of its ecstatic enactment.[1]

The black essay as a textuality, a materiality, of black being and becoming.

I want to consider two examples, each by a poet who is also a superlative essayist. Indeed, over the next few pages, I will linger deliberately with two essays to try to render them nearly as fully as one could a short poem, residing thoroughly in their poetic habitat.

First Reginald Shepherd's singularly dazzling "On Not Being White": Shepherd is known for five award-winning poetry collections published before his death in 2008, including *Some Are Drowning*, *Otherhood*, and *Angel, Interrupted*, though "On Not Being White" remains notable because of its inclusion in Joseph Beam's 1986 *In the Life: A Black Gay Anthology*. The best I can do to summarize "On Not Being White" is to say that the essay travels along a speaker's meditation through various anecdotes of his desires for erotic and affective connection with white men, particularly gay white men. In its focus on desires, Shepherd's text navigates both a yearning for recognition and the incompleteness of the articulation of yearning, especially this unspeakable interraciality. It is a tumultuous, luscious undertaking that requires the capaciousness of a black world orientation.

Here is how the essay begins:

> I'd like to speak of a young man of my acquaintance. All his friends call him Little Wing, but he flies rings around them all. That's not my line, of course. I'm just searching for the words to make him real to you, an objective correlative to give these aimless desires some sense of shape. They have object but no reason for existing; he's beautiful but I don't know him. His name is Pablo, he looks younger than he is. He lives in my neighborhood. All of this means nothing to you; it's everything to me. I want you to know how this comes about. His name could be anything, David or Ross or anyone. I could list his names but they're only words. Hugh. Shane. Arthur. Eric. I write down the names of my desire to make them real, tokens or talismans. Today his name is Pablo. Little Wing, don't fly away. I must set you down in words and keep you there, the only way I will ever have you. The way I keep you in desire, whatever your name this time. (46)

There is so much liveliness in the persona here, this voice that opens in invocation, as if calling to order an audience for an occasion. Almost, but not quite, since the first sentence doesn't say "you" and thereby leaves the direction of address wide open: "I'd like to speak of" rather than "I'd like to speak to *you* of." This slyness seems to acknowledge the likely failure of speaking ("I'd like to speak" but I can't) even as the hesitancy clears a space for exploration without sanction. Moreover, in this case, "I'd like to speak" also means I am going to speak regardless. The complexity of address amplifies how we might read the direction of voice here. That is, as the speaker uses the second-person pronoun—particularly in the strikingly direct "All of this means nothing to you" in the paragraph's middle—we could recognize that the rhetorical effect is of a subject thinking out loud to himself through an imagined scene. Notice, for example, that by the end of the paragraph, the speaker is in conversation with Pablo, the idea and ideal of his affection, the one he is trying to keep, capture, remember.[2]

These aesthetics of address allow the voice to slide around the paragraph and dislocate the expectation of audience. I might even say that this opening constitutes the speaker's dialogue with himself, his asking permission to speak of himself and his desires: to explore this ordinary thing of his being that is not necessarily ordinary in its politics. Indeed, the speaker articulates this query through the subjunctive ("I'd like to speak"), which heightens this moment as an imaginative inhabitance. The essay's beginning sets a scene of exceptional awareness, of fraughtness, especially when Shepherd writes, "Call this a definition by example of the difficulty I find in expressing myself directly on a topic so fraught with dangers" (47), this directive that vocalizes the speaker's self-consciousness in the midst of the exposure.

What a tender deliberateness, this "I'd like to speak of," tender for all the obvious reasons, deliberate because the speaker is aware of the essay genre and its perfect inarticulateness: "The things I have to say in this essay are not all things I would wish to say; they are certainly not things many would wish to hear, or if so, they wish to hear them for the wrong reasons. *But I want to be honest this once, if only for my own sake*" (47; emphasis added). This statement declares the speaker's cause, his deploying of the essay as a trial where truth is fleeting and where experience—the being in the happening—is supreme: "But this is only an attempt, the root of the word essay, an attempt at definition which can serve as a self-definition, an identity with which I can live. So here I am thinking of myself on paper, in the hope that some of my obsessions might fruitfully provoke a response in a possible reader" (47). Don't be distracted by this reference to the reader, since the critical point is the conceptualization of the essay as a genre of relation and subjunctivity, as a text of encounter between the writer and himself. Shepherd's "On Not Being White" materializes a speaker whose telling *creates* and *invokes* a version of himself, such that the speaker gets to inhabit the happening by encountering his earlier self. (The speaker, then, is also his own reader.) The essay instantiates and installs the speaker as both subject and object of being who exists in the expansive nowhere of the textual world.

I love "On Not Being White" for the ways Shepherd exemplifies the phenomenon of aesthetics, the aliveness in using the first person to enact and inhabit the poetics of distance. For example, this is how the paragraph quoted earlier concludes:

> "Myself" being in this context a twenty-two year old black gay man (how odd to think of myself as a "man"; isn't it always the others who are *men*?) with an obsessive attraction to white men. A black man who deeply fears most other black people, primarily other black men. A black man, also, afraid of white men and deeply resentful of their power over me both sexual and social. A gay man afraid of men. Naturally concomitant is that I'm afraid of myself. Every fear is a desire. Every desire is a fear. (47; emphasis in the original)

The speaker sets the reflexive pronoun ("myself") in quotation marks, exaggerating the citation not only for the sake of troubling identity but also toward extenuating the relational praxis of his self-study. To my reading, this relationality authorizes the speaker's vulnerability of looking at himself; and in this regard, one doesn't have to make a defense of his desires since the speaker himself names the fear that constitutes his most definitive subjectivity: "I'm afraid of myself," a fear that includes but surpasses the terms of gender or race or sexuality, a fear that belongs to a deeper register of being.

Shepherd's essay is a masterpiece of exposed being and indulgent interrogation, a text that co-opts the reiterative practice of telling so as to uncoil its speaker into vital feeling. Such expressiveness coheres partly through repetition, as in the case of the chiasmus that closes the foregoing paragraph: "Every fear is a desire. Every desire is a fear." More than a statement of ambivalence or equivalence, this chiasmus reflects the intersubjective dynamics of the speaker's encounter with himself, the possibility of transcendence to be had in the immanence of self (now) meeting self (then). Chiasmus, the literary scholar Dagmawi Woubshet tells us, is a rhetorical idiom of crossing or magic, where one thing gives into and becomes another. Indeed, as the terms of Shepherd's chiasmic equation intersect, the speaker's fear of self translates as a *desire* of self.[3]

The excellence of "On Not Being White" resides in its lavish aesthetics, its abundant form-moves that animate the speaker's being-on-the-page. The performativities are plentiful: in the essay's title, which embraces display and elision, where "on not being" enunciates presentation and absence; in the deferral legible in the syntax "I'd like to speak of," which opens the work; in the way the speaker regales in an accomplished conversational tone that ripples with wryness and exaggerated confession ("Actually, Pablo's not really white; he's Hispanic. So I'm making progress after all" [46]). Shepherd's performativity lives also in the way he riffs through literary allusions to Audre Lorde, Susan

Sontag, T. S. Eliot, and William Faulkner, allusions that are at once organic to and self-conscious for one who notes that Hades and Sybil are "words [that] are supposed to be alien to [him]" (48).[4] Or in the superlative artful artifice as the speaker proclaims that to survive not being white, he "sought . . . to shed the few ghetto idioms [he] had," followed two sentences later by a vernacular idiom, "Yesterday don't matter if it's gone" (49).

This is high aesthetic style, a revelry in prose mastery. But style and mastery should not be equated with control, at least not exclusively so, especially since the essay exemplifies the speaker's encounter through and *with* language as a praxis of self-pursuit. The aliveness of style here represents play and pleasure, a fantastic inhabitance that transports the essaying one into another field of being, another register of experience. I think of such doing as in accord with the right to revel in the saying, to be of and become through the word, the pleasure of "living as an *aesthetic being.*"[5]

The most striking formal move in "On Not Being White" might be the use of repetition, not only the chiasmus quoted earlier but a dramatic moment when the speaker reprises himself:

> Perhaps I have been too abstract; if so, it is only in self-defense. Let me begin again, attempt this time to provide a context for my ramblings. What contextualizes more than history? What traps us more irredeemably? I've learned something since I was a child.
>
> I was born and raised in New York City, afraid of everything. Specifically (yes, let us be as specific as possible), I was raised in the Bronx, never the South Bronx but bad neighborhoods nonetheless. I suppose my home was stereotypical for a gay youth: I was raised by my mother, my father was an occasional negative mention and every few months a "weekly" child support check. The overriding facts of our lives, the shadow that determined everything we did or did not do or longed to do, was poverty. Though we did our best to ignore or deny or transcend it, . . . we were poor and we were black and all our efforts could not overcome those conditions. (50)

In this instance, the speaker seems to confess against and apologize for his abstract meditations on fear and desire, and offers another telling that is more conventionally and concretely biographical ("stereotypical") even as he seems to question the utility of biography (the ironic question, "What contextualizes more than history?"). Of course, the expression of regret is performative, since Shepherd could have started the essay with precisely this reprised narrative. The performativity, then, dramatizes a delicate nuanced thing the speaker is trying to do: to introduce the particularity of his experience of black life without that particularity being consumed by a generic ideology of black privation. Imagine, for example, that Shepherd had begun the essay with the paragraph that begins, "I was born and raised in New York City. . . . I was raised by my mother, my father was an occasional negative mention." Such an opening, however honest, would conflate his story with ready narratives about blackness, overwhelmingly so, and would almost foreclose the worldness of a *singular* black speaker set loose in revelry and aesthetic wildness.

In this way, the reprisal privileges the speaker's oneness. That is, if the abstract telling and the more concrete one are both matters of his essaying, then this reprisal is chiasmic—one version of being erases and becomes another as the speaker gets to be of human breadth rather than being hampered by the treachery of discourse. "Let me begin again," he says, a performativity that inspires another unfurling, like a palinode—a poem that revises a view expressed in a previous poem. "Let me begin again," he says as he abides the process of his essay packed full of aliveness, his voice shimmying all over the page and into the air, twirling.[6]

The dynamism in "On Not Being White" reflects the fact that transparency eludes the speaker himself, and the sequence of repetitions and evasions constitutes subjunctivity. Indeed, Shepherd's speaker directly references subjunctivity in a passage where he considers further the idea of the past:

> I sought to shed the baggage of history as easily as I shed the few ghetto idioms I had, to shed even the baggage I didn't even know I carried. I wanted to erase the past and the present and live in the future. It wasn't *my* past, after all: all those dead people. Things are different today. Yesterday don't matter if it's gone. The operative word is "if." William Faulkner, that closet Confederate apologist, wrote that "the past is never gone. It is not even the past," but I have always been an adherent of the philosophy of "as if," more so than of "if only." But black people don't read Hans Vaihinger, do they? (49; emphasis in original)

Characteristic of the essay, a lot happens in this brief moment, though I am interested centrally in the citation of "as if" as a way to navigate the impositions of a collective black past. This "as if" is drawn from the work of German philosopher Hans Vaihinger, whose monograph *A Philosophy of As If* (1911) argues that people invent narratives and discourses—ideological realities—so as to organize what is incomprehensible and unknowable of the world.[7] In one regard, the speaker's casual reference to obscure philosophy is another example of performativity. And yet, it is not merely performative, since the speaker's ethos—

using rhetorical inventiveness to sustain unknowability—seems like an inverse of Vaihinger's hypothesis. (I love, too, how Shepherd explicates the philosophical formality of "as if" through a distinction with the commonplace—and vernacular—"if only.")

Overall, the subjunctive in "On Not Being White" reinforces the speaker's rejection of authenticity and his engagement of blackness as a conceit, as the fascinating floating signifier it is.[8] We see an example of this interface with blackness-as-idea in the conclusion of the foregoing passage; again:

> But black people don't read Hans Vaihinger, do they? They probably don't even read Faulkner. Black people are poor and uneducated and shiftless and poor (again) and *are never going to get anywhere.* I don't know where I've gone but I don't live in the projects anymore. So I couldn't be one of *them.* So (the logic is impeccable) I will behave as if I were not. Not that it ever mattered; everyone at my various private schools knew I was different: black and poor, and weird too. Everyone knew what I couldn't admit to myself. Don't talk about it and it will go away. "Don't look, it's ugly. It's a monster." The monster in my mind was always me. (49; emphases in original)

I'll come back to the four concluding sentences later on, though I quote this in full now because of the elegant rhythm of Shepherd's study in distance. Notice, for example, how the speaker articulates these ideas about blackness in plural, such that "black people" become characterized idiomatically as a lot of depravity. This pluralization idealizes these ideas, sets them in relief so that the speaker can encounter them; notice also how this dynamic is enhanced by sarcasm (the tag "do they?"), repetition (of "poor" for emphasis and distinction), and italicization (which materializes antiblack pejorative). All of these aesthetic moves indicate a speaker who is citing his process of distanciation and objectification.

"I don't know where I've gone," the speaker proclaims, but he is, regardless, becoming.

In the spirit of the essay genre as a black world, we are less likely to misread this passage as self-hatred, since the speaker is free to do what perhaps every black person does and has to do: to grapple with the annotations of our racial name. Shepherd's speaker doesn't control his encounters with the ideas of himself, be they biographical or historical; but neither does he have to be representative of or sustain fidelity to any of these ideas. Instead, the speaker of "On Not Being White" is held in suspension with himself, not toward resolution, but simply toward the bombard of encounter and the discovery it affords.[9]

Identity and its seemingly easy politics are not akin to the habitat of relation—this Shepherd's speaker knows and enacts.

And where are the anecdotes of this essay? They are told obliquely and vaguely, through high-styled feeling. Consider again the opening meditation on Pablo / Little Wing that flits around the page as a wispy description of a happening between the speaker and another man. Sure, there is no framing that indicates the heft of a specific incident, nothing that sets a scene as might occur with a proper anecdote, but the iteration seems like a piecemeal recall. Or consider this moment from the essay's second half:

> It's strange how willing white men become to approach me or be approached by me once they have seen me with another white man: if I like one I must of course like them all. The reverse is true as well; often when I have once seen a man with a black man he becomes more attractive or at least more interesting to me, simply because he has thus entered the realm of the possibly available: if he likes one he must of course like them all. Of course, I am not "black" enough for some of them: nothing cools the ardor of some white men "attracted" to black men more quickly than a large vocabulary. Then again, this is Boston; I have eyes. The great majority of the black men I see in clubs are with white men, and conversely far too many of the white men I see in those clubs look at me as if to say, "I couldn't sleep with *you*. You're *black*." (54; emphases in original)

One almost misses that this is an anecdote writ large except, perhaps, for the specificity of "this is Boston," which signals the speaker's inhabiting a particular place and time. Reading the passage closely, one notices the narrative frame of the opening sentence, something specific in the description of queer interracial approach. But the speaker doesn't offer details and instead leans on repetition (again, chiasmus) to expose the thinking to which he himself acquiesces: if I/he like(s) one, he/I must like them all. I love that Shepherd avoids making an argument here and lets the speaker remain entangled in the scene of objectification as the recollection moves in and out of his awareness of his hypocrisy. This entire sequence reeks of the speaker's processing through his existing in a happening, such that "It's strange" gives way to "The reverse is true"—an acknowledgment that seems of surprise—followed by "Of course" and finally "Then again." The speaker is processing experience—its harms, its meanings, its conundrums.

In Shepherd's essay, the anecdotes are stylized into eluding strokes that sustain tension, facilitating the speaker via a poetics of force, movement, captivation, and especially abjection. Such attention to the negative embraces the speaker's commitment to behold his ugliness and to use distance so as to be of his own terribleness. Indeed, what else is "On Not Being White" (the title, the essay) but an extended encounter with the vulgar and terrible? What else are those chiasmic phrases but the terror of being undone and remade through the holy syntactical exchange of one name for another? We might want to read these undertakings as political naïveté or something worse—racial treachery— but they might also be understood as the electricity of doubt manifest. The speaker, he who is on the make and replete with a performance of display, he is the hero of this essay, which studies through his bad and "ugly feelings"— ambivalence, reluctance, indifference, cowardice, and embarrassment.[10]

I love this essay's fine black aesthetics as I love its audacity. Every black one of us has a right to face the terror and beauty of blackness in our own way. And if we are to be able to behold Shepherd's speaker, we must be willing to give him room to be in and of relation with blackness, his delicate despairing dance. Such a thing could not be called self-hate since it is obsessed with—even in love with—blackness.

Shepherd's singular essay is home to a speaker who negotiates the happenings of blackness *personally*, even as the personal might be an insufficient reckoning. I don't mean to imply anything careless or naïve or superficial here (again: the personal is not the individual), but to say that the speaker orients toward his becoming such that the elisions and evasions sustain his alive being rather than support an argument.[11] His is a lyrical inhabitance. Consider this early and important moment in the essay:

> I've had notions, negative each one, images of what it is to *seem* black: to look black, to talk black, to walk black, to dress black; need I list the stigmata further? The language of culture and education was not among those seemings. I've shaped for myself a manner of appearing quite other than those seemings. If one didn't say those things, wear those things, if one didn't do things that way, then one would never, could never, be branded with that word, that awful word; though of course one was. That word does not appear in this essay. (48–49; emphasis in original)

It is that last sentence that matters most, the astuteness of the speaker to his own rightness and the refusal to name that word out loud. Another person might well feature that word as an epithet in their engagement of being—this doing might work for another person, but not in this speaker's process. The statement, "That word does not appear in this essay," pulls the speaker out of his voice and into the realm of direct address, but notice, too, that the address is capacious, divine, even—it is said definitively by the one in authority, addressed to no one and meaningful to all.

This moment always breaks my heart: I love the exquisite tenderness of the speaker toward himself, how his not-saying declares the direction of his performance. In this moment, "On Not Being White" clearly exists as the black speaker's habitat—an imperfect belonging, sure, but one that is inclined ever toward the essential privacy of a black one. That word is a public term with historical stakes and a legacy of grievances; it is not capable of the grief and beauty that bespeak this precise moment.[12]

What gorgeousness.

Earlier, I quoted a passage where the speaker names his own monstrosity, a proclamation that comes right before he restarts the telling: "Everyone knew what I couldn't admit to myself. Don't talk about it and it will go away. 'Don't look, it's ugly. It's a monster.' The monster in my mind was always me" (49). Again, the speaker aestheticizes the terrible, this time by rendering it as externalized speech. This doing enlivens the scene and lets the speaker reside as a character in its moment. Moreover, one isn't sure of the referent for the pronoun "it," which eludes clarity even in context of the full passage: Is "it" racism, or blackness, or the speaker as a young person in the world of whiteness? Is it weirdness, or queerness? What seems exceptionally clear is the declaration of kinship with monstrosity, which holds the speaker in the intimacy of his encounter with his own ambivalence, holds him in all the difference that is his oneness.[13]

In "A Politics of Mere Being," poet Carl Phillips argues for "an instancing—an enactment—of being as not only mere, but wildly various." We might think of mereness as the habitat of the essay, the essay as the approximation of black experience as *merely* aliveness. Such is Shepherd's attempt in "On Not Being White," where there is no triumph or completion to be had via the telling: just a scene of being. Here, then, is how the essay ends, falling into dissolve and into the very modest confession that, indeed, the speaker is not healed in the journey:

I just want to be me, but who would that be? So I can't live there, in that other realm of freedom. Freedom's just another word for being nothing. What and who would I be without the burden of the past, the past which I am constantly attempting to discard but also the past which I must reshape into something with which I can live, from which I can draw sustenance? Without it, I certainly wouldn't need my shining blond knight, and how could I live without him?

I read a very moving response to a question in *The Hite Report on Male Sexuality* of all places, a response to the section on gay men: "I used to call it 'love' when I was feeling pathologically afraid and inferior to another person. Now I call it love when I feel free and comfortable to be myself

with another person, and the emotion is joy instead of fear." I'm afraid I
have yet to reach that point, though I hardly spend my life in sackcloth
and ashes. The Special AKA sing: "If you have a racist friend / Now is the
time for your friendship to end." I have a friend like that, a friend I call
desire. Sometimes I don't know where he ends and I begin. Sometimes I
wish I could forget his name, but it sounds too much like mine. (57)

The personification at the end converts the speaker, finally, into desire and
its trembling messy porousness . . . its hungry entangled illogic. The speaker
maintains a certain incomprehensibility even to himself, appropriate enough
since "each individual is essentially strange. There is . . . a portion of ourselves
that we never fully comprehend."[14]

"On Not Being White" honors its black speaker's aliveness. All of its
dynamics—the chiasmic repetitions, the negations, the high-style performativity—
all of these can be read as attempts to authorize the speaker's own authenticity, not authenticity for the sake of corroborating one or another idea about
blackness, but authenticity as if to say: *these are my wicked and incommensurate*
coordinates; this is all the human I am. What a fantastic textuality, a black essay
where the speaker is the ideation of blackness on behalf of the being who is black,
where the aim is not to be free of blackness—being free of blackness might not
be possible or even desirable—but to be free *within* it, to be free in one's regard
to being of blackness.

One could call it a kind of exploitation—that the speaker exploits the idea of
blackness for himself. The word "exploit" might seem harsh or even dramatic,
but it also recalls Patricia J. Williams's description of her writing: "I deliberately sacrifice myself in my writing" (92). "Exploit" is the precise word, especially in regard to ravishment, exploiting as a reckless appreciating that leaves
everything possible, as in, that, too, could be me . . . exploiting as a textuality
of blackness through the capacious imaginary alighted by the imperative "Let
me tell you something that happened to me."[15]

The black essay as I am explicating it here does not pursue optimism or
achievement; it does not respond urgently to the social peril of blackness; it is
not a celebration of the yield of hard work, since there is nothing promised by
hard work other than more hard work.[16]

It is of the working that is of pleasure, just the doing . . . the difficult beauty
of being, the beauty of doing one's work.

If there are reservations about the freedom I am advocating via the essay as
a black genre, perhaps they generate from the anxiety of audience and representation. In "The Site of Memory," Toni Morrison describes this anxiety as

an exemplary burden of black American literary history, especially in regard to the position of the speaker of a slave narrative: "Whatever the style and circumstances of these narratives, they were written to say principally two things: One: 'This is my historical life—my singular, special example that is personal, but that also represents the race.' Two: 'I write this text to persuade other people—you, the reader, who is probably not black—that we are human beings worthy of God's grace and the immediate abandonment of slavery'" (66). In Morrison's estimation, the black speaker is inaugurated via the expectation of representativeness and is imagined to address a reader suspicious of the speaker's humanity. Morrison further argues that such burdened narratives deploy an aesthetic of modesty, a veil, refusing to be explicit in describing horrible happenings.

Morrison's thesis confirms that it is nearly impossible for the black first person to be able to enact full immersion into the essay genre's freedom, into the free being of voice. Indeed, there is another complication for the black writing subject, which Morrison explains in *Playing in the Dark: Whiteness and the Literary Imagination*: that the very words we might use to portray transformative experience are racialized, that "blackness" itself becomes a metaphor of encounter for the nonblack subject. Conceptually, blackness functions as "excitable speech" and therefore is always addressable externally, a figuring that warps how we understand black writing as an encounter with chaos, ignorance, inexpressibility.[17] These entanglements of audience leave little room for relationality in the personal essay, a genre that scholar Gerald Early describes as being overwhelmed by the doubleness of insider-outsider as well as of writer-reader: "The black essayist is caught between acting and writing, between seizing the instrumentality and being trapped by the fact that he is inescapably an instrumentality" (*Tuxedo Junction* xii–xiii). In the wake of this conundrum, Early celebrates the black essay's capacity to elude the nonblack reader or, alternately, as a text that brings the nation to racial reckoning.

Figured as a public intellectual, the black essayist is indeed "caught" ineptly in regard to the genre's vitality. In the excellent *On Freedom and the Will to Adorn: The Art of the African American Essay*, Cheryl A. Wall is clear that even as "the essay offers its creator intellectual freedom—the freedom to work around, with, and through an idea" (1), the black essayist always has to reconcile the public matter of antiblackness and racial subjection. As such, the genre doesn't necessarily offer its writer freedom but instead operationalizes a consideration of freedom *for the race*. Gerald Early confirms Wall's assessment in the introduction to his two-volume *Speech and Power: The African American Essay and Its Cultural Content from Polemics to Pulpit*:

(Few black writers have written what might be strictly called belles lettres-style essays.) The conditions under which many black writers felt they had to write (and live), and their coming to terms with these conditions, have constituted their most driving intellectual obsession. Thus, the black essay has been, in truth, a political provocation and a flawed example, if not a full representation, of a philosophical rumination even if the work itself was sometimes entangled in a thicket of sociological detail. Black writers could not help but see their writing as political, since they saw their *condition* in these terms and their writing and their *condition* have been largely inseparable. ("Gnostic or Gnomic?" x; emphases in original)

Early's and Wall's hedging of the black essay's capacity for wild freedom resonates with Vinson Cunningham's argument for the American essay as a particularly combative genre.[18] In "What Makes an Essay American," Cunningham pushes against John D'Agata's declaration of the essay as "neutral attempt" and advances the argument that "most of us Americans are Emersons: artful sermonizers, pathological point-makers." Cunningham makes the case that "conflict is elemental to America and to its creative expression; that a well-crafted argument is art, not its opposite; . . . that the more fiercely . . . our sensibilities clash, the better off our country might be."

In their appraisals of American literary tradition, Cunningham, Early, and Wall rightly declare the (black) essay as the domain of the public intellectual. And yet in this framing, they seem to surrender the capacity of the essay to political imperative, conscripting the genre as only (or largely) a surrogacy of racial politics, rather than attending to the essay as a potential circuit of wandering. This construal is overdetermined, I think, by the impositions of audience in and beyond US constructions of blackness and antiblackness.[19]

I don't mean to be obstinate to the fact of literary history where black essaying exists coterminously with the exigencies of social and political freedom. Indeed, in the enduring state of the world, it is hard to imagine—and even harder to manifest—the right of neutrality for a black speaker (writer) in the essay genre. But that imagining becomes more possible in *reading as if in a black world*. Essayists as varied as James Baldwin, Marita Bonner, Ta-Nehisi Coates, Ralph Ellison, Roxane Gay, Zadie Smith, and Patricia J. Williams all argue, in their own ways, against the burden of audience and representation—and all, variously, try to inhabit the freedom of essaying on the behalf of a black speaker, toward the philosophical oneness that is constitutive of the human.[20]

Could we undo audience as the fundamental instantiating principle of black expressiveness, not only audience as an interracial imprisonment but also the expectation that a black speaker speaks to and for a black audience? Could we imagine that a writer could sometimes—just sometimes—admit, "I don't know what political discourse needs but I know the need of this speaker (me) to feel through this thing"? Could we use the "imagine" of the essay to make untrue this gospel from the poet Cornelius Eady: "Presenting one's emotional truth is difficult enough. But unlike white writers, black writers are also expected to solve the problems they present in their work"?[21]

I am advocating for the heterogeneity of us that is possible in a textual world where there is no imperative of audience—at least not audience as such is over-determined by the needs of racial fidelity established in regard to antiblackness. In such an imaginary, the speaker tries to speak on their own behalf. A blackness without audience, where the display is not *of* the speaker and *for* the reader, but is display of and for the speaker, display of the speaker's undoing and beholding . . . of a figure of black being, open and subjectable to trial, where "trial" infers neither indictment nor conviction nor harm but simply means effort without conclusion. To try, which is the human praxis of being, every day to try; that is the habitat of the essay, and it can also be proxy for and of black being.

I am describing the idea of an essay's speaker as witness of a self, the speaker's own, on the page. As such, the speaker is writer *and reader* of the self who unfurls in the telling, which is a way to conceptualize the essay's "contradictory desires for recognition and freedom," what literary scholar Francesca T. Royster might call its performative black eccentricity (40). That is, in the ethos of the essay, the impetus for recognition is not necessarily exterior—not a public negotiation of worth—but instead the recognition that is possible via the vagary of relational oneness.[22]

The essay is the office of oneness, a scene of poetic inhabitance in the ways it lurches toward feeling and the incommensurate, its ecstatic use of language that exists as and creates a world for delicious, terrifying knowing. This commitment to the essay's poetic intelligence revives Audre Lorde's arguments about embodied knowing—Lorde, who, like Shepherd, was a poet. Indeed, one excellence of poetry rests in its mobilization of voice, "the way that the intimacy of a single voice speaking across time and space can become a call to empathy," in Natasha Trethewey's formulation.[23] This phrasing, "intimacy of a single voice speaking across time and space," appoints the essay's praxis of telling, how the speaker is reaching toward their own self-in-imagination, and how this reaching is dynamic in its travel and compounded in its intimacy. Yes, this is it. At its most capable, most affecting, most transformative, the first-person essay is a genre that revels in the whirlwind of that "single voice speaking," the dervish-like mess and grace of self-study. The essay might be a prose genre, but its logics are poetic, a bite-size affective fleshy thing that is awry of argument and replete with voice . . . and it can belong to a black one.[24]

The memoiristic essay can't sustain the needs of the collective. Maybe if we put together one thousand such essays by each writing person we'd have . . . one thousand essays by each person. The essay gives nothing but its scene to the speaker; it cannot be expected to give anything but its scene to the speaker. (It can be affecting to the reader, but we should not displace affect with intent or expectation. That is, its doing is beautiful and will inspire but it ought not be judged on its capacity for that.) The essay's happenings—its encounters with shame or fear or heatedness or doubt—are scaled to the world of the one . . . this is its aliveness.

The essay as an intimacy of black being, an openness of self-study that is not authority but something wilder and more fragile.[25]

I know that the legacy of racial blackness makes it nearly impossible to imagine a black speaker engaged in being without constituting that being as an argument in regard to antiblackness. That is, it is hard to imagine the black speaker being of the "neutral attempt." But it *must* be possible that if black people live lives full of everyday human confusion, then it is also possible that a black speaker, on the page, might be of or be oriented toward being in the trial . . . not as a one free of blackness but as a one who is free *within* blackness—as a figure who is able to be free within their regard to being of blackness.

Like the speaker in Toi Derricotte's "Beds."

Derricotte is the author of five poetry collections, most notably 1999's *Tender*, and cofounded Cave Canem (with Cornelius Eady), that superlative black poetry workshop. She also wrote the memoir *The Black Notebooks: An Interior Journey*, a *New York Times* Notable Book of the Year in 1997, so her foray into prose is not a detour. Indeed, Derricotte's oeuvre delights in the interior, in the affective trajectories of shame and regret and fear that she narrates as "poignantly realized details of feeling."[26]

"Beds," anthologized in the 2011 edition of *The Best American Essays*, is a collation of twenty-seven brief scenes each indicated by a Roman numeral. (There is also an italicized afterword.) The title as much refers to the fact that some of the episodes occur in sleeping quarters as it represents the essay's attention to the threat in seemingly innocuous domestic settings where full-bodied trauma is afoot. Derricotte's anecdotal telling, then, sketches life in a household where a father's violence terrorizes mother, daughter, and dog, though the focus is on the speaker (the daughter) as a narrating witness to her becoming. Indeed, this attunement is signaled by the essay's epigraph from Franz Kafka: "You say

I should go down further still, but I am already very deep down and yet, if it must be so, I will stay here. What a place! It is probably the deepest place there is. But I will stay here. Only do not force me to climb down any deeper." Kafka's speaker struggles against the call to go deeper, a call made by an unnamed other, though in truth, the speaker and the authoritative voice are really one. As such, the speaker names the fear that fuels and impedes essaying—that descent, falling and falling into, takes effort. It does not just happen; one also has to do it. Such is the context that frames our appreciation of the young black female speaker in "Beds."[27]

The essay proper begins with an impossible memory:

I.

The first was a bassinet. I don't remember what it was made of; I think it was one of those big white baskets with wheels. When I couldn't sleep at night, my father would drag it into the kitchen. It was winter. He'd light the gas oven. I remember the room's stuffiness, the acrid bite of cold and fumes.

My father didn't like crying. He said I was doing it to get attention. He didn't like my mother teaching me that I could cry and get attention. Nothing was wrong with me, and, even if I was hungry, it wasn't time to eat. Sometimes, I screamed for hours, and my father—*I do remember this*—would push his chair up to the lip of the bassinet and smoke, as if he was keeping me company.

After a few nights, he had broken me, but when he put the bottle to my lips, I was too exhausted to drink. (49; emphasis added)

Because the opening sets the speaker as a baby in a bassinet, it amplifies the imprecision of remembering, particularly any recollection done through family happenings. The authority of the speaker's telling wobbles further because of the father's voice, which crowds in through free indirect speech: "Nothing was wrong with me, and, even if I was hungry, it wasn't time to eat." As the speaker's voice mingles with the father's in a kind of ventriloquism, ambivalence permeates the memory. Surely the child experienced these happenings, but how much could she remember in this precise language? "Beds" commences with this tussle between the infant speaker and her recalcitrant surveilling father, though the speaker interrupts the ambivalence to assert the authority of her becoming: "I do remember this." This declaration is vital, and it reminds us that the (adult) speaker is watching as well as reinhabiting the threshold scene of her baby-self, that it is the speaker's mattering that matters.

The next episode confirms the speaker's reflective viewpoint: "My second was a crib in the corner of my parents' room. We moved to the attic when I was 18 months old, *so it must have been before that*" (49; emphasis added). In this moment, framed by archival doubt, the speaker recalls her sleeplessness and imagines the father as a gray monster and a tree. From these first two episodes, we almost expect a sequence of tellings marked by one bed and then another ("the first was," "my second was"), but what becomes apparent by the third sequence is that the idiom bed is metaphorical, an item of furniture that conjures a spatial concept of repose, rest, fitfulness, vulnerability, dreaming, perhaps the innermost intimate locale in a home:

III.

My aunt brought home a present for me every day when she came from work. I'd wait excitedly by the kitchen door as soon as I could walk. Sometimes, she'd fish down in her pocketbook, and the only thing she could find was a Tums, which she called candy. But mostly she'd bring colored paper and pencils from the printing press where she worked.

When I was 2 or 3, I began to draw things and to write my own name. I wrote it backward for a long time: "I-O-T." I drew houses, cars, money, animals. I actually believed everything I drew was real; the house was a real house, as real as the one we lived in. I held it in my hand. It belonged to me, like a chair or an apple. From then on, I did not understand my mother's sadness or my father's rage. If we could have whatever we wanted just by drawing it, there was nothing to miss or to long for. I tried to show them what I meant, but they shrugged it off, not seeing or believing.

(The sideways escape—the battle between my father's worst thought of me and this proof, this stream of something, questioned and found lacking, which must remain nearly invisible—pressed into what leaks out as involuntarily as urine, a message, a self, which must be passed over the coals, raked, purified into a thin strand of unambiguous essence of the deep core.) (49-50)

There is no bed portrayed here, though we get the first characterization of female subjects other than the speaker—the aunt and the mother—as well as the implication that bed is an idiom of the speaker's interior and creativity. Notice, for example, that in addition to recalling the aunt's inventiveness such that Tums become a gift of candy, the speaker slips into a parenthetical voice to describe her "sideways escape"; that is, the speaker narrates her creativity in a performative syntax of creative indirection.

Increasingly, Derricotte recounts the speaker's subjectivity in terms of creativity, resonant of Kafka's notion of descent-as-encounter. In this way, Derricotte's essay becomes a meditation on discovery, and it elevates the speaker's *thinking* as an act of divination:

> Thinking was the thing about me that most offended or hurt him, the thing he most wanted to kill. (Episode VI, 50)

> Sometimes, I believed that the things in the world heard your thoughts, the way God heard prayers. When I was very young, not even out of my crib, I'd ask the shades to blow a certain way to prove they heard me. (Episode XI, 52)

These passages showcase a persona who revels in the exploration of her irrepressible wandering thoughts on all that happened, whose ambition is to pursue intimacy. The speaker tells us as much in episode VIII, after a quotation from a newspaper article on abused children who abuse animals (the newspaper reports that "such children can only achieve a sense of safety and empowerment by inflicting pain and suffering on themselves and others"):

> *I am trying to get as close as possible to the place in me where the change occurred*: I had to take that voice in, become my father, eternally vigilant, the judge referred to before any dangerous self-assertion, any thought or feeling. *I happened in reverse*: My body took in the pummeling actions, which went down into my core. The voice is no longer his. It is my voice asking, before any love or joy or passion, anything that might grow from me: "Who do you think you are?" I suppress the possibilities. (51; emphases added)

This moment articulates the trial of the essay, the attempt to develop proximity to a discursive process animated by distance, deferral, and delay. "I am trying to get as close as possible," the speaker exhales as an homage to her thinking, suppressed thing that it has been in the past and still is now. But the real gem of the passage is the encapsulation "I happened in reverse," a terrific equivocation that reminds us that the speaker is mobilizing distance on her behalf. That is, this phrase of orientation could refer to the speaker's contemporaneous happening in the face of revisiting these sequences of childhood being. Or it could be synonymous with the "sideways escape" of earlier, as a term of an indirect, circular, irregular route of coming into one's relation. Whatever the case, "I happened in reverse" declares the speaker's becoming through the object case, as a subject displaced from the center of her own being (the displacement is both in the happening and in regard to telling the happening). This sense of displacement connects to all the ways the speaker is set, and sets herself, in relief through various instances of pervasive domestic danger. Moreover, Derricotte's description of delay—the "reverse" of the speaker's happening—makes us aware of the essay as a habitat of time, where the speaker encounters a past self in a present.[28]

These aesthetics of distance and displacement frame the domestic peril in "Beds," particularly the erotic tension and violence cultivated through the father's harming behavior toward his daughter. Rather than criticize or rationalize such awfulness, the speaker exists *in regard* to the happenings: "Life is something you have to get used to: what is normal in a house, the bottom line, what is taken for granted" (episode XIV, 53). Which is precisely what the speaker is doing—becoming familiar ("get used to") with the experiences of her being, engaging in reading herself as she thinks through the past. Such an open orientation reinforces the episodic quality of the essay's intensities:

> He was the ruler of my body. I had to learn that. It had to be as if he were deep in me, deeper than instinct, like the commander of a submarine during times of war. (Episode V, 50)

> My father and I shared a new bedroom, and my mother slept on the pullout in the living room so that she couldn't wake us when she got dressed in the morning for work. We slept in twin beds, pushed up close together, as if we were a couple.
>   I could have slept with my mother in the bedroom. . . . I could have slept on the pullout. (Episode XV, 53)

> My mother shopped after work every Thursday, so my father would come home and fix dinner for me. . . . He'd bring it [the steak] home and unwrap the brown paper . . . like someone doing a striptease. (Episode XVI, 54)

> I was never happier than when I was with my father and he was in a good mood. . . . He was so handsome that I felt proud when people noticed us. . . . I had dressed up as if I were his girlfriend. (Episode XVII, 54)

The sequence here is progressive without being cumulative, such that there is no conclusion that sexual abuse occurred, even as the speaker resides in the clutch of these influential occurrences. We might want a more argumentative case made in defense of this black girl, but what organizes the voice of the essay is the speaker existing in the poise of watching her exposedness, as in a moment from episode XIX where she describes offering to dance for her father:

> I thought, maybe, if he saw I was almost a woman and could do what beautiful women do, he might find a reason to love me.
>
> At the end [of the dance], I spun around and around until most of the drapes, towels and my mother's nightgown fell to the floor. I don't remember what remained to cover me. (55)

This is a dreamy and discomfiting scene, iterative of fantasy. Here, the speaker doesn't resolve the moment and instead leaves her (young) self exposed in that last line, "I don't remember what remained to cover me," where the forgetting resonates with the elusive covering and with the connotative heft of the word "remained": something left, abandoned, lost; something resilient. She, the speaker, watches herself there, *remains* to watch herself; her force materializes in the recognition to be had in the telling of this pointed scene. Said another way, the speaker watches; she becomes a one in the object case, an example of third-person being in the first-person essay.[29]

Derricotte's "Beds" exemplifies the essay genre as a habitat of black aliveness: the dramatization of the world of a black one, of the encounter between self and other self that manifests relational being; the negotiation of past (something happened) and present (I am happening) into a subjunctive fabulation that surpasses the logics of chronology and argument; the capacity to tingle in the creativity and surprise of being. In these ways, we might understand the essay as *the opulence of a black mind* . . . a speaker's thinking that is reflective of one's embodied intelligence, that encompasses the world scale of happening such as is present in this sequence of twenty-seven scenes that think through and reckon with experience. Moreover, Derricotte's doing renders the first-person essay as an approximation of a speaker's interior, where the term "interior" resonates more with Édouard Glissant's opacity than with any fallacy of integrity or transparency. Yes, the essay tries to stylize *thought* as a materiality of one's being, as if lines of thinking, on the page, would be put in quotation marks just as lines of speech might be.[30]

I love how "Beds" gathers as an imperfect site of holdings and a site where beholding happens—an archive of the impossible. That is, in light of confrontations with the inevitable failure of archives, the essay generically bypasses historical telling and coheres as a repository of something undone. I read Derricotte's catalog, this storehouse of knowing, as a useable stash of memories that assumes incompleteness. We see this incompleteness in the adverbs that temporalize some of the scenes—for example, "once," which opens episode

XIX, and "sometimes," which commences episode XX. We see it also in the speaker's dynamism near the essay's end, first speaking of herself in the third person universal—"You would think that the one treated so cruelly would 'kill' the abuser, throw him out of the brain forever" (episode XXVI, 58)—and then admitting how entangled her father's worldview is with her own:

> In the deepest place of judgment, not critical thinking, not on that high plain, but first waking judgment, judgment awakened with perception, judgment of the sort that decides what inner face to turn toward the morning sun—in that first choosing moment of what to say to myself, the place from which first language blossoms—I choose, must choose, my father's words. . . . There is no inner loyalty, no way of belonging. I cannot trust what I feel and connect to. . . . I do this to myself in remembrance. (59)

This reflection on judgment, perception, and language, these essential human doings that have consumed philosophers over time, come to no resolution except perhaps a fidelity to the state of being unfinished. "I do this to myself in remembrance," the speaker proclaims, since to assay through this archive is to hold one's being in regard, in suspense, in ordinary honor.[31]

The incompleteness is amplified by Derricotte's final episode, which returns to a scene from her youth—"The time I had the migraine, after my father had beaten me, he made me bathe"—and which the speaker summarizes thus: "Maybe he had some idea of how much he had hurt me. I knew that, sometimes, men beat their women and then make up. I didn't know what to believe" (episode XXVII, 59). The essay ends with enduring confusion, a speaker who remains immersed in this (past) feeling observing a girl child who is ensconced in a domestic idiom of female subjection. The openness here ("I didn't know what to believe") is vocalized in past tense but resides in the speaker's contemporaneous time—as a present happening—in the italicized afterword, where the speaker's voice sits in exceptional relief: *"I hear in myself a slight opposition, a wounded presence saying, 'I am me, I know who I am.' But I am left with only a narrow hole, a thin tube of rubber that the words must squeak through. Where words might have gushed out as from a struck well, I watch it—watch every thought, every word. It wasn't my father's thought that I took in; it was the language. It is the language in me that must change"* (59). Here, finally, the speaker renders her watching in theatrical and embodied terms, and describes her essaying as a pageant of gushing, squeaking words, visible and tangible. If this afterword resolves, it does so as a moment of relationality where the speaker suspends in regard to herself, where the conclusion remains eternal as a charge for now: to think and inhabit the present, vivaciously, vis-à-vis the past and what may come.[32]

There is no meaning to deduce from this essay except that it was written, that its aesthetics are superb, that its speaker speaks dynamically. (The writer might have something to say about the "after" of the essay, but that is different from our beholding its worldmaking aesthetics.) So Derricotte's "Beds" arrives as a textuality that figures the tender being and becoming of a black female speaker, a terrain through which the speaker can proceed, not necessarily forward or upward . . . descent, as Kafka might say, as an instance of one's deepening. ("I happened in reverse," she says.) In Derricotte's scene-scape, the anecdotes exist as a sequence of shimmering bits and the speaker becomes unrecognizable as a self, maybe even unrecognizable to herself, at the center of these instances of her invention and inventiveness.[33]

(What a joy it is to engage essays up close, to perceive their structural fineness.)

Simply, and not so simply, the essay aims to tell a story around a thing that happened. The story is not meant to be representative, or prescriptive; it is, after all, just one story, and human life cannot be reduced to signs on a page. Instead, each story's value is found in its telling, its speaker's surrender to the world possible in her specificity. The essay, then, is an invitation to look at and through the idiom of one's self, a thrall, a performative act of black rightness. And the freedom to be had through the essay is the freedom to be of encounter, freedom as the orientation of the one who is object, subject, author.

Of course, the difficulty of these ideas lies in their breadth—freedom, even as we know better than to think any human in the modern world is free; the fallacy that the essay can manifest as space of unfettered being, given its performativity and its display (it is, after all, a genre of publicness). I don't mean to disregard this complexity, though I mean to suggest that we can read the essay through oneness, and that such a reading can be meaningful to thinking about black relationality as such is possible in a black world orientation.

The speaker of the essay begins her thinking thus: *I am alive. No matter what else can be said about the condition of my being, I am alive. Aliveness is of me.* Even if this preface is performative, it is an enunciation that aims to establish the speaker as one to whom things happen, as a one who happens. Again, to be free in blackness, to be free in regard to one's alive being of blackness.

Every human animal has in them perfect intelligence; that is, in every human is full feeling, hunger and ripeness and lethargy and unease, all of it in a rhythm that is as it is. Such intelligence is perfect in that it is rightly of the being—again, it is as it is, and one can know through it. For this reason, in "Form-of-Life," philosopher Giorgio Agamben argues for thought as the habit or character that constitutes what is indefinable about life. Not thought as "the individual exercise of an organ or of a psychic faculty, but rather an *experience*" (9; emphasis added).

Agamben advocates for thought, thinking, as a phenomenological act, an unrepresentable case of being human. And in this way, life is of one who thinks, where thinking is not a privileged intellectual act: life is of one who thinks; one who thinks has and is of life. What disturbs the rightness of this knowing and thinking is the need to try to communicate with or cohere through sociality (even as sociality, via relation, also makes possible more knowing).[34]

The essay is of the open totality of this knowing. It swoons in the imperative-subjunctive of "imagine this," that worldmaking invocation, the immanent and transcendent self-ensnarement. I find inspiration in the way that the first-person essay tries to dispense with argument and tarries instead in the study of a moment. (Sigh: I am aware of the irony of making an argument using the example of essays.) I find inspiration in the way that the essay doesn't explicitly substantiate (evidence) though its aestheticization and approximation of experience make—or try to make—something evident.[35] The essay, this genre of black thinking rendered as a thrilling materiality; the essay as aliveness, as a practice of aliveness that holds ethical implications because it is a deepening of one's capacity of being. Indeed, in paying close attention to Derricotte's and Shepherd's speakers, I am trying to highlight the exquisite work of studying, their trying to stay with their version of the human question, how to be, a question that cannot be asked from a place of deficit, a question that has no predetermined answer and that cannot be fulfilled by identity, a question that must be pursued from the grace of one's capaciousness.

(This chapter is dedicated to Hilton Als, whose cultural criticism works through the essay form superbly, whose narrative personas try to engage the black freedom possible in the genre.)[36]

5 ALIVENESS

AND ETHICS

"It was the right thing to do, but she had no right to do it."[1] This is the borrowed line that Toni Morrison uses to summarize Sethe's consequential action from *Beloved*, the attempt to kill her three young children rather than see them returned to the horrors of slavery, an unsanctioned sanctified act that succeeds with one child, the middle daughter. I love how Morrison's chiasmus expresses the unresolved and unresolvable matter of ethics, the impossibility of Sethe being able to orient herself rightly in an antiblack world. And yet Morrison's comment also maintains that the disavowal of black ethical possibility does not surpass the importance of understanding Sethe as an ethical subject. Pivoting on two different meanings of "right," Morrison's summation acknowledges the terrible fate for enslaved children (what makes infanticide potentially a right thing) as it asks us to behold Sethe as human and, as such, responsible to questions about being—an imagining where Sethe's thinking and doing are philosophical in caliber.[2]

"It was the right thing to do, but she had no right to do it."

In an antiblack world, the black subject is essentially nonrelational. In an antiblack world, there is no ethical possibility for the one who is black: there is no figuring through one's humanity because one's humanity is figured already as marginal, subjected, diminished. Said another way, if the ethical conceptually depends on one's instantiation as *a one*, the discourse of antiblackness hinders such instantiation, for as James Baldwin reminds us, "the American triumph—in which the American tragedy has always been implicit—was to make black people despise themselves."[3] In the face of an imperative for self-despisal, the only orientation possible is either acquiescence to being wrong or antagonism to the hypothesis of wrongness. An antiblack imaginary presumes to have nullified the question "how to be," since we either are whatever the world says we are or are enmeshed in refusing that imposition. Of course, acquiescence is intolerable, and though defiance is essential, it is not sufficient enough to honor ethical inhabiting. In either instance, the black one is *turned away* from rather than *into* herself, alienated from the site that might generate ethical rendering.

Baldwin's declaration comes in an open letter to Angela Davis as she awaited trial in 1970, though the conditions of black being that he articulates reverberate beyond this context. For sure, the terms of self-despisal constitute a hitch in the common understanding of social justice, where, at best, black being—disregarded, harmed, or killed being—is the object lesson that inspires justice and spurs racial reckoning for the nation-state, as well as for the person who is not black. This is the metaphorical use of black life as a scene of social thinking, a scene that excludes and exempts blackness from the conditions of life itself: the proverbial canary in the coal mine; the killed or harmed one whose cry or pain becomes the impetus for an antiblack world to try to confront itself. Such dynamics cannot withstand the black one as a subject of being and therefore as a subject of the ethical question; such dynamics are not the condition of black livelihood.[4]

Sigh: One can only undertake the ethical in a context where orientation remains open, such as the relationality constituted in a text's invocation of a black world. That is, as a question, "How am I being/becoming?" cannot be figured through the terms of worth and value on which antiblackness is predicated. Simply, every black one is already worthy since they are on earth and worth is a human legacy. And embedded in this claim is the companion notion that every human being is called on to manifest their worth—to believe it, to act of its accord, to negotiate its parameters and fall short of its obligation, over and again: this is what might be called grace, the work of trying every day to be engaged in an investigation of one's being. I know that the historical denigration of blackness troubles any suggestion that one has to *reckon with, earn,* one's worth. And still, the invitation to reckon must be countenanced without being anchored to an ideology of black nonvalue.[5] Reckon we must, since the reckoning with being human is ours to bear: "Our humanity is our burden," Baldwin reminds us, "we need not battle for it; we need only to do what is infinitely more difficult—that is, accept it."[6] One does not have to display one's reckoning to another so as to have it be verified or confirmed; one does not have to be of a certain manner or tethered to a normative idea of what constitutes ethical encounter. One must reckon, over and again.

"It was the right thing to do, though she had no right to do it."

Morrison's willingness to behold the ethical recalls the idiom of care articulated by literary theorist Christina Sharpe as wake work: "What happens when we proceed as if we *know* this, antiblackness, to be the ground on which we stand, the ground from which we to [sic] attempt to speak, for instance, an 'I' or a 'we' who know, an 'I' or a 'we' who are" (7; emphasis in original). Sharpe's declaration refuses the fallacy of thinking black ethics in any normative frame, since the normative is antiblack, and her emphasis on proceeding "as if we *know*" is akin to instantiating a black world orientation. Morrison's chiasmus and Sharpe's theorizing represent a black feminist poethics in the way philosopher Denise Ferreira da Silva means the term, a creative praxis that abandons the creeds of the antiblack world toward "the ethical mandate of opening up other ways of knowing and doing" ("Toward" 81). Again, Morrison doesn't elide the ethical; instead, she authors it in the black world of a novel where ethical weight can fall humanly, rightly, on a black and female one. As such the question isn't only about the legality of murder or the wrath of slavery's terror, but also a high order of self-assessment embedded in confronting Sethe and her doing. I take Morrison's insight as inspiration for exploring the black ethical through the language of ordinary examples.[7]

"How to be" is as essential a question as it is unanswerable, especially because its interrogative is more wide open than "what" (what to do, what to be).[8] "How" indicates manner, condition, and means—it is a discernment that includes thinking about one's instance and capacity of being, as in: what am I feeling, what resources do I have, what do I need, what can I do, what might be its impact. The scale of the question "how to be" is a profoundly personal one, which is how it appears in a disagreement about goodness in the last conversation that Sula has with Nel. The exchange—an argument, really—comes while Sula is in pain on her deathbed; Nel visits to pay respect but also to seek an explanation for Sula's infidelity with Nel's husband, Jude. Their conversation runs for six pages, and it crackles as a scene of philosophical dialogue between the two, each repeating the other's short phrases in ways that expose the competing understanding in each woman's positionality. Sula's illness does nothing to dull the audacity that allows her to imagine and pursue rightness of being, and at the end,

> embarrassed, irritable and a little bit ashamed, Nel rose to go. "Goodbye, Sula. I don't reckon I'll be back."
>
> She opened the door and heard Sula's low whisper. "Hey, girl." Nel paused and turned her head but not enough to see her.
>
> "How you know?" Sula asked.
>
> "Know what?" Nel still wouldn't look at her.
>
> "About who was good. How you know it was you?"
>
> "What you mean?"
>
> "I mean maybe it wasn't you. Maybe it was me." (Morrison, *Sula* 146)

There are no more words between them after this moment—Nel takes "two steps out the door and close[s] it behind her." I want to appreciate Sula's "How you know?" as a genuine query in her consideration of goodness. Earlier, Sula is more resolute in declaring that "being good to somebody is just like being mean to somebody. Risky. You don't get nothing for it" (144–145). Indeed, she makes the comment as a retort to Nel's suggestion that one's goodness matters in the abstract and can be adjudicated outside one's self. "It matters," Sula says of good-doing, "but only to you. Not to anybody else" (144). Here, Sula dismisses a notion of goodness as an inflection of domestic respectability since an ethical framework can't be given to you; instead, she advances a starker concept of ethical *pursuit*. For her, goodness is a lifelong query, an unsettled and unsettlingly personal one. So when she says, "Maybe it was me," we can consider the statement not only as sarcasm, as if Sula intends to say, "Of course it was me," but also in regard to the chapter's depiction of a character who is caught in the surprise of what dying means, as a person reckoning again with the quality of how she has lived. As such, "How you know?" expresses Sula's speculative ethos, her investment in her right to be alive and to be of the questions afforded by aliveness. Sula can bear the open-endedness of these questions because of the faith she has in her rightness of being and its invitation to surrender to the ambivalence of knowing. That this doing is personal doesn't abdicate the consideration of care or relationality. Indeed, an ethics of goodness can account for harm, but only as much as the harming one can behold the harm they have done, only as much as the harmed one can speak—to themself at least—the name of said harm. Ethics is the site of self-beholding, and therefore Sula is not invoking the apparatus of the state to adjudicate the possibilities of goodness, since the state could not recognize her or Nel, nor their righteous actions toward being of a life. She is grappling with—unsettled in—her thinking about being and how to be, about the life she inhabits and its force in the world, including its force with, between, toward Nel.[9]

I call again on *Sula* because of my commitment to oneness as the name for a subject of philosophical significance, a self-centered idiom of the human being engaged in her living. And though Sula's self-centeredness might seem unethical, such interpretations overlook the relational praxis of her audacity. Who else but Sula thinks through the wealth of being and occupies each day oriented by "how to be"? Sula, she who realizes that there is no ethical compass offered by an antiblack and antifemale world, even as the need for an ethic pulses within: "Because each had discovered years before that they were neither white nor male, and that all freedom and triumph was forbidden to them, they had set about *creating something else to be*" (52; emphasis added). This is the novel's—and its title character's—figuring of the ethical imperative through the relationality of black female oneness.[10]

The black text is a black world where a black one can navigate the ethics of being, the question of how to be.[11]

The authority of Sula's thinking recalls Audre Lorde's ideas, which I have co-opted for defining aliveness. Remember that in "Uses of the Erotic," Lorde directs us clearly toward the ethical as being held in feeling:

The erotic is a measure between the *beginnings* of our sense of self and the chaos of our strongest feelings. It is an internal sense of satisfaction to which, once we have experienced it, we know we can aspire. For having experienced the fullness of this depth of feeling and recognizing its power, *in honor and self-respect we can require no less of ourselves.* (*Sister Outsider* 54; emphases added)

For the erotic is not a question only of what we do; it is *a question of how acutely and fully we can feel in the doing* (54; emphasis added)

In Lorde's formulation, self-interrogation is key to a meaningful living practice. She extends this notion in two later passages:

Beyond the superficial, the considered phrase, "It feels right to me," acknowledges the strength of the erotic into a true knowledge, for what that means is the first and most powerful guiding light toward any understanding. Any understanding is a handmaiden which can only wait upon, or clarify, that knowledge, deeply born. The erotic is the nurturer or nursemaid of all our deepest knowledge. (56)

When we begin to live from within outward, in touch with the power of the erotic within ourselves, and allowing that power to *inform and illuminate our actions* upon the world around us, then we begin to *be responsible to ourselves* in the deepest sense. (58; emphases added)

What is conceptualized here is not solipsism but a relational practice of study where the initial sentiment ("It feels right to me") ushers in another "understanding"; that is, the rightness of one's feeling—of inhabiting and interrogating feeling—gives way to a deeper appreciation of one's being in the world. The force of contemplative engagedness, rather than closing off the contemplative one in rabid isolation and individualism, inspires more capacity. I could cite again the opening of "Poetry Is Not a Luxury" to reinforce that the interrogative "how" coheres in Lorde's work: "The *quality of light by which we scrutinize our lives* has direct bearing upon the product which we live, and upon the changes which we hope to bring about through those lives" (*Sister Outsider* 36; emphasis added). Indeed, this sequence of passages exemplifies that the imperative of Lorde's thinking is toward *principled being*, toward the ethical, a tumbling movement into more and more consciousness that we might call studying.[12]

Throughout this project, I have used the words "study" and "studying" to describe the attentiveness of an alive one. We might think of studying as the special province of the academy, but here I mean studying as a human endeavor, the way that Lorde or Baldwin or Sula invites us to pursue intelligence by giving attention to what troubles and what intrigues. Studying, in this vernacular, constitutes being a holy philosopher of one's inhabiting of the world, what Socrates named as the vitality of examining one's life.[13] It *might* involve books and a nudge from a mentor, as in the anecdote from Nikky Finney's National Book Award acceptance speech, where in giving thanks for the gift of encouragement, Finney recounts an efficient anecdote from her college years: "Dr. Gloria Wade Gayles, great and best teacher, you asked me on a Friday, 4 o'clock, 1977, I was 19 and sitting on a Talladega College wall dreaming about the only life I ever wanted, that of a poet. 'Miss Finney,' you said, 'do you really have time to sit there, have you finished reading every book in the library?'"[14] I want to be clear that the urgency here is not particular to the institutional, but instead comes from what it means to have fidelity to the doing. Studying is ordinary, and Finney, whose poetry regularly invokes scenes of instruction,[15] characterizes this everydayness through a love of pencils:

I was raised in a land of pencils and pencil users. I was reared around people who worked with their hands: seamstresses, tailors, carpenters, teachers, butchers, coaches, painters, farmers, electricians, plumbers. These small town folk were close inside my life and within my eyeshot. I noticed them and how they did their work in the world. As they kept an eye on me, I noticed their pencil habits. Pencils were a part of their tool belts and jewelry. It was not unusual how they kept pencils so near their lives, just inside a purse, in an overalls pocket, on a cash register, on a string dangling from a nail in the wall, over an earlobe. As a girl, not only did I like to write with pencils but I also liked to read them and imagine the places they represented: Jimmy's Hog Heaven, Dent's Undertaking Establishment, The Silver Moon Café, Johnson's Nursery, Miss Mable's Frozen Pies and Custards. Pencils got me going about words and the work worlds of human beings. Pencils in my girlhood were tiny handheld billboards; they were jumbo pencils with knife-carved points; cigar-size pencils with teeth marks speckled all down their backs, evidence of a nervous mouth; early morning computation; or an evening with lunations found in the almanac.

As a girl, I tied pencils to sweat and hard work. I associated them with calculations and contemplation. People who worked with their hands and their heads used pencils. *People who made mistakes and understood the power of second effort reached for pencils.* (215–216; emphasis added)

This passage, from an essay titled "Inquisitor and Insurgent: Black Woman with Pencil, Sharpened," describes "pencil habits" as a manner of being and working in the world, a habitat of worldly existence where one is attentive and has regard for possibility. The labor and the trial described here constitute studying as an ethic for and of the black one.

Part of thinking about study is a rethinking of our understanding of work, to make the term "work" or "labor" usable again. That is, in the logic and critique of racial capitalism, the notion of work seems corrupt and irredeemable. And still, here in these poems and essays—and in the invitation for the black one to be of/in relation with the phenomenon of her reading—is a wealth of *work*, the craft or poiesis where what is being made is the self's project of inhabiting life rather than a product that confirms systems of capital. The work I mean here animates rather than degrades or violates the black one. "I want to make myself" (92), Sula says, not as an overdetermined sense of completion but as an articulation of a will toward becoming, the certainty that can withstand uncertainty. Work, effort, will, labor: all these words seem inept, though what I really mean by them is the poetic happenings of one, the possibilities for study illuminated by one being engaged in the circuits of one's being. Work as an iteration of oneness, as a thing that happens on one's behalf rather than against the one—a relational dynamic of the one, similar to the Old English connotation of the word "craft" as "a form of knowledge, not just a knowledge of making but a knowledge of being" (Langlands 7).[16]

It is terrifying, this work that is a descent into knowing, a terror rendered beautifully in James Baldwin's singular essay "Nothing Personal":

> It has always been much easier (because it has always seemed much safer) to give a name to the evil without than to locate the terror within. And yet, the terror within is far truer and far more powerful than any of our labels: the labels change, the terror is constant. And this terror has something to do with that irreducible gap between the self one invents—the self one takes oneself as being, which is, however, and by definition, a provisional self—and the undiscoverable self which always has the power to blow the provisional self to bits. It is perfectly possible—indeed, it is far from uncommon—to go to bed one night, or wake up one morning, or simply walk through a door one has known all one's life, and discover, between inhaling and exhaling, that the self one has sewn together with such effort is all dirty rags, is unusable, is gone: and out of what raw material will one build a self again? (384)

Ah, Baldwin: Baldwin goes right to the heart of aliveness, its responsibility and its tenuous tender edges. He imagines the "terror within" as a source of energy for being in one's life. And his syntax, that exceedingly long and wandering final sentence of tumbling lyrical sublimity, mimics the terrifying quality of feeling. Both the syntax and claim reflect Baldwin's ideological voluptuousness, the way that he hardly ever concludes an argument—there is rarely ever a pithy summary or a sense that the speaker has won the day—but instead sustains in the righteous pursuit of knowing.[17] Here I am implying a crucial distinction between righteous and self-righteous: self-righteousness elevates the self-righteous one above others and is nonrelational (because I believe this, I am better than you), whereas righteousness exists in regard to one's studying, is a call to act from and in regard to that which one believes. The orientation of the righteous is toward becoming, toward inhabiting being rather than toward the denigration of an other.

The righteousness of trying to learn (from) the things one already knows, of trying to *know* what one already knows, a deepening of insight, a humility and ferocity of pursuit: this I believe and by this I shall try to live rightly.

Studying is ordained righteously, and it is also lonely—the feeling and the work of pursuance is lonely. Think back to the invitation in Lucille Clifton's "won't you celebrate with me" and the reiterated imperative in closing, "come celebrate / with me." That invitation constitutes a lonely practice, lonely not only because of the question and the enjambed clause that seem to separate the speaker from her audience, but even more so because the poem aestheticizes an invocation of the one by the one. Again:

won't you celebrate with me
what i have shaped into
a kind of life? i had no model.
born in babylon
both nonwhite and woman
what did i see to be except myself?
i made it up
here on this bridge between
starshine and clay,
my one hand holding tight
my other hand; come celebrate
with me that everyday
something has tried to kill me
and has failed. (427)

The vocative energy here designates a speaker in reflection, and the tender clarity of the killing threat—that invitation to come celebrate—marks the speaker as one on the cusp of newly arrived knowing (the clay enrobed by not sunlight but "starshine"). Clifton's verse often dramatizes the call to do one's solitary work, as is the case in many of her Lucifer poems, Lucifer being the figure of the poet herself since both are named for light. Here I am thinking of the eight-poem sequence "brothers," which includes the following note at the start:

(*being a conversation in eight poems between an aged Lucifer and God, though only Lucifer is heard. The time is long after.*) (466; italics in original)

The first poem is titled "invitation" and commences stunningly:

come coil with me
here in creation's bed
among the twigs and ribbons
of the past. (466)

We might notice the echo between this invocation and the one in "won't you celebrate with me," as well as the excellent verb "coil" that characterizes perfectly Lucifer's habitat and longing. And since we know that God doesn't speak in these poems, since *the silence of God is God* (469; italics in original) as Clifton tells us in a later epigraph, Lucifer's invitation is toward himself. There is no response to the entreaty to "coil," and throughout the eight lyrics, Clifton showcases Lucifer's voice moving through anger, regret, and then resolution, alternating between his speaking directly *to* God, speaking *of* God, and sometimes speaking as if to himself. In the final poem, Clifton repeats the epigraph about God's silence—it is a line from a Carolyn Forché poem—with a signal difference:

8.
". . . . . *is God.*"

so.
having no need to speak
You sent Your tongue
splintered into angels.
even i,
with my little piece of it
have said too much.
to ask You to explain
is to deny You.
before the word
You were.
You kiss my brother mouth.
the rest is silence. (470)

The title's indication of absence, that long line of conjoined ellipses, reinforces God's immanence, which has already been established and need not be repeated. But I love, too, that this syntax opens up the possibility that *anything* might be akin to God, that one might complete the blank space with any word or phrase. This punctuation is a sign of and a doorway to work—as in, fill in the blank. Indeed, we get evidence of Lucifer's work in the poem's opening line, "so.," a word that suggests the conclusion of one era of his discerning and the commencement of another: "so.," appended with a period and therefore akin to an apostrophe, an exclamation; "so.," a vernacular dismissal of God's dismissing silence; "so.," a word that locates accountability as a contingency of the relation—not achieved, not a demand, just this moment of Lucifer concluding for now what he can conclude. This single word "so." is a term of orientation, and it initiates the final poem with the sense that all that matters is the orientation, the effort to try to be of regard relationally. As such, no reconciling is necessary as Lucifer speaks *for* God (who is addressed here as throughout in the relational You, properly capitalized) and puts to rest his own yearning in a crisp closing sequence: "You were," "You kiss," "the rest is silence." In this finale, Lucifer constructs himself as the one to whom the ecstatic happens—that kiss, which, in its emphatic present tense, contrasts with God's other actions in the poem, which are noted in the past tense. (Again, because God never speaks in the eight poems—he is a presence but is not legibly present—Lucifer describes happenings from before the fall.) Lucifer *recalls* the kiss (Judas-like?) from their days of being boys together but chooses to narrate it in the present: "You kiss" rather than "You kissed," which means that the relation is forever, which secures Lucifer to a relationality of studying that begins in and stays with Lucifer, he who radiates toward a sharper understanding of being.[18]

It is a lonely telling, this reckoning that Lucifer must do alone, announced and reconciled in the opening "so.," reminiscent of another Clifton poem that is too beautiful not to pass on, "lucifer speaks in his own voice":

sure as i am
of the seraphim
folding wing
so am i certain of a
graceful bed
and a soft caress
along my long belly
at endtime   it was
to be
i who was called son
if only of the morning
saw that some must
walk or all will crawl
so slithered into earth
and seized the serpent in
the animals   i became
the lord of snake for
adam and for eve
i   the only lucifer
light-bringer
created out of fire

illuminate i could
and so
illuminate i did (402)

We could read the poem along its balance of subjunctive assertion, such that "sure as i am" is revised as "so am i certain." In this repetition, the surety of the first statement conditions the second as the syntactical order is inverted: "*sure* as *i am*" becomes "so *am i certain.*" This inversion, nearly chiasmic, puts verb before noun in the second clause and, in so doing, intensifies the weight of the adverb "so." (Again.) The clarity, then, of Lucifer's knowing resides in the relation between the first sureness and what may come from that, as if certainty could propel the capacity to withstand more certainty and even uncertainty. In Clifton's slim poem, Lucifer's subjunctive moves are quiet and sly, including the "if" clause, which adds hesitation to his status ("i who was called son / if only in the morning"), and the perfect modal magic at the end: "illuminate i could / and so / illuminate i did." What strikes me here is the inverted syntax again, where Lucifer's speech delays the first-person referent, which has the effect of emphasizing the action as well as emphasizing the authority of the speaker—almost like a case of thrown voice: not "i can and will illuminate" but "illuminate i could / and so / illuminate i did." Clifton dramatizes subjunctive agency in depicting Lucifer as a figure of trembling, Lucifer as hosting a willfulness that radiates with hesitation . . . not a rash or arrogant speaker, but a considered lonely studier of his condition, determined, yes, but also wide open. In Clifton's poetics, the call to illuminate is work, and this work of inhabiting the pursuit of one's fire is ontological (as it is with Sula). Notice, for final example, the incredible clause, "it was / to be," where the line break stages the presentation of two statements of being: it was (as in something happened or is instantiated), to be (as in something is and is becoming). This is Cliftonian excellence, and I love the breaks of line and the fractured space left open—those edges and suspensions that gape before Lucifer as he inhabits the "sure" subjunctive work that he alone, "the only lucifer"—with that "i" separated by a chasm!—could undertake: that brilliant illuminating arriving he does as a vocation that no one might understand.[19]

This is holy poetics: "sure as i am" begets "so am i certain" begets "it was / to be" begets "illuminate i could / and so / illuminate i did." I love how Clifton's Lucifer inhabits encounter even without an interlocutor, how he remains in studying's lonely enterprise. This Lucifer recognizes the impossibility of relation, the simple fact that we are never met fully by—never fully meet—the other. In this way, we are always impossible toward each other, and the meaning of "impossible" depends less on the prefix ("im-") and more on the fact that the meeting *might* exist, if not now, in some other instance, some other attempt. This explication might seem convoluted, but I am drawing from a particular way in which Clifton uses "impossible" in an untitled poem, "a woman who loves," that comes pages before "lucifer speaks in his own voice." The untitled poem considers "a woman who loves / impossible men" (354) and though the idiomatic woman doesn't triumph over her misplaced loving, it is the characterization of the men as "impossible"—a vernacular idiom that repeats six times—that gives me pause. Clifton's syntax elides the stereotypical language that frames black female-male relationships, such that the men here are not failed or slack or worthless but are *impossible,* such that the woman's shortcoming is about repeated attempts to behold relation. The term "impossible" conspires with subjunctivity and, rather than render definitive judgment of a person, seems more to assess the relating: it doesn't exist now, doesn't seem as if it might ever exist, though it might . . . there is always possibility in the impossible of relation. This is surely a difficult way to live, this sustained openness to what might seem closed, but such is the aspiration of relational inhabitance.

I say all this to contextualize Lucifer's loneliness, his outreach to God (ah, as an impossible man), his declaration of his being "the only lucifer" who must illuminate this way, this wildly, because he could. Lucifer's impossibility echoes Sula's audacity during her illness and isolation before her eventual death. Recall, for example, the passage quoted in an earlier chapter after Ajax leaves and Sula wakes from a deep sleep with an unfamiliar melody in her head. She quickly remembers the song's provenance after misbelieving she had created it, and this tiny occasion yields a meditation:

> She sat on the edge of the bed thinking, "There aren't any more new songs and I have sung all the ones there are. I have sung them all. I have sung all the songs there are." She lay down again on the bed and sang a little wandering tune made up of the words *I have sung all the songs all the songs I have sung all the songs there are* until, touched by her own lullaby, she grew drowsy, and in the hollow of near-sleep she tasted the acridness of gold, left the chill of alabaster and smelled the dark, sweet stench of loam. (*Sula* 137; emphasis in original)

"Audacity" might be the only word to describe this willful doing, Sula's inventiveness with a small moment such that it expands into a meditation on life—that there is nothing new; that every exceptional thing is common; that even in this regard, one can illuminate, can be alive. I love how much Sula's song-making undermines the absence it names (impossibly), how the existential intelligence here is not that Sula has answered—or presumes to have answered—one of her life's central questions, but more that she has approached the question and exists in its terrifying solitude. Illumination to be sure.

And isn't loneliness the indictment that Nel makes of Sula's life—"Lonely, ain't it?" she asks in the argument where Nel wants Sula's contrition? In this moment, Nel thinks she has uttered a damning assessment, but Sula's reply shifts the stakes of loneliness and also, potentially, offers a way for Nel—for any of us—to envision aliveness: "Yes. But my lonely is *mine*" (143; emphasis in original).

To claim loneliness, to inhabit it as a consequence and quality of being in one's experience of being: studying, then, is lonely because the hunger and struggle of pursuing a question—of even knowing that the question is one's question—cannot be shared, not fully or properly, with another. Its relationality cannot yield, is not transactional, cannot be made to express. Indeed, the inhabiting of the question and its imperative on one's breathing never materializes in a way that one can possess or commodify or present. We neither own nor command our inquiry, though we are called to be of regard to its humming vibration. We may know, but even in the knowing we exist with ineffability. Lucifer and Sula are of reckoning's ecstasy; they both recognize the eternal loneliness of studying's praxis, that the sweet revelation not only is incomplete but is beyond one's dominion. "There is a loneliness that can be rocked," Morrison tells us in the coda of *Beloved*, and "then there is a loneliness that roams": "No rocking can hold it down. It is alive, on its own. A dry and spreading thing that makes the sound of one's own feet going seem to come from a far-off place" (274). This wandering loneliness—it is relational, so it travels and encounters—this fantastic suspension, this terrifying boldening . . . this is studying, a synonym for Baldwin's love or reckoning, our holy call, the ethical invocation embedded in the question how to be. "To study," the director Anne Bogart tells us, "you enter into a situation with your whole being, you listen and then begin to move around inside it with your imagination. You can study every situation you are in" (2). In this regard, studying is a force of, a force within, a force toward—though it is not a force against; its relationality moves the one and moves the one in the world.

Studying is possibility, an "adventure of [one's] own existence."[20] In advancing this claim, I am echoing the previous chapter's case for *thinking* as a phenomenological act of the human, such that life is of one who thinks, and one who thinks has and is of life. I'll end, then, with Baldwin, who sutures being and doing as a self's moral obligation to itself: "I think all theories are suspect, that the finest principles may have to be modified, or may even be pulverized by the demands of life, and *that one must find, therefore, one's own moral center and move through the world hoping that this center will guide one aright. I consider that I have many responsibilities, but none greater than this: to last, as Hemingway says, and get my work done*" (*Notes of a Native Son* 9; emphasis in original).[21] Baldwin's distillation of the call to write (which is the call to reckon with being) echoes the singularity of studying as an ethical undertaking, studying that is a loneliness that radiates within but also outward, offering to the world the widened self of the one in study.[22]

Oneness returns ethics to the philosophical capacity within each of us. Isn't this what Lorde was advocating so brilliantly in "Poetry Is Not a Luxury" and in "Uses of the Erotic"? Yes, this is our aliveness, a condition of relation that a black world makes possible, where the absence of any argument about human worth sustains the imperative to engage in being of one's worth. We could name this the subjectivity of "regardless" in accord with Alice Walker's language in the third entry of her definition of womanism: "3. Loves music. Loves dance. Loves the moon. *Loves* the Spirit. Loves love and food and roundness. Loves struggle. *Loves* the Folk. Loves herself. *Regardless*" ("Womanist" xii; emphases in the original). "Regardless," italicized and singular, is such a fine word to describe an orientation of the one in the world: one is in the world as it is, at the same time that one's astuteness to being exceeds the world. So much of my thinking about aliveness has been inspired by the notion "being of regard" that it might seem antithetical now to celebrate regardlessness. But I take Walker's use to be vernacular such that it means superlative *regard* for one's instance in the world: it is at once a dismissal of the world's terms, as it is an acknowledgment of the world's conditions (including its terrible) that reinforce the essentiality of care.

I feel a bit self-conscious in articulating what seems like unbridled and naïve optimism, when what I really want to say is that though everything may not be possible, no human manner of being is impossible. It is an idea that is both terrifying and exhilarating, this capaciousness that makes necessary the work of "how to be." I think, again, of this beautiful and complicated fact: that one adult enslaved black person made a doll for a child who was also black and enslaved. In truth, archaeologists and scholars have confirmed that this must have been done many times by many enslaved peoples. *Regardless* could describe the orientation of the doll-making one, who instantiated a world through their doing, whose doing was an ordinary, small force that resided in and far, far beyond the antiblack world of slavery.

Beautiful, and complicated, hence I am reluctant to exemplify this example, which could be used facetiously to try to underplay the horrors of slavery or to support an argument about personal responsibility in the face of structural violence—as if anything personal can ever resolve the enduring structures of terrible. What I can say is that I find this example compelling, that it allows me to organize a black world reading for a scene and happening that did not occur in a black world but that occurred in the profoundly antiblack world of transatlantic slavery. Considering this example allows me to get closer to beholding the dignity of black being as ever always there, just there. That this happening, and its unaccountable bigness, makes me speculate anew about ways of being—about how the scope of conversations about being are too narrow for understanding this discernment, this doll-making and doll-giving. And I want to be clear that there can be no torqueing of this fact of doll-making to do antiblack work. (I know that I am using this example for the case I want to make, and therefore this injunction is probably false.) Simply, bigly, an adult person made a doll for a child, an act that reflected a world of being and that also inspired—made—the world anew; an adult person made a doll for a child, and the philosophical meaningfulness of this doing lives with me.[23]

I read Walker's "Regardless" as a name for human dignity that is not indexed to how one behaves or comports oneself or is assessed, a dignity that is inherent and that can inspire one's exploration of the question, how to be. No one can judge for you the manner of your reckoning with that dignity. It is as it is, as one is of regard to it. Again, I turn to Lorde: "[The erotic] is an *internal sense of satisfaction to which, once we have experienced it, we know we can aspire*" (*Sister Outsider* 54; emphasis added). Notice that the erotic is constitutive and transformative, evident and aspirational, an interior well-spring that compels action or pursuit. And Lorde names this feeling and doing as *excellent*, such that "to encourage excellence is to go beyond," an inclination that comes as a result of "having experienced the fullness of this depth of feeling" that is the erotic (54). This sterling capacity is the ambition and inspiration of being in one's life. The best example I know of this ideology is when Baby Suggs, holy, calls the people into the Clearing in Morrison's *Beloved*:

> She did not tell them to clean up their lives or to go and sin no more. She did not tell them they were the blessed of the earth, its inheriting meek or its glorybound pure.
>
> She told them that the only grace they could have was the grace they could imagine. That if they could not see it, they would not have it.
>
> "Here," she said, "in this here place, we flesh; flesh that weeps, laughs; flesh that dances on bare feet in grass. Love it. Love it hard. Yonder they do not love your flesh. They despise it. They don't love your eyes; they'd just as soon pick em out. No more do they love the skin on your back. Yonder they flay it. And O my people they do not love your hands. Those they only use, tie, bind, chop off and leave empty. Love your hands! Love them. Raise they up and kiss them. Touch others with them, pat them

together, stroke them on your face 'cause they don't love that either. *You* got to love it, *you*! . . . This is flesh I'm talking about here. Flesh that needs to be loved. Feet that need to rest and to dance; backs that need support; shoulders that need arms, strong arms I'm telling you. And O my people, out yonder, hear me, they do not love your neck unnoosed and straight. So love your neck; put a hand on it, grace it, stroke it and hold it up. . . . The beat and beating heart, love that too. More than eyes or feet. More than lungs that have yet to draw free air. More than your life-holding womb and your life-giving private parts, hear me now, love your heart. For this is the prize." (88–89; emphases in the original)

Morrison imagines Baby Suggs engaging the subjunctivity of imagine ("the only grace they could have was the grace they could imagine") in an exceptional way: the invocation of imagine is how Baby Suggs comes to regard herself and her beloveds as ones in the world; and it is this regard that she recites as a prayer. Said another way, *Baby Suggs is regard, imagines regard, and then articulates regard through an imperative to have regard.* And in this instance, regard—or self-regard—doesn't mean "self-concept, as in self-esteem," Patricia J. Williams reminds us. Instead, such regard connotes the work of beholding, "the view of the self which is attained when the self steps outside to regard and evaluate the self" (66). Self-regard as the work aestheticized via the syllogism "If they could not see it, they would not have it."

Come celebrate, Baby Suggs says, come be of the becoming of the virtuous ordinary you are.[24]

In making this argument about ethics, value, and the everyday, I am drawing on the intellectual tradition of black womanist ethics, particularly as articulated by the late Katie Geneva Cannon, where every human being has to earn her humanity as much as her humanity has to be taken for granted. This notice that humanity has to be earned is a necessary caution against forswearing the work we are called to do, the slow work of getting close to what one feels and of trying to act from the integrity of such knowing on behalf of one's goodness. In saying this, I do not mean to infer any prescription of how one should act, look, be. The question "how to be" is too dynamic to be relegated to norms, too humbling to sustain judgment of another person's inhabitance. It is work of the one. Notice that Baby Suggs doesn't begin with a claim to specialness or deprivation; that she makes only brief reference to an "out yonder" that might correlate to the nation-state, the plantation, the modern Western project. Baby Suggs anchors her thinking in the realm of the spiritual and its vernacular language of human existence.

Again, I am cautious of the ways that a turn to the everyday might evoke dis-courses of personal responsibility as well as exempt an account of the structural; I mean neither the exemption nor the alliance. (As I understand it, there are at least two levels of reckoning—institutional and personal—though these are not always discrete from each other. And since the force of institutionality works against the human, institutional actors always have a responsibility beyond the terms of relation, a responsibility to be accountable to their power and its destruc-tive normativity—think, for example, of a parent in a family or a director of a company, never mind agents of the state.) I am making a case for ethics through the capacity of oneness, through the philosophical possibility legible in the aes-thetic worlds of black texts and somewhat in the tradition of what V. Denise James calls "black feminist pragmatism." In oneness, the question of the ethical is phenomenological: its temporality is now ("now," which holds subjunctivity), the time of the body sensorially; its recourse is not to the pronoun "we" as a matter of political ideology and critique but to the "one" of relational being.[25]

The ethical of black aliveness remains open, ushers an invocation toward (more) awareness, an invitation for the one to inhabit self-regard. I know that our social worlds probably can't withstand such openness, but I also don't want to be limited by the world we live in. I am studying with and through a tradition of phi-losophers who are creative writers, thinkers who are largely black and female and who are working through the question of being. I turn and return to their think-ing, this cohort of human beings: Clifton, Morrison, Lorde, Brooks, Finney, Bald-win, Jordan, Shockley, Kincaid, Shepherd, Awkward-Rich, Derricotte, Walker, Toni Cade Bambara, she who said that the revolution must be irresistible, which I take to mean that one could pursue the beautiful, that one should be moved since moving is feeling is being in the work of one's doing.[26] In a black world imagi-nary, one can embrace relation as an invitation to stay open through the wonder, smallness, hostility that happens. Relation, which summons the one to be ever of becoming, an ongoing habitat, "being human as praxis."[27]

"Everything can be done with a little grace," Gwendolyn Brooks writes in *Maud Martha* (66). To me, this use of "grace" connotes engagedness, such that in everything, in every state or practice of being, one can be of attentiveness: if one is angry, mean, being petty; if one is feeling deeply some ugliness, all of this can be inhabited with an attentiveness to the thing. That attentiveness, however particular, is one's grace, a "measure" of awareness in regard to a mo-ment of one's being-on-earth.[28] In this way, the question how to be is an inflec-tion of "how am I" as an occasion to consider one's self, to feel and be of one's viscerality. In this way, the world of being is open-ended, and in that wideness, the question is not "how to be *perceived*" but "how to *be*." It is an abundance, this question, akin to the quality of the speaker in Ross Gay's poem "Catalog of Unabashed Gratitude":

> Friends, will you bear with me today,
> for I have awakened
> from a dream in which a robin
> made with its shabby wings a kind of veil
> behind which it shimmied and stomped something from the south
> of Spain, its breast aflare,
> looking me dead in the eye
>
> . . .
>
> it was telling me
> in no uncertain terms
> to bellow forth the tubas and sousaphones,
> the whole rusty brass band of gratitude
> not quite dormant in my belly—
> it said so in a human voice,
> "Bellow forth"—
> and who among us could ignore such odd
> and precise counsel? (82–83)

This two-page opening is one long, continuous sentence, a flare of feeling that swells from a dream scene where a cargo-carrying bird traveling from Spain to Indiana prompts the speaker awake into awareness. Notice immediately that the enjambment in the second line emphasizes the completed state (in the present perfect tense) of the speaker's commencement: "for I have awakened," not only from a specific dream or on a specific morning but in timeless perfection. "I have awakened," he says. In this utterance, we might conclude that the speaker speaks to a congregant of one, capaciously, calling himself into formation, aestheticizing the call and the astuteness via the swooping rise and fall of that long, breathless sentence, erotic and luscious as it is. (The scope and sweep of the address—from one to one—recall Morrison's Baby Suggs in the Clearing and the salutation of Celie's final letter in Walker's *The Color Purple*.)[29] In Gay's poetic landscape, the invocation incites a tumbling into repeated apostrophes of grace: "thank you," the speaker exclaims over and again, as in

> and thank you for taking my father
> a few years after his own father went down thank you
> mercy, mercy, thank you (84)

What I want to highlight is how these expressions of gratitude constitute an aesthetic liveliness in the poem, not only the way that the words unfurl textually (the poem is eleven pages long, and its line and stanza breaks bear no discernible pattern), but also in regard to the poem's present tense. This intensity of present tense refers both to the verb case and to the speaker's instantiation of the poem as happening *now*. Moreover, being of gratitude, a feeling in the broadest sense of that term, is an act of attentiveness that is consonant with the act of writing this particular poem. It is as if the speaker is experiencing the words as they form on the page:

> And thank you the tiny bee's shadow
> perusing these words as I write them.
> And the way my love talks quietly
> when in the hive,
> so quietly, in fact, you cannot hear her
> but only notice barely her lips moving
> in conversation. Thank you what does not scare her
> in me, but makes her reach my way. Thank you the love
> she is which hurts sometimes. And the time
> she misremembered elephants
> in one of my poems which, oh, here
> they come, garlanded with morning glory and wisteria
> blooms, trombones all the way down the river.
> Thank you the quiet
> in which the river bends around the elephant's
> solemn trunk, polishing stones, floating
> on its gentle back
> the flock of geese flying overhead. (86–87)

This is aliveness, the way that the speaker's immanent experience of writing cavorts with the arrival of another experience, one that breaks open the poem being written. Notice, for example, the signal exclamation, "oh, here / they come," which recognizes the coming of decorated poetic elephants in a place where they were not before, elephants that are heralded by the sonic pairing of "blooms" and "trombones." Notice, too, how the repeated exclamation is not appended by a preposition ("thank you *for*") but is a "thank you" that is wedged right up against its referent: "Thank you the tiny bee's shadow," "Thank you what does not scare her," "Thank you the quiet." I love this syntax, which creates a merged expressiveness where the speaker is not divorced from or in control of the thing being spoken of; I love to think that this syntax characterizes the pulse of the speaker being in regard to the feeling of this sequence of compiling gratitude, this catalog of awareness. There is something of the magic of alive being in the poem, how openness is both an arrival and a departure, how the speaker's verse-traveling ensues because of and beyond the trajectory of his being. "Abundance" might be the only word for it.

Gay's aesthetic of gratitude includes the terrible, since abundance consti-tutes every possible—and impossible—thing:

And thank you the baggie of dreadlocks I found in a drawer
while washing and folding the clothes of our murdered friend;

. . .

. . . thank you
the way before he died he held
his hands open to us; for coming back
in a waft of incense or in the shape of a boy
in another city looking
from between his mother's legs (89)

In this sequence, where the image of a killed beloved morphs into the visage of a shy boy, the speaker describes and performs conjuring; that is, the scene materializes through its doubling, which is another instance of its abundance.

What a poem of aliveness, even more so because the speaker's exclamations, "thank you" and "mercy," are elliptical speech where the expression omits part of the clause (as in "*I* thank you," "____ have mercy"). I love the way that this omis-sion enhances the force of the speaker's presence, since the one who says these holy terms is made, via the syntax, into a one . . . rendered as an immanent figure whose speaking does not require a self-referent. Moreover, that Gay uses these two phrases interchangeably reinforces our appreciation of "thank you" as a syn-onym of gratitude, as an expression not necessarily directed to the other but as an articulation and inhabitance of oneness. (To be able to say "thank you," truly, is to be of a feeling at least as much as it is a kindness to the other.)[30]

It is hard to discuss this poem other than through the language and insights of affection: I love that the poem's address orients toward the one speaking, he who is subjectless, deeply intimate and local, cosmological. In "Catalog of Unabashed Gratitude," the speaker is alive, tumbling through his becoming as such is realized both in the moment of experience and in the feeling of being filled by attentiveness to experience. "Thank you," he says to his lover, to the reading/listening one encompassed by the poem's first word, "friends" ("and

you, again you, for hanging tight, dear friend"), to a whole host of people and
things; and in the instance of speaking so fully, he speaks of himself:

> . . . Soon it will be over,
>
> which is precisely what the child in my dream said,
> holding my hand, pointing at the roiling sea and the sky
> hurtling our way like so many buffalo,
> who said *it's much worse than we think,*
> *and sooner*; to whom I said
> *no duh child in my dreams*, what do you think
> this singing and shuddering is,
> what this screaming and reaching and dancing
> and crying is, other than loving
> what every second goes away?
> Goodbye, I mean to say.
> And thank you. Every day. (93; emphases in original)

This gratitude, which closes the poem, aestheticizes the speaker dressed in attentiveness, winding through the catalog of all that he is and is becoming, even
and especially through the terror of extinction. Gay's "Catalog of Unabashed
Gratitude" articulates through a speaker who is of poetic relation, who says
thank you as an expression of the unfolding self of his encounter. *Thank you
for what I am and what is possible through my being, this largess that is of a black being
in the world.*

What an achievement, this poem that animates through its speaker's aliveness, a voice that exists as one trying to attend to its formation. "In my attentiveness, I am becoming possible to myself," the speaker seems to say in Gay's
poetic rush of grace, a studying that is lonely, and abundant.

Another example, this time Tracy K. Smith's ironically titled "Political Poem":

> If those mowers were each to stop
>   at the whim, say, of a greedy thought,
>   and then the one off to the left
>
> were to let his arm float up, stirring
>   the air with that wide, slow, underwater
>   gesture meaning *Hello!* and *You there!*
>
> aimed at the one more than a mile away
>   to the right. And if he in his work were to pause,
>   catching that call by sheer wish, and send

back his own slow one-armed dance,
        meaning *Yes!* and *Here!* as if threaded
    to a single long nerve, before remembering

his tool and shearing another message
        into the earth, letting who can say how long
    graze past until another thought, or just the need to know,

might make him stop and look up again at the other,
        raising his arm as if to say something like *Still?*
    and *Oh!* and then to catch the flicker of joy

rise up along those other legs and flare
        into another bright *Yes!* that sways a moment
    in the darkening air, their work would carry them

into the better part of evening, each mowing
        ahead and doubling back, then looking up to catch
    sight of his echo, sought and held

in that instant of common understanding,
        the *God* and *Speed* of it coming out only after
    both have turned back to face to the sea of *Yet*

and *Slow.* If they could, and if what glimmered
        like a fish were to dart back and forth across
    that wide wordless distance, the day, though gone,

would never know the ache of being done.
        If they thought to, or would, or even half-wanted,
    their work—the humming human engines

pushed across the grass, and the grass, blade
        after blade, assenting—would take forever.
    But I love how long it would last. (54–55; emphases in original)

Everything vital to this poem is encapsulated in that final line, which stuns with its first-person self-reference and which makes us aware of the speaker, who, all the while, has been imagining and absorbing the tense, quiet action of the scene. "But I love how long it would last" upends the poem's construct of twoness, the dialectic between one man and another, and instead trains attention on the relational inhabitance of the one who beholds the scene. The poem, then, is neither about the political signaled in its title nor about the possibility of these two men; indeed, the work that is being celebrated here is the speaker's witnessing subjunctivity.

Let's begin with the fact that "Political Poem" is a verse of *work*, not only because that word is used twice; not only because it describes two men in domestic labor; but especially because it speaks to the diligence and engagedness of being open. We could notice, for example, how rife the poem is with deliberate slowness, its cascade of prepositional clauses and commas and enjambments that encase or make up its swaying, almost overlapping rhythm. In the very beginning, the fantasized thought is broken by a line break and by characterization: "If those mowers were each to stop / at the whim, say, of a greedy thought, / and then the one off to the left . . . ," where the speaker's interjection of "say" enhances the spoken quality of the line and also adds to the embellishment of "stop" and "whim"—the interruptive "say" enacts a whimsical stop itself. Such syntactical dynamics resonate throughout the poem, including near the end, in the last two stanzas when the speaker comes back to the wish noted earlier: "If they thought to, or would, or even half-wanted, / their work"—and then rather than complete the thought, the poem wanders off for fifteen words, bracketing again the speaker's stylishness, the speaker who is the "humming human engine" described in the clause. The poetics here are superb, as Smith's language reinforces deliberation and hesitancy, this half-wanting that is preceded by two other verbs ("thought to," "would"). Again, this syntax enacts the poem's conceptualization of work as it also points us to a speaker whose language, notice, and effort are so keen that they match the scene the speaker is imagining.

What fine inhabiting, this speaker, who is unafraid to acknowledge the enduring quality of being in study. If they wanted to, the speaker says, this work could and "would take forever." "Work" here is physical for sure, but it is also affective and psychic, of relationality; we might be inclined to think of—and critique—work as a synonym of modernity and its state formations, but that would be a superficially political understanding of a term that really, in this context, constitutes an ethic of relation.[31]

Notice, too, that the poem's exploration of work turns on the subjunctive—the poem begins with an "if" clause, and narrates something that has not happened but that exists as a possibility in the imagination of the speaking one. This wishfulness amplifies the speaker's doing, for if we think about how *much* work the speaker performs to conjure up exclamations and greetings, to create and compel the subtlety of each man's yardwork, to travel through the capacities and hunger of each—if we behold that effort, we can no longer fixate on the two mowing men. The marvelous here is *the effort of the speaker's attentiveness*, which spins into a world of abundance. And the more one appreciates the speaker's endeavor, the more one realizes that the slow-drag quality of the imagined yardwork becomes a synecdoche for the speaker's own poetic doing. As such, Smith's speaker exists not outside the scene of these two but as the third—and centering—force of the poem, the figure of oneness in this text of reckoning that unfolds over twelve form-full tercets. Look again at the third and fourth stanzas: "catching that call by sheer wish, and send // back his own slow one-armed dance, / . . . as if threaded / *to a single long nerve.*" The line breaks here are fantastic, creating swerve and mimicking the threading work as the lines pull back and forth in sequence with the stanza's wavery indentations. And the notion of a "single long nerve," that tendril of capacious being that seems to encase both men and the speaker, that tendril speaks of oneness. Smith sustains the metaphor of relation in the eighth stanza: "each mowing / ahead and doubling back, then looking up to catch / sight of his echo." These lines seem to describe the poem's undulating structure, each of its stanza's three lines indented at a different point; it also names the tussle of relation, of being flung between habitats of one's being. Indeed, the referent for this metaphor is the speaker, who, engaged in the lush inhabiting of a world, is "mowing / ahead and doubling back" in aliveness, becoming expansive through the tingly threshold of the poetic scene.

In this regard, the poem's hesitant subjunctivity, all of its half-wanting trembling, is not a discourse of difference, but instead constitutes the breath of black aliveness—the push and pull and undoneness of being. I know that there is nothing racially specific in Smith's poem, but I am making this claim to resist the way that "Political Poem" has invited a commonplace reading: that the poem speaks to our current political climate of divisiveness. At various public events, Smith's interlocutors have seized on the specter of the poem's two (male) protagonists positioned across a proverbial fence, and have advanced an interracial interpretation that also suits the larger arc of Smith's collection, *Wade in the Water.*[32] But what if we could read the poem not as a tension between the two protagonists but on behalf of its speaker, who unveils themself so strikingly at the end? We might take a clue here from Smith's admission that the poem was originally titled "Mowers," in ode to the Robert Frost poem "Mowing." As such, we might recall that Frost's speaker grapples with what can be learned from his "scythe" dancing over the ground, that the animating matter in Frost's "Mowing" is the revelation to be had by the one in a steady act of back-and-forth doing. Frost's and Smith's verses amplify the quotidian, and Smith's, especially, warns against felicitousness (the irony of her title). I can understand how the symbolism of two men and a fence would garner critical purchase, but the aesthetic moves of "Political Poem" seem to require attending to its speaker.[33]

Indeed, such attending is nearly mandated by the poem's final line, that glorious sentence, "But I love how long it would last," a sublime statement of human capacity, especially for a speaker who has already done the work to conjure possibility. In this clause, the speaker expresses fidelity to being undone by the small and forever of work (the conjunction "but" and the auxiliary verb "would" both indicate forever), to staying in relation to being, no matter how fleeting. But most of all, there is the verb "love" in audacious present tense, enduring as if love is happening in the moment for which love is awaiting. This is the line in which the speaker reveals themself as the figure who animates "Political Poem." Moreover, it is an exceptionally subjunctive revelation, since the syntax enacts love for a moment that hasn't happened, since it uses the work of imagining to revel in feeling now for something that has yet to come. "But I love how long it would last," whenever—if ever—it comes, this whatever ("it") that is small and simple and terrifying, a call of preparedness.

Again, what fineness: in Smith's "Political Poem," the tension and reaping of relationality belong to the one, the beautiful speaker doing that beautiful beholding and imagining, the one who could say and bear the capaciousness of "But I love how long it would last," enduring as if love is happening in the moment for which love is awaiting—the speaker who arrives in the moment for which they are awaiting.

Aesthetics makes the ethical possible via the invocation of a textual world where a black one can live in a relation of rightness. In this way, the idiom of a black world inspires rather than forecloses the ethical question since the imagining of such a world does not presume to have solved the human problem of being.

Here, I am making a case for an ethics of aesthetics, for an appreciation of the capacity that resides in paying attention to form, shape, style—all the vibrancies of the made-text. Aesthetics is not a surface matter; indeed, as philosopher Martha Nussbaum explains, "style itself makes its claims, expresses its own sense of what matters. Literary form is not separable from philosophical content, but is, itself, a part of content—an integral part, then of the search for and the statement of truth" (3). This commitment to art's philosophical vitality characterizes the advocacy of the Black Arts/Aesthetic movement, most explicitly in Larry Neal's declaration that "your ethics and your aesthetics are one" ("Black Arts Movement" 31). Neal's conspiration between ethics and aesthetics describes the condition of being an artist, where the exploration of life's questions happens via the imagination. In this regard, Neal seems to reprise James Baldwin's 1963 essay "The Artist's Struggle for Integrity," which suggests that "the artist's struggle for his integrity must be considered as a kind of metaphor for the struggle, which is universal and daily, of all human beings on the face of this globe to *get to become human beings*" (50–51; emphasis added). Compellingly, Baldwin exemplarizes this becoming as the work of poets, "(by which I mean all artists) [who] are finally the only people who know the truth about us" (51), poets whose doing he conceives as ethical engagedness.[34]

In my embrace of the poetic, I mean to address the black poem as a world left wide open for encounter, our literature as an apparatus of suspension. That is, in thinking about ethics through oneness and studying, I am interested in the black reader who is instantiated via "imagine a black world," in what is possible for that reader by the invocation of such a world. I am compelled by the work that the reader must do to behold and to be beheld by their engagement with the page. Such commencement of work materializes in Lorde's instruction about poetry, right there in the first sentence—"the quality of light by which we *scrutinize* our lives" (*Sister Outsider* 36; emphasis added). Here, aesthetics is a site of relation, and we can inhabit the ethical summons of oneness through the materiality of the text, through its very "texture of being."[35] This conceptualization appreciates black aesthetics for its vitality as well as its collation with freedom, akin to the broad case philosopher Paul C. Taylor makes in *Black Is Beautiful: A Philosophy of Black Aesthetics*. Throughout this project, I have embraced black literature as an apparatus of black aliveness, which is precisely what literary theorist Barbara Christian describes in "The Race for Theory." Christian, in this essay published in 1987 at the height of arguments about canons, exclusion, and theory, asserts unflinchingly, "My folk . . . have always been a race for theory" (52). For Christian, theory does not exist distinct from the artistic production of black (women) writers; instead, theory constitutes and is constituted in the creative deployment of abstraction and eroticism in black arts. In Christian's conceptualization, black literary criticism—like black literature itself—is phenomenological and epistemological, an invitation to encounter being and becoming: "For me literature is a way of knowing that I am not hallucinating, that whatever I feel/know *is*. It is an affirmation that sensuality is intelligence, that sensual language is language that makes sense" (61; emphasis in original). Here, the literary is a world of and for the black one, a textuality for feeling and orienting; in this way, Christian is in conversation with Audre Lorde's argument in "Poetry Is Not a Luxury" (indeed she cites Lorde) as well as with Hortense J. Spillers, who, in a reevaluation of black intellectualism, notes, "It seems to me that the only question that the intellectual can actually *use* is: To what extent do the 'conditions of theoretical practice' pass through him or her, as the *living site of a significant intervention*?" (456; emphases in the original). Spillers coheres intellectual doing to the body, akin to the embodied consciousness that Lorde argues and that I have deployed throughout this book. Moreover, in Christian's, Lorde's, and Spillers's formulation, the work of studying is a praxis of the living one, an ethical inhabiting of how one does what one does.[36]

It is common wisdom in black literary studies—in black culture writ large—that words can effect profound change. I am interested in considering this capacity for change, not through the public, but through the *one*: What is the call that the literary work makes to the black one reading it? And how is this call ever an ethical invitation?[37]

As before, Lucille Clifton offers two good examples, which I want to engage briefly; first, "the times":

the times

it is hard to remain human on a day
when birds perch weeping
in the trees and the squirrel eyes
do not look away but the dog ones do
in pity.
another child has killed a child
and i catch myself relieved that they are
white and i might understand except
that i am tired of understanding.
if this
alphabet could speak its own tongue
it would be all symbol surely;
the cat would hunch across the long table
and that would mean time is catching up,
and the spindle fish would run to ground
and that would mean the end is coming
and the grains of dust would gather themselves
along the streets and spell out:

these too are your children   this too is your child (545)

Let's consider this poem through the subjunctive invocation ignited by the speaker's admission, "i might understand except / that i am tired of understanding," a claim that sends the poem careening on an if clause ("if this / alphabet could speak its own tongue"). The imaginary here converts the instance of terrible happening, of exhaustion and fear, into an imperative for the human one. I love how the speaker's reluctance is textualized by their delayed arrival as a subject in the poem's second sentence . . . that it is seven lines before the speaker says, "i catch myself." Yes, the speaker gets beheld by themself in this moment where we might assume they should be oriented toward the other, the killed and killing ones in the world. This "i catch myself" allows the speaker to become subject and object of the happening, and thereby to recognize themself as an astute human who sees birds and trees and squirrels and dogs and who, therefore, can also be of and can recognize human pain. Said another way, "i catch myself," in its repetition and circularity, performs embrace and nudging; the reckoning with the ethical happens *through* the speaker's being, not as a displacement of that being. And the poem ends with a declaration emphasized via exaggerated spacing—"this too is your child"—that doesn't resolve the speaker's dilemma of understanding. As if to say, the world is open for you to be in it—you, too, are a subject of this becoming that is marked by harm and its seeping risks, that is marked by the possibility of and need for care.

Throughout her body of work, Clifton offers invitations to black oneness. In her poetic worlds, we are obligated to read as if the one who is speaking and the one who is being figured, is black, often black and female. Clifton's doing, to me, is a black world aesthetic, these textual habitats of oneness that tingle with possibility for studying. Again, in aliveness, one exists as the subjective case and the objective case; ethical being arrives in the steady reconciliation between being the subject of one's object, being object of one's subject. In aliveness, ethicality resides in your capacity to engage your relation. Such inclination toward oneness operates even in a poem like "blessing the boats," where the speaker seems to be offering a prayer to another:

blessing the boats
  (*at St. Mary's*)

may the tide
that is entering even now
the lip of our understanding
carry you out
beyond the face of fear
may you kiss
the wind then turn from it
certain that it will
love your back   may you
open your eyes to water
water waving forever
and may you in your innocence
sail through this to that (405)

I like reading "blessing the boats" in sequence with "the times" because of the way each poem helps to expose the other's philosophical trajectory: In "blessing," the speaker seems to address the reader in the catholicity of the second person ("may the tide / . . . / carry you out") and seems to share the occasion with the addressee ("the lip of *our* understanding"). And yet, it could be that the speaker addresses themself through the second person—that they are the "you" speaking to themself, in whisper—and that the pronoun "our" indicates a generic larger community. However one explicates the site of address here, "blessing" is a relational offering: I love the way its wishes for leave-taking are articulated in broad, straightforward language ("and may you in your innocence / sail through this to that"), as if the wish could be inhabited by anyone who has to move from a "this" to a "that." I love, too, the subtle music of its repetition, as in "face of fear" or "you in your" or the v's and w's of "water / water waving forever," a cascading quality that reinforces the precision of this imprecise thing. That mix of breadth and exactitude matches the poem's relationality, where the speaker is offering not answers but a world for the intimacy of encounter, a text of thresholding that means possibility and doubt. Again the subjunctive, the ethos of bearing what may come, a surrender that includes terror, as is notable in this poem's diction and images that gesture to the abyss: tide, the being carried out, fear, all that water. But into the abyss we are called with the tender blessing of "may" and "may" and "may" and finally "may."[38]

Clifton's thinking conceptualizes blackness through a cosmological orientation located in the habitat of one's being, a grandeur of the small.[39] The pervasive terms of racial capitalism cohere individualism, accumulation, and withholding into a violent logic through which we often think of selfhood. But the call here, in Clifton's poetry, is about relation, relation that moves in (one's) oneness and moves toward (more) oneness. I study oneness through Clifton's imagination, through the way I understand her to construct relation as a dialectic of the one. This ethical thresholding that Clifton undertakes so singularly recalls the efficient explication of work that Sara Ahmed offers in *Queer Phenomenology*: "Even when things are within reach, we still have to reach for those things for them to be reached" (7). Such fidelity to doing, to trying, resonates with the blessed intelligence of Clifton's thinking, her investment in the terms of relation, which can be described no better than in her own comments at the end of an interview:

> I have this friend, and she changed her name—when everybody was changing their names to African names—hers was Jeribu. And I thought that was the most beautiful name because it means "one who tries." If ever I were going to change my name I would like to be known as Jeribu,

one who tried. I would like to be seen as a woman whose roots go back to Africa, who tried to honor being human. And who tried to do the best she could, most of the time. My inclination is to try to help. ("I'd Like" 328)

That is Lucille Clifton, the philosopher, a one who lived and knew aliveness. It is in this regard that we could read anew the aesthetics of distance in her poem "reply" as an ethical invitation: again, this marvelous poem that begins with terribleness:

[from a letter written to Dr. W. E. B. Dubois by Alvin Borgquest of Clark University in Massachusetts and dated April 3, 1905:

"We are pursuing an investigation here on the subject of crying as an expression of the emotions, and should like very much to learn about its peculiarities among the colored people. We have been referred to you as a person competent to give us information on the subject. We desire especially to know about the following salient aspects: 1. Whether the Negro sheds tears. . . ."]

reply

he do
she do
they live
they love
they try
they tire
they flee
they fight
they bleed
they break
they moan
they mourn
they weep
they die
they do
they do
they do (337)

Reading this poem again, over the arc of thinking about aliveness, I understand its roll call of possibility as a subjunctive imagining. Such subjunctivity resides both in the world made by the poem and in the ethical instruction via that black worldness, as if to say: black one, *this is how you are, this big and this small, this is how you can be.* The phrase "imagine" is unspoken here, but it is implied in the breath and breadth of life showcased through the poem and in the lingering echo of "they do / they do / they do."

I could read this poem forever and find each time something else of its bewildering aliveness. This poem reminds me that to read via the inevitability of black oneness is an ethical orientation: in such reading, I am thrown into the possibility that I, too, could be a one and could figure being through aliveness. This poem, all the poems in this book, are in our hands, are a world of invitation in one's hands.[40] This is what a poem does: it orients you into openness, into being capable of the openness that is rightly yours.

How to be: be like an artist, the one making art of one's self, as in Maud Martha in Gwendolyn Brooks's novel. Study one's self, study away from what is quantifiable or what can be indexed by achievement, since the cosmic of oneness moves against such measurements. Again the instruction comes from Patricia J. Williams: self-regard as "that view of the self which is *attained* when the self steps outside to regard and evaluate the self" (66; emphasis added). Be as an artist of one's self, this pursuit that can be an ethical inhabiting.[41]

Be of one's aliveness as such is manifested in and by the materiality of texts, where the question, how to be, is possible, is open and wondrous and terrifying too—where there is grace in bearing the rigor of the question every miserable day. Black aliveness, which calls the black one to be of their abundance and smallness; black aliveness, which says: do not think only of your deprivation, though deprivation surely is yours; be of humility and of grandeur too . . . all of this is your aliveness, all of this is an invitation to study, to study regardless of the things of the world, to study because you are black and alive and human.

Be like a poem—like the poetic inhabitance of Audre Lorde's argument, like the ambling of the speaker in the first-person essay, who is random and brief and unyielding in commitment to the pursuit of a clarity that is never singular, never promised, always, always worth the pleasure and struggle of the doing. Lorde, in "Poetry Is Not a Luxury," instructs us well: "I feel, therefore I can be free. Poetry coins the language to express and charter this revolutionary demand, the implementation of that freedom" (*Sister Outsider* 38). Yes, yes, that "revolutionary demand" for freedom is chartered in poetic inhabitance. Yes: be like a poem, like Beulah in Rita Dove's *Thomas and Beulah*, she who is described this way: "Like all art / useless and beautiful, like / sailing in air" (48). Has ever our normative language permitted black female subjectivity to be "useless and beautiful"? Well, regardless, be like that, useless, beautiful, like a poem. "Black people . . . Are poems," said one writer; "*Black people you are Art. You are the poem*," followed another.[42]

In a black world, the black one can be like a poem.

CONCLUSION

AGAIN, ALIVENESS

If this book is anything, it is a process, not an answer: not a recipe for how to be, certainly not a chastisement to any of us, but a study, a determination to try to think about the being of one's being. And I have been deliberate not to call this work black *life*, since I did not want to invoke personhood per se, but instead I wanted to set the idea of aliveness in relief. We, black people, have been studied plenty; we'll be studied more, some of it for the good, but I didn't want to replicate that here.[1]

Black Aliveness is of relation, and as such it revels in the heterogeneity of us, the vagary of black being that cannot be cataloged. That capaciousness resonates with Édouard Glissant's phrase "consent not to be a single being," where "consent," as Fred Moten argues, "is not so much an act but a nonperformative condition or ecological disposition" (*Black and Blur* xv). Moten's phrasing tries to acknowledge Glissant's consent as a force or domain, an orientation in or to the world. In this way, I read Glissantian consent as aliveness, as a manner of *being* of aliveness that also means *becoming* that aliveness.

Our aliveness is heterogeneous.

In making an argument for aliveness through the aesthetics of texts, I want to be clear that aliveness cannot be captured in writing—that, at best, it can be approximated. I would not want to betray the ineffable excellence of being. Moreover, aliveness doesn't exist because it is public or legible; indeed, I mean aliveness to describe a state of being that moves beyond the trouble of a public-private binary as well as beyond the logics of an antiblack world. It might be better to think of aliveness as a philosophical habitat that sustains being, propelling the one into any possible manner of existence; again, black aliveness resides in relation's open tussle of being and becoming. Ecological, Moten says, or cosmological, like Audre Lorde's depth of feeling that constitutes a privacy that also radiates out into the world of one's company. A black *world* is not a black *public*—it does not exist in response to a problem; it is not a black *nation* intended to cohere right blackness. It is an orientation to reading that inspires an orientation to being.

A black world is of relation, and relation unsettles rather than affirms identity—relation invites one into the world of becoming. Racism and antiblackness make essential that we have to figure our being through the language of community, but the oneness of relation is also our right. We need both; we need the world-making of oneness too. Sigh: I am trying to be clear that neither oneness nor relation nor black worldness equates easily to the idea of community, while I am also trying to honor that relation is intersubjective—that it calls the one toward more and more connection. In this attempt at balance, I hope to bypass the interraciality that overwhelms political conversations about intersubjectivity, especially in a US context. I think again about James Baldwin, whose writing often analyzes reckoning as a complicated interracial relationality—Baldwin, who in "The Hallelujah Chorus" proclaims, "But Amen is the price." I love this idiom of Baldwin's, which comes from a narrative interlude of the 1973 concert performance with Ray Charles, a performance chronicled beautifully and extensively by poet and scholar Ed Pavlić in *Who Can Afford to Improvise?* Pavlić reads "Amen" as a term of intersubjectivity, such that "one must say amen to life, forgo delusions of personal safety, and accept the twists and turns of experience in attempts to remain in touch with others doing the same" (167). Later, Pavlić assesses that for Baldwin, who had recently returned to the United States and who was creating his part of "Chorus" "during an era of widespread political violence"—in that context, for Baldwin, "to say 'Amen' [is] to implore people to be present in their lives and works in ways that go beyond the taboos and divisions" (169). (By "taboos and divisions,"

Pavlić means the boundaries of racial difference.) There is no quibble with Pavlić's glossing here, not only because of his substantial study of Baldwin's canon and his effort to bring renewed attention to "Chorus," but especially because his assessment reflects Baldwin's inclination to think about reckoning through a discourse of national racial belonging, "to achieve our country," as Baldwin himself phrases it in *The Fire Next Time* (105).

What happens, though, if we co-opt the notion of "Amen" from its entanglement with community, black or interracial, such that being able to say "Amen" at the end of each day is the only price the black one ever has to pay? Baldwin certainly meant the phrase as a statement of interracial salvation, but Baldwin also often suspended his language of national reckoning to speak directly to a black us about our being human. (Again, as in the previous chapter: "Our humanity is our burden, we need not battle for it; we need only to do what is infinitely more difficult—that is, accept it" [*Notes of a Native Son* 23].)[2] As such, I want "Amen" to belong also to the black one, as if it were a line in Sula's deathbed song, Sula alone and of intimacy in her broad "ecological disposition" (Moten, *Black and Blur* xv), Sula, whose relational ethic produces a life, a dying, and a death that embeds her into a deepened connection with others around her, without sacrificing the vitality of her self-regard. What would it mean if each of us, each black one of us, could live with "Amen" as our horizon, such that the doings of each day, however modest, would be anchored by the reflective invitation in being able to say, "Amen" . . . such that this saying reflects the habitat of the human, the disposition of right and of humility, the beautiful case of becoming.

I can be even clearer still: in addition to the assumption of interraciality noted earlier, I am also sensitive to the tug of *community* as a guarding and authenticating function, community that coheres as a political response to the state's profound antiblackness. In making a case for the *world* of black aliveness, I am eclipsing *community* in favor of the idea of a *commune* or a *commons*, akin to the way Stefano Harney and Fred Moten describe shared being in *The Undercommons*, their articulation of a collective that "perseveres as if a kind of elsewhere, here, around, on the ground, surrounding hallucinogenic facts. Meanwhile, politics soldiers on, claiming to defend what it has not enclosed, enclosing what it cannot defend but only endanger" (18). This characterization envisions collectivity through relation's wide berth rather than through the narrow language of politics, and it helps me to affirm, again, that the call to oneness is not an abdication of a black collectivity that enrobes us in joy and pain, as in that fantastic roll call in Lucille Clifton's "reply"; the call to oneness is a call of a black world, a call that exists and vibrates beyond the scope of the rule of the world as we know it—an imaginary that inflects how we *can* behold ourselves and each other.

Relation is and makes a world, and when we move in relation, we move with trust, with regard for (our) one that manifests regard for (each) one. We can trust the freedom of a black world, and its free-mindedness can enliven more and more. And more.

A good example here might be Toni Morrison's Nobel lecture, where relation—and its rigorously earned trust—is at stake in the narrated fable: an old woman who lives on the edge of town is approached by some children who seem to want to tease her. She is blind, and they ask her to tell them whether the bird in their hands is dead or alive. She refuses their question, first with no response, then with this reply: "I don't know whether the bird you are holding is dead or alive, but what I do know is that it is in your hands. It is in your hands" (199). Morrison tells us that this story circulates in many cultures, but "in the version I know the woman is the daughter of slaves, black, American" (198); she uses this provocation to organize a lecture in two parts—first, the speaker (Morrison herself) muses on what the old woman's refusing gesture and her modest comment can mean; then the speaker asks us to imagine that, rather than attempting to trick the old woman, the children wanted to be engaged, to be heard. What is striking in this latter case is that Morrison's speaker doesn't speak for the children but rather the children speak for themselves—we get to read their indictment of the old woman's silence in their furious words. This structural apparatus is vital because while Morrison's speaker uses the old woman's few words—and the gap produced by their smallness—to ignite a meditation on language, violence, racist and colonial plunder, misogyny, and political hope, the speaker gives the children the stage for and to themselves. And they inhabit it fully, railing against what they perceive as the old woman's arrogance in declining to engage them, especially since she has bequeathed them a ruined world. "You trivialize us and trivialize the bird that is not in our hands. Is there no context for our lives?" they ask and then implore her, "Tell us what it is to be a woman so that we may know what it is to be a man. . . . What it is to live at the edge of towns that cannot bear your company" (205, 206). The whole lecture is glorious, but I am interested in the way things end:

> It's quiet again when the children finish speaking, until the woman breaks into the silence.
> Finally, she says, "I trust you now. I trust you with the bird that is not in your hands because you have truly caught it. Look. How lovely it is, this thing we have done together." (207)

"I trust you now," she says as she directs attention to their collective hands, to work—"this thing we have done together." The "thing" is relation, the being engaged with each other through the dissonance of unknowing or fear, through the presumption of thinking that they, old woman and children, could know the you beforehand. The gift of relation is trust, but the gift is also work—the effort to inhabit the capacity to meet and be met.

This exchange of trust happens in a black world; in a black world, oneness enables trust because relation is a praxis of precisely that: to be able to say "you" without fear. Such an understanding of fear, trust, and collectivity informs my consideration of ethics in the previous chapter, especially my determination that the ethical question can't be answered collectively (it can't be answered at all). But this truth should not obscure that each *one* in a black world can be ethically engaged, and that collectivity, as such is possible, comes and becomes through the relationality of each one.

Racism and antiblackness make essential that we have to figure our being through the terms of community but oneness is also our right, oneness that is not antithetical to collectivity, oneness that is a term of relation. Amen, indeed.[3]

"Imagine a black world" is the invocation that makes it possible to be invested in ideas that might seem naïve or uncritical but that remain vital, ideas like being human. I take my cue here from Sylvia Wynter, whose own work characterizes what David Scott names as "a demand for, a hope for, a search for, a new universalism" (Wynter, "The Re-enchantment of Humanism" 196). Wynter, in conversation with Scott, affirms this framing:

> Yes. One [a new universalism] whose truth-for will coincide with the empirical reality in which we find ourselves, the single integrated history we now live. You see, the problems that we confront—that of the scandalous inequalities between the rich and the poor countries, of global warming and the disastrous effects of climate change, of large-scale epidemics such as AIDS—can only be solved if we can, for the first time, *experience* ourselves, not only as we do now, as this or that *genre* of human, but also *as* human. A new mode of experiencing ourselves in which every mode of being human, every form of life that has ever been ever enacted, is a part of us. We, a part of them. (196–197; emphases in original)

Wynter compels us to imagine a possibility where one exists not as "this or that *genre* of human, but . . . *as* human," an appeal that recognizes the structural ravages of the orders of modernity. I read Wynter's overture as a relational call to an openness that is not precisely optimism since an optimistic orientation presumes that better is forthcoming or is inevitable. (The reverse might be said of pessimism too.) Relation does not assume to predict what might be and does not foreclose possibility; simply, relation invites the one to be open to being as well as to be open to the undoing of being. Such relational thinking thrives in Toni Morrison's oeuvre—in the "make me, remake me" of *Jazz*, in Sula's embrace of her oneness (*Sula*), in Baby Suggs's sermon in the Clearing (*Beloved*), in the Nobel lecture cited earlier. It is there, too, in Audre Lorde's theorization of embodied being, and in Lucille Clifton's worldmaking verses. These three writers are philosophers of being, and each of them, in their differing registers, embrace this bit as gospel: every human being has to earn their humanity as much as their humanity has to be taken for granted. This doing is the very meaning of ethics, of goodness as "the acquisition of self-knowledge."[4]

"Imagine a black world" is a gambit to return the subjunctive to blackness, akin to the verb phrase in the title of Whitfield Lovell's beautiful 2011 charcoal drawing *Kin XXXIII: May I Assume Whatever Form I Want, in Whatever Place My Spirit Wishes*. Here, the verb "assume" and its mood ("may") indicates a timeless aspiration, a magic spell in the way it announces a question and also commences an invocation of the one becoming the assumption. Like Lovell's prayer, I use "imagine a black world" as a thought experiment intended to make space for one to engage black being-in-the-world beyond the imperatives of antiblackness and the restrictions of ideas about blackness. Again, poetic being is experimental being, poetic being is being experimental.

"May I assume whatever form I want . . ."

Earlier in *Black Aliveness*, I flirted with the claim that every black person lives under the terror of antiblackness. This statement is true—I believe it to be true—but I want to be cautious of its sayability, since to claim subjection as the definitive fact of black life is to establish a threshold of authenticity, maybe even to imply that there is a certain quality of subjection—a quality of responding to subjection—that confirms black being. To do this would be to undermine the case I am exploring for black aliveness. To say this is to make a declaration about us to someone beyond us—the forever problem of audience. It is undeniable that every historical thing, including the days of summer 2020, reminds us that blackness, terror, and death are synonyms in the world. That sentence needs to stand alone, and so does this next one: in the world of a black person's being, death is both a fact of antiblack threat and a fact of being alive (this latter fact is the death that countenances the human's ordination of living).[5]

In a black world imaginary, we can think of death more capably than in the stark terms offered by an antiblack world. Glissant, in *Poetics of Relation*, reminds us that "the active violence in reality distracts us from knowing" the poetic force of being (159), that the violence of subjugation interferes with one knowing how and what one knows. We can't will the violent reality away, nor can we not incorporate its impact. We have to live in the world and also live in the world of imagine.

In a black world, black people are human without qualification. In a black world orientation, there is no need to verify blackness along any measure, especially since such a world is not instantiated in response to a problem. A black world *is*, is of "Blackness stern and blunt and beautiful, / organ-rich Blackness telling a terrible story" (Gwendolyn Brooks, *Blacks* 431).

Black aliveness is. It is. And the study in this book is an attempt to realize something about a sequence of writing that stirs (up) such aliveness of being.

Sigh: This is a book by one black person about reading (and) blackness. It is also a love letter to myself, made as if in a black world where the capacities of being can be taken for granted. Indeed "imagine a black world" is a love gesture that says to the one: *Be as you are. You will become and you will undo. As you are, you are and are worthy—inhabit that and unfurl in and into the world.* In this way, the invitation to imagine a black world requires enduring work. It is a call to relation that means it is a call to suspend in the heft of its work, an invocation of ethicality that resides in the capaciousness of one's figuring through one's oneness, discerning every day how to be in the world. "I am what the world and I have never seen before," Audre Lorde writes of herself in *The Cancer Journals* (48), that ecstatic statement of newness and determination and surprise . . . and rightness—a statement of the right to be becoming. Such a statement might be misread as individuality but it is not that; it is relational, black aliveness as the whole world of being. (Again, individualism is a bankrupt idea and it is incompatible with black life in an antiblack world; moreover, black aliveness is relational, not individual.)

We deserve the inspiration of oneness that the textual makes possible—we deserve that inspiration, and here I am pressing on the denotation of breath in the word "inspiration." We deserve the force of alive being and how it can enable each of us, each day, to imagine how we want to be in the world and then to move toward that being. I know we have to engage the antiblack world and to host conversations of our being in the realities of that world; I also believe that we need the imaginary of a black world and its gentle nudging welcome—*come, baby, sit here and do this piece of your work*—that we never get from the world as it is.

Were I to start this book over now, I'd say that my claim is this: when black literary characters say "I" or "you," they can also mean "one"; that when black speakers speak, they are in pursuit of the oneness that is of a human being philosophically oriented to a problem that is theirs to pursue. Even when they seem to be speaking toward the audience of antiblackness, their furious doings could be read for what they mean to the one of black being. As such, I am making a case for an equanimity of syntax—I, you, one—that conscripts the black reader into a manner of reading. I am interested in the black reader who is instantiated via "imagine a black world," in what is possible for that reader by the invocation of such a world, the *work* the reader must do to behold and to be beheld by the world of the work. In short, "imagine a black world" is an invitation to study that a black text makes to a black reader. This being conceptualized by reading as if in a black world—this is what I mean by black aliveness as a poetics of being. It is a notion of study that resonates with bell hooks's *Sisters of the Yam: Black Women and Self-Recovery*, a book that taught me how to read literature for (my) black becoming, a book that begins with a superb invocation of black world instantiation: "Sisters—and you who are our friends, loved ones, and comrades—I greet you in love and peace" (1). Such astonishing poetics here.

Aliveness is a world, a pursuit, and—most of all—an ethical habitat that doesn't traffic in debt, as in what we owe to the other. What we owe is to ourselves—love and generosity, the will and willingness to be better in our being.

Such is the exploration in this book.

I've chosen a very specific archive for this project—poems and essays, mostly written since 1970.[6] And except for the foregoing reference to Lovell, I have not engaged the visual arts. Two readers of this manuscript questioned this exclusion, so I feel compelled to explain briefly: in *Black Aliveness*, I want to undermine as much as possible the representational imperatives for black being, since the logics of representation so often constitute limits to how blackness is imagined. Even in the case of first-person essays and poems of relation, my investments remain with the quality of feeling, the materiality and dynamism of the speaker as a textual endowment of oneness. I am interested in the abstracting capacities of literary blackness as a harbor of aliveness. Of course, it is possible to think with abstraction in the visual, or even to "think like a work of art" in Stephen Michael Best's idiom, which means attending to sensation and experience rather than securing argument. As critic Darby English writes, "Some art—particularly the possibilities certain art rehearses by presenting concepts, images, actions, and ways of being not yet expressed in instituted culture—points to a way forward" (xi). Here, English means that art can help us describe and contend with living in an intensified climate of racial terror. But English cautions us against any easy understanding of the visual, since "art like this exercises its critical function at a distance from the everyday and the real. *At the end of the encounter, it's we who must return and face the day*" (xi; emphasis added). I appreciate English's reminder of the profound gap between art's representative capabilities and the life invoked (as subject or as viewer) by its presence. To me, English's argument, his investigation of what it is "to describe a life" (his book's title) hinges on abstraction. And indeed, one of the reasons I adore Lovell's work is that his drawings of black faces privilege the capacity for abstraction without undermining the rich singular life that might be constellated via a charcoal image on paper. I could say the same thing about work by Lorna Simpson, Arthur Jafa, Carrie Mae Weems, Kara Walker, Amy Sherald, Kehinde Wiley, Simone Leigh, and so on.[7]

In thinking with the literary, I wanted to keep my terms of aliveness from arcing toward the fallacy of representing life itself. In *Black Aliveness*, I wanted to indulge in abstraction's generous wake, in the breadth to be had in imagining blackness as everything and nothing, in eluding the discursive limits of representation. Such is the abstraction mobilized in the textual examples throughout the book, and the prodding to think visually gives me the occasion to consider the cover image, Shinique Smith's sweeping *Prayer for Grace*, where dimension is produced through fabric pieces and ink lines. In Smith's distinctive use of calligraphic practice, blackness is idiomized as something sculptural, like a new animal form with swooping antennae and radial shell made by snatches of material. And yet I read in this image less a form and more a map, a map of and for one's traveling—dimension; in this way, *Prayer for Grace* composes a worldliness via its small collaged pieces.

As is the occasion with Gwendolyn Brooks's *Maud Martha*, the invocation of and traveling through grace belongs to blackness.[8]

Smith's *Prayer for Grace* is an apt complement to an image that holds my heart, Jacob Lawrence's *Migration Series* panel 46 (see fig. C.1). No work moves me more than this one, this staircase or ladder or tracks for a train that signals both ascent and descent, the possibility that movement might happen—this approximation of deepening, of force left open, a trail that doesn't offer direction. And that window with a moon visible—or is it a green door with a golden knob? Astonishing. I love how blackness here is figured not as a legible subject but as an energy or capacity, a poetic. Thrilling and terrifying. I love Lawrence's gorgeous slim color palette and modest gestures, this abstracting aliveness that invites one to engage the threshold of paying attention, the way the image's perspective constitutes one as a subject in the visual scene rather than presenting the subject themself. The black one gets to ride or fall or rise in the scene, not be captured by it.

Lawrence's colorful modified cubist style revels in abstraction and therefore complicates how we read representationally. That is, before we get to the figureless panel 46, his aesthetic in the *Migration* sequence showcases figures that lack extensive representational detail. In that regard, shape and color and angles do the work of approximating and importing breadth and specificity to his characters. This abstracting praxis intensifies in panel 46, one of the few paintings in the sixty-piece series that does not include a human figure. Moreover, though the panel's caption—"Industries attempted to board their labor in quarters that were oftentimes very unhealthy. Labor camps were numerous"—offers important

46

FIGURE C.1. Lawrence, Jacob (1917–2000) © ARS, NY. Industries attempted to board their labor in quarters that were oftentimes very unhealthy. Labor camps were numerous. 1940–1941. Panel 46 from *The Migration Series*. Tempera on gesso on composition board, 18 × 12″. Gift of Mrs. David M. Levy. © 2020 The Jacob and Gwendolyn Knight Lawrence Foundation, Seattle / Artists Rights Society (ARS), New York. Digital Image © The Museum of Modern Art / Licensed by SCALA / Art Resource, NY.

historical context, this context does not totalize the capacious scene of ladder (or track?), door (or window?), moon (or knob?). The caption is essential historically and is resonant of the narrative arc of the series, though it is not determinative of what we see and feel and know through apprehending panel 46.[9]

Panel 46 is all sky—when I recall it, I often remember it as all sky, as being oriented to and suspended in sky.

This piece, in its poetics, strikes me as about as Brooksian an art piece as there is. What I mean is that Lawrence's abstracting aesthetic relates well to the way in which Gwendolyn Brooks wrote about and characterized black people, especially in the long poem *In the Mecca*, with its compounded subject clauses full of unusual adjectives situated next to surprising nouns. Here, for example, is how the poem presents Mrs. Sallie Smith, black mother and domestic worker, as she returns home and climbs the stairs to her fourth-floor apartment:

S. Smith is Mrs. Sallie. Mrs. Sallie
hies home to Mecca, hies to marvelous rest;
ascends the sick and influential stair.
The eye unrinsed, the mouth absurd
with the last sourings of the master's Feast.
She plans
to set severity apart,
to unclench the heavy folly of the fist.
Infirm booms
and suns that have not spoken die behind this
low-brown butterball. Our prudent partridge.
A fragmentary attar and armed coma.
A fugitive attar and a district hymn. (*Blacks* 407)

This language is superb: the use of "hie" to describe hasty movement, "sick and influential" to denote a staircase, the exceptional balance of "eye unrinsed" with "mouth absurd," where the poetic iteration deforms the normal adjective-noun pattern and thereby elevates the scene of this ordinary woman, tired and resilient and moving. Brooks's diction dramatizes the simple fact of heavy breath and crusty eyes, makes it unfamiliarly known. We *feel* the heft and loveliness of this "prudent partridge" of a woman who casts a long shadow. Indeed, the poetic characterization is enhanced by the way each of the last three lines cleaves along a caesura, the break in a line where one phrase ends and the following phrase begins, as if to imply balance and separation, as if each line holds a twinned description of Mrs. Sallie: "low-brown butterball" paired with "our prudent partridge"; "a fragmentary attar" with "armed coma"; "a fugitive attar" with "a district hymn"—all three prefaced by the earlier tethering of "eye unrinsed" with "mouth absurd."[10] The diction of *In the Mecca* is compellingly unusual, nearly absurd in its use of specificity to abstract the specific. Take, for example, the rapturous conclusion of "The Sermon on the Warpland":

"My people, black and black, revise the River.

. . .

Build now your Church, my brothers, sisters. Build
never with brick or Corten nor with granite.
Build with lithe love. With love like lion-eyes.
With love like morningrise.
With love like black, our black—
luminously indiscreet;
complete; continuous." (*Blacks* 451–452)

Notice that this declaration of doing swirls on a series of *l*'s and *i*'s ("lithe love," "love like lion-eyes"), and the impressive chiasmic repetition in the last two lines as "lumin*ous*ly" adheres with "continu*ous*" and "indisc*reet*" with "compl*ete*." It is further evidence of the way blackness is narrated in Brooks's aesthetic, how her mouthy syntax wriggles away from simplistic rendering even as she is very much interested in the simple, how her syntax marries words to densify the expressed thing. Brooks's rich, quirky language—what scholar Gloria T. Hull describes as "idiosyncracies [*sic*] of manner" (281)—enacts abstraction and disrupts our belief that we know, can know precisely, black people. People are unknowable; we are lucky if we get close enough to be moved by their breath and breadth, but they are unknowable. So Brooks's poetry, as much as it chronicles and describes black characters, also seems to refuse a kind of knowing.[11]

Gwendolyn Brooks writes love songs for black life, a gift to us. I read her syntax and its abstraction as kin to the wide-open magic in Lawrence's *Migration* panel 46, an invitation for us to imagine.

I'll say it again: No work moves me more than this staircase or ladder or tracks for a train that signals both ascent and descent, this approximation of deepening, of force left open as well as the force of being left open. (Indeed, the dynamism in panel 46 is a bookend to the calligraphic grace of Shinique Smith's image on the cover.) This, to me, is aliveness, the way it constitutes one as a subject in the visual scene rather than presenting the subject themself. Here, in this instance in Lawrence's world, the black one gets to ride or fall or rise in the scene, not be captured by it. I am moved both by trying to imagine Lawrence imagining and making this, as I am moved in beholding myself as the one in the scene of the work—as the one who is reading and can be read in the scale of this ladder, this window, this moon.

Aliveness: in thinking through poetry and the poetic, I am leaning on words to *go there*—for words to withstand the unsayable expressivity of being. Like Fred Moten, I want to advance poetics as a capable case for aliveness, poetics that is elusively blurring and still present and of presence. "I feel, therefore I can be free," Audre Lorde tells us in "Poetry Is Not a Luxury," this repeatable bit of wisdom: "I feel, therefore I can be free. Poetry coins the language to express and charter this revolutionary demand, the implementation of that freedom" (*Sister Outsider* 38).[12]

If this is prayer, then I hope Reginald Shepherd and Audre Lorde and Lucille Clifton and James Baldwin know how much we rejoice in the example of their study, the relation-of-being evident in their thinking. If this is prayer, I hope they know this. I hope that all the ones whose work moves here know this. If this is prayer, I hope it lands on Toni Morrison too. I am a grateful student of these thinkers, especially Clifton and Morrison and their sustained investment in the force of one's self-regard. Morrison, and Clifton, she who, in the poem "grandma, we are poets," revises the definition of autism from its pathologies—"*a state of mind / characterized by dreaming*," a "*failure to use language normally*," "*ritualistic and repetitive / patterns of behavior / such as excessive rocking and spinning*" (374–375; emphases in original)—so as to theorize a notion of ethical inhabitance in being of one's self:

> say rather
> i imagined myself
> in the place before
> language imprisoned itself
> in words
>
> . . .
>
> say rather circling and
> circling my mind i am sure i imagined
> children without small rooms
> imagined young men black and
> filled with holes imagined
> girls imagined old men penned
> imagine actual humans
> howling their animal fear
>
> . . .
>
> say rather i withdrew

to seek within myself
some small reassurance
that tragedy while vast
is bearable (375)

I could present and gloss the whole beautiful poem (including how the past tense yields to the present in the line "imagine actual humans"—oh my), but "say rather" that Clifton's call to a language-of-being and to the withdrawal that is an ethical enactment of the will to be alive—"say rather" that this call is a subjunctive declaration of aliveness.[13]

(If this is prayer, then pray also that it finds my grandmother, my mother's mother.)

For as long as I can remember, I have seen the world in and through black women's understandings of blackness. In my study, to be in relation to black femaleness is to be in relation to blackness, which is also what it means to be in relation to black aliveness. This black femaleness is ecumenical, which in its root means "the whole inhabited world."[14]

If I could, I would have called this book "Aliveness." If I could, I would have dropped the qualifier; I could speak of us—of any one of black us—as being of aliveness and it would be discursively self-evident. I could study this same collage of poets and essayists and thinkers, and the title "Aliveness" would make perfect sense. If I could, this book would not need to exist.

These works tell us that aliveness is personal, not individual, personal in the way that James Baldwin means that word in his tour-de-force essay "Nothing Personal": as a term of reckoning with the condition of being on earth, alive and therefore responsible. We have in us aliveness. We are of aliveness and indeed our aliveness can help us navigate being and being (alive) in the world, including that ethical question, how to be, which so often is troubled by antiblackness. *Aliveness is the repertoire of having an ethical orientation in a world that is not ethically oriented.*

We are not the idea of us, not even the idea that we hold of us. We are us, multiple and varied, becoming. The heterogeneity of us. Blackness in a black world is everything, which means that it gets to be freed from being any one thing. We are ordinary beauty, black people, and beauty must be allowed to do its beautiful work.

We do not live in a black world, this is true. But the as-if of such imagining can inspire how we might navigate the world that we indeed live in, the one that is antiblack and that resists and resents and despises our being. We do not live in a black world, but in a poem there is an orientation of such being waiting for us, these poems in our hands as a world of invitation.[15]

This being is poetic and we are of its aliveness.

ACKNOWLEDGMENTS

First there are poets, by which I mean the ones mentioned here as well as those who are uncited, that cohort of artists whose work has helped me to think about poetics as a frame for being (this includes my eldest sister, Cindy). Then there are black writers in general (essayists, novelists, scholars), musicians and visual artists, dancers and actors—could I just say thank you to the whole wide world, since it is worth mentioning too those people (some of them new to me) who asked questions or nudged me along during talks, or students (graduate and undergraduate, especially those in Race and Love) and faculty colleagues who held space open for thinking, strangers in everyday moments who helped me appreciate another inflection of these ideas? It is hard to imagine a page wide enough to bear acknowledgments. Indeed, many of the people who might be acknowledged here are noted in the endnotes, which I take seriously as a chance to be able to name names. And still, it is not possible to name everyone whose interest or attention has propelled me along. I am grateful; as Ross Gay might instruct, I will just say, broadly, thank you.

Thanks to colleagues at Smith College (Africana Studies, the Program for the Study of Women and Gender) and Brown University (English Department, Africana Studies), as well as colleagues and audiences at Connecticut College, Dartmouth University, Hamilton College, Hampshire College, Harvard University (especially that dazzling American Studies graduate cohort), Pomona College, Tulane University, UCLA (especially Sarah Haley's black feminist working group), the University of Cincinnati, the University of Massachusetts at Amherst, the University of Miami, the University of Michigan, the University of Pennsylvania, and Vassar College.

Particular gratitude goes to Dr. Maryemma Graham for organizing a National Endowment for the Humanities summer study in black poetry (at the

University of Kansas) and to all the colleagues there from whom I learned much (especially Monifa Love, Sequoia Maner, Claire Schwartz, and Derik Smith); this book came to its aliveness there.

These people have been my company in this studying, both in their manner of being and in the fineness of their ideas: Aliyyah Abdur-Rahman, Jafari Sinclaire Allen, Donn Boulanger Jr., J. Kameron Carter, Lyrae Van Clief-Stefanon, Devon Clifton (especially), Soyica Diggs Colbert, Margo N. Crawford, Madhu Dubey, Ann duCille, Nikky Finney, Temar France, Warren Harding, Bonnie Honig, Catherine Imbriglio, Ricardo Jaramillo, Joyce Ann Joyce, Jacques Khalip, Daniel Kim, Airea Dee Matthews, Dennis Miehls, Diego Millan, Rolland Murray, Claudia Barbosa Nogueira, N'Kosi Oates, David Osepowicz, Emily Owens, Dixa Ramírez D'Oleo, J. T. Roane, Kiran Saili, Dorin Smith, Eric Sorenson, Hortense J. Spillers, L. H. Stallings, Mecca J. Sullivan, Britt Threatt, and Andre C. Willis. As students and now as colleagues, Quinn Anex-Ries and Nasir Marumo have been especially dear to me; as inhabitants of "the black alcove," so have Kristen Maye, Cole Morgan, and John Casey. (Has there ever been a finer reader than John Casey?) At various moments, Fabrizio Ciccone, Erin Prior, Adanne Ogbaa, and Nora Daniels worked tenderly with me on parts of the project. Thanks, also, to Courtney Berger, whose enthusiasm was so genuine and generous that it caught me off guard, and to the staff at the press (especially Courtney Baker and Sandra Korn). Thanks to Melody Negron and the folks at Westchester Publishing Services. Thanks to Benita J. Barnes and Jennifer Randall for full-life living; to Mike King, whose thinking and studying and being-with is rapture; to Matt Ashby for conversations about Audre Lorde the philosopher. Thank you to the company of black women, none of whom are academics, who came to lectures and who engaged me afterward (the engagement was always away from the formal scene of the talk): these specific women, each of whom I met only once, all of whom I have been writing for and thinking with the past ten years: thank you. Similar gratitude goes to Daphne Lamothe for believing in the radical right for black study and for all the days of writing side by side, so severely, so singularly.

I could say thank you forever: Thank you to Lucille Clifton, Gwendolyn Brooks, Audre Lorde, Toni Morrison, James Baldwin, Monique J. Savage; thank you to Sula Mae Peace. Thank you to Jacob Lawrence. Thank you to my three sisters and my parents. I never take it for granted that anything particular will manifest from studying; I am just studying. For support in this orientation, among other things, thank you, dear Peter Riedel, my guy; and thank you, forever, to Miss Esther P., my mother's mother, my first and best teacher, poet human she was.

NOTES

Introduction

1   My use of "rightness" here echoes Sylvia Wynter's argument about "wrongness of being"; see the essay "On How We Mistook the Map for the Territory, and Re-imprisoned Ourselves in an Unbearable Wrongness of Being, of *Desêtre*: Black Studies toward the Human Project," in *Not Only the Master's Tools: African-American Studies in Theory and Practice*, ed. Lewis R. Gordon and Jane Anna Gordon (London: Routledge, 2006), 107–169.

2   All my references to Clifton's poems are from *The Collected Poems of Lucille Clifton, 1965–2010*, ed. Kevin Young and Michael S. Glaser (Rochester, NY: BOA Editions, 2012).

3   I could mention, too, that the long *e* sound resonates with the short *i* of "live" because of the sonic play of the consonants in that word, which is another way of saying that sonic entanglement is rife throughout this poem. Gratitude to Mike King, who used the word "waltz" in a discussion with my Smith College students in 2015 and who engaged me in conversations about black sonic and verse practices. Thanks also to Herman Beavers, who alerted me to Michael S. Harper's poem "Deathwatch," which makes reference to the DuBois query.

4   Frantz Fanon, *Black Skin, White Masks*, trans. Charles Lam Markmann (London: Pluto, 2008), 82. Thanks to Heather Williams for an astute question about the vernacular inflection of "he do / she do."

5   See Daphne A. Brooks, *Bodies in Dissent: Spectacular Performances of Race and Freedom, 1850–1910* (Durham, NC: Duke University Press, 2006), especially the introduction, as well as her engagement of Brechtian distanciation in "Nina Simone's Triple Play," *Callaloo* 34, no. 1 (2011): 176–197; in both instances, Brooks reminds us to attend to the black performer more than to the presumptive white audience, to listen to and for blackness. My discussion of looking here could be described by the term Elin Diamond, a performance studies scholar, uses: "looking-at-being-looked-at-ness." Elin Diamond, *Unmaking Mimesis: Essays on Feminism and Theatre* (London: Routledge, 1997), 52. For more on distance, looking, and black subjectivity, see Hortense J. Spillers's consideration of the black specular in "Mama's Baby,

Papa's Maybe: An American Grammar Book" ("*being* for the captor" as a "distance *from* a subject position" [*Black* 206; emphases in original]) and "'All the Things You Could Be by Now, If Sigmund Freud's Wife Was Your Mother': Psychoanalysis and Race," in *Black, White, and in Color: Essays on American Literature and Culture* (Chicago: University of Chicago Press, 2003), 203–229, 376–427; bell hooks, *Black Looks: Race and Representation* (New York: Routledge, 2015); Nicole Fleetwood, *Troubling Vision: Performance, Visuality, and Blackness* (Chicago: University of Chicago Press, 2011); Elizabeth Alexander, "'Can You Be Black and Look at This?' Reading the Rodney King Video(s)," *Public Culture* 7, no. 1 (1994): 77–94; Jasmine Nicole Cobb, *Picture Freedom: Remaking Black Visuality in the Early Nineteenth Century* (New York: New York University Press, 2015); Leigh Raiford, *Imprisoned in a Luminous Glare: Photography and the African American Freedom Struggle* (Chapel Hill: University of North Carolina Press, 2013); Kimberly Juanita Brown, *The Repeating Body: Slavery's Visual Resonance in the Contemporary* (Durham, NC: Duke University Press, 2015); Courtney R. Baker, *Humane Insight: Looking at Images of African American Suffering and Death* (Urbana: University of Illinois Press, 2015); Krista Thompson, *Shine: The Visual Economy of Light in African Diasporic Aesthetic Practice* (Durham, NC: Duke University Press, 2015); Simone Browne, *Dark Matters: On the Surveillance of Blackness* (Durham, NC: Duke University Press, 2015); and Kalpana Seshadri-Crooks, *Desiring Whiteness: A Lacanian Analysis of Race* (New York: Routledge, 2002), which describes race as a "regime of looking" (2). That this list reflects only part of my encounter with a subset of works in this area suggests the potency of matters of blackness and looking.

6   The dynamics of address are multiplied when "reply" is read in regard to the poems that precede and succeed it in *Quilting*: "memo," which is dedicated to Fannie Lou Hamer, where the speaker addresses Hamer directly and includes herself in the "us"; and the aptly named "whose side are you on," where the speaker, in the first person, declares allegiance with a woman trying to get on a bus before its door closes.

7   Gilles Deleuze, *Difference and Repetition*, trans. Paul Patton (New York: Columbia University Press, 1994), 2–3, emphasis added. In the longer passage, Deleuze uses the terms "general" and "ordinary" in ways that might seem in conflict with my thinking about the quotidian excellence in Clifton's verse. I take my cue on Deleuz-ean time from John Rajchman's introduction to Deleuze's *Pure Immanence: Essays on a Life* (New York: Zone Books, 2001); Rajchman notes that for Deleuze, "We are always *quelconque*—we are and remain 'anybodies' before we become 'somebod-ies'" (14). For more on Deleuze's thinking, see Daniel W. Smith, *Essays on Deleuze* (Edinburgh: Edinburgh University Press, 2012); and John Protevi, *Political Physics: Deleuze, Derrida and the Body Politic* (London: Bloomsbury, 2001). I am also drawing on Michelle M. Wright's argument about time, phenomenon, and epiphenomenon in *Physics of Blackness: Beyond the Middle Passage Epistemology* (Minneapolis: University of Minnesota Press, 2015). Finally, in regard to my comment about the orthography of the repetitive "they do," see Jennifer DeVere Brody's consideration of ellipsis as a black sign in *Punctuation: Art, Politics, and Play* (Durham, NC: Duke University Press, 2008), chap. 2.

8   This Finney citation is from her National Book Award acceptance speech, included at the end of *Head Off and Split* (Evanston, IL: TriQuarterly Books / Northwestern

University Press, 2011), n.p. My comment about utopia references Clifton's *Quilting: Poems, 1987–1990* (Rochester, NY: BOA Editions, 2000), the collection that contains "reply" and that is inundated with iterations of subjunctivity where time and history are on the make. For more on conceptualizations of utopia, see José Esteban Muñoz, *Cruising Utopia: The Then and There of Queer Futurity* (New York: New York University Press, 2009); and Jill Dolan, *Utopia in Performance: Finding Hope at the Theater* (Ann Arbor: University of Michigan Press, 2005).

9 I am riffing here on Amiri Baraka (LeRoi Jones) and Billy "Fundi" Abernathy's photographic verse collection, *In Our Terribleness (Some Elements and Meaning in Black Style)* (Indianapolis: Bobbs-Merrill, 1970). I am also acknowledging that many of Clifton's poems are invitation poems in the tradition that Erik Gray explores in his essay "Come Be My Love: The Song of Songs, *Paradise Lost*, and the Tradition of the Invitation Poem," PMLA 128, no. 2 (2013): 370–385. This point will be explored further in chapter 1.

10 I am using the phrasing here from Saidiya Hartman, *Scenes of Subjection: Terror, Slavery, and Self-Making in Nineteenth-Century America* (New York: Oxford University Press, 1997).

11 I am referring to Wynter's essay "On How We Mistook" and to Margo Natalie Crawford's *Black Post-blackness: The Black Arts Movement and Twenty-First-Century Aesthetics* (Urbana: University of Illinois Press, 2017). The worldmaking that Wynter advances as a feature of the intellectual project of nascent black studies complements the case that Crawford makes for experimentation and abstraction as central to the Black Arts movement's intellectual commitments. As a complement to Crawford's work on expanding how we understand Black Arts, also see Evie Shockley, *Renegade Poetics: Black Aesthetics and Formal Innovation in African American Poetry* (Iowa City: Iowa University Press, 2011); James Smethurst, *The Black Arts Movement: Literary Nationalism in the 1960s and 1970s* (Chapel Hill: University of North Carolina Press, 2005); Howard Rambsy, *The Black Arts Enterprise and the Production of African American Poetry* (Ann Arbor: University of Michigan Press, 2011); Cheryl Clarke's conceptualization of circles in *After Mecca: Women Poets and the Black Arts Movement* (New Brunswick, NJ: Rutgers University Press, 2004); and GerShun Avilez, *Radical Aesthetics and Modern Black Nationalism* (Urbana: University of Illinois Press, 2016). Indeed, the era's worldmaking instinct is legible in the example of the renaming of *Negro Digest* as *Black World* in 1971, the return to Négritude as an ideology of the black subject's "being-in-the-world" (Jean-Paul Sartre, *Black Orpheus* [Paris: Présence Africaine, 1963], 41), or the think-tank Institute for the Black World, founded in 1969.

The reference to Wynter is intended to signal her superlative contribution to the power of narrative in inventing worlds; see, for example, "The Ceremony Must Be Found: After Humanism," *Boundary 2* 12, no. 3 (1984): 19–70. Scholarship on black worldmaking is vast, including Paul C. Taylor, *Black Is Beautiful: A Philosophy of Black Aesthetics* (Hoboken, NJ: Wiley-Blackwell, 2016), which offers a thorough consideration of blackness, aesthetics, and black life-worlds; Zakiyyah Iman Jackson, *Becoming Human: Matter and Meaning in an Antiblack World* (New York: New York University Press, 2020), which explores black writers' "imaginative practices of worlding" that refuse liberal humanism's terms of the human (1); and Anthony Reed's reading of "textural and textual" "worldliness and wordliness"—via Martin Heidegger and Black Arts theorists—in *Freedom Time: The Poetics and Politics of Black Experimental Writing* (Baltimore: Johns Hopkins University Press, 2014), 31. Also see studies on Afrofuturism and cosmopolitanism—for example, André M. Carrington, "The Cultural Politics of Worldmaking Practice," *African and Black Diaspora: An International Journal* 8, no. 2 (2015): 1–13; Carrington, *Speculative Blackness: The Future of Race in Science Fiction* (Minneapolis: University of Minnesota Press, 2016); and Alex Zamalin, *Black Utopia: The History of an Idea from Black Nationalism to Afrofuturism* (New York: Columbia University Press, 2019). For studies on aesthetics and cultural history, see works such as Imani Perry's reading of "I'll make me a world" in *May We Forever Stand: A History of the Black National Anthem* (Chapel Hill: University of North Carolina Press, 2018); and Mark C. Jerng, *Racial Worldmaking: The Power of Popular Fiction* (New York: Fordham University Press, 2018). For performance studies, see works such as Malik Gaines, *Black Performance on the Outskirts of the Left: A History of the Impossible* (New York: New York University Press, 2017); and Tavia Nyong'o, *Afro-fabulations: The Queer Drama of Black Life* (New York: New York University Press, 2018). For black gender studies, see, for example, Kimberly Nichele Brown, *Writing the Black Revolutionary Diva: Women's Subjectivity and the Decolonizing Text* (Bloomington: Indiana University Press, 2010); and L. H. Stallings, *Funk the Erotic: Transaesthetics and Black Sexual Cultures* (Urbana: University of Illinois Press, 2015). For works on the black radical tradition, see Robin D. G. Kelley, *Freedom Dreams: The Black Radical Imagination* (Boston: Beacon, 2002); Ashon T. Crawley's notion of dreaming and otherwise in *Blackpentecostal Breath: The Aesthetics of Possibility* (New York: Fordham University Press, 2016); and Barrymore Bogues's "radical imagination" in "And What about the Human? Freedom, Human Emancipation and the Radical Imagination," *Boundary 2* 39, no. 3 (2012): 28–46. For work in black political cultures, see Richard Iton, *In Search of the Black Fantastic: Politics and Popular Culture in the Post–Civil Rights Era* (Oxford: Oxford University Press, 2008). This partial list explores what Greg Thomas summarizes well in *The Sexual Demon of Colonial Power: Pan-African Embodiment and Erotic Schemes of Empire* (Bloomington: Indiana University Press, 2007): "The world put in place by colonialists is not the only world that has ever been. It is not even necessarily the only world that is. It is most assuredly not the only world that can be" (154).

Suffice it to say, also, that the discourse of worldmaking is expansive in humanist theory, including Nelson Goodman, *Ways of Worldmaking* (Indianapolis: Hackett, 1978); Goodman, *Of Mind and Other Matters* (Cambridge, MA: Harvard University Press, 1987); Jean-Francois Lyotard, *The Postmodern Condition* (Minneapolis: University of Minnesota Press, 1984); Maurice Merleau-Ponty, *The World of Perception* (New York: Routledge, 2004); Ludwig Wittgenstein's notion of language and worldmaking in *Tractatus Logico-Philosophicus* (San Bernadino: Decades, 2019) ("*The limits of my language* mean the limits of my world" [5.6, p. 123, emphasis in original]); Toril Moi's engagement of ordinary language theory and worldmaking in *Revolution of the Ordinary: Literary Studies after Wittgenstein, Austin, and Cavell* (Chicago: University of Chicago Press, 2017), esp. chaps. 1, 2; Nicholas F. Gier, *Wittgenstein and Phenomenology* (London: Routledge, 2018); Stephen Mulhall, *On Being in the World: Wittgenstein and Heidegger on Seeing Aspects* (London: Routledge, 1993); Jacques Rancière's construction of heterotopia in "The Senses and Uses of Utopia," in *Political Uses of Utopia: New Marxist, Anarchist, and Radical Democratic Perspectives*, ed. S. D. Chrostowska and James D. Ingram (New York: Columbia University Press, 2016), 219–232, and "The Aesthetic Heterotopia," *Philosophy Today* 54 (2010): 15–25; and Charles W. Mill's interrogation of the worldmaking of racial ideology in *The Racial Contract* (Ithaca, NY: Cornell University Press, 1997). Finally, worldmaking has also been important conceptually to thinking about aesthetics and narratology; see, for example, Jerome Bruner, "Self-Making and World-Making," *Journal of Aesthetic Education* 25, no. 1 (1991): 67–78; Daniel Yacavone, *Film Worlds: A Philosophical Aesthetics of Cinema* (New York: Columbia University Press, 2014); and Pheng Cheah, *What Is a World? On Postcolonial Literature as World Literature* (Durham, NC: Duke University Press, 2016), which includes the beautiful phrase "literature that worlds a world" (10).

12   Baraka's verse use of emotion (anger, rage) is consistent with Sara Ahmed's argument about emotions as worldmaking; see *The Cultural Politics of Emotion* (Edinburgh: Edinburgh University Press, 2004). I read this closing call, in its turn to the cosmic, as a utopian performance, "a manifesto [as] a call to a doing in and for the future" (Muñoz, *Cruising Utopia* 26). For further discussion of the unusual quality of "let" as an imperative, see Rodney Huddleston, "Clause Type and Illocutionary Force," in *The Cambridge Grammar of the English Language*, by Rodney Huddleston and Geoffrey K. Pullum (Cambridge: Cambridge University Press, 2002), 851–945, especially the discussion of directive and open imperatives on 934–937. I am grateful to Neal Whitman's blog *Literal-Minded* for the reference. The imperative in Baraka's "Black Art" situates the invocation in all-time, even outside time, such that there is not ever a moment when one cannot imagine a black subject feeling or living through or speaking this call. It is important that Baraka's speaker does not orient blackness via a past or a future (the line is not "Let black people understand that they were or will be"), since these are the common time registers for conceptualizing black subjectivity. Instead, Baraka's speaker speaks through the time of sensibility and feeling, surpassing the logics of what Michelle M. Wright has called "Middle Passage time" so as to focus on "the phenomenology of Blackness—that is, when and where it is being imagined, defined, and performed and in what locations, both figurative and literal" (*Physics of Blackness* 3). In this regard, Baraka's is a time of the being in embodiment. For more on time and phenomenology, see Sara Ahmed, *Queer Phenomenology: Orientations, Objects, Others* (Durham, NC: Duke University Press, 2006); Mark Hansen, "The Time of Affect, or Bearing Witness to Life," *Critical Inquiry* 30, no. 3 (2004): 584–626; Brian Massumi, *The Politics of Affect* (Cambridge, UK: Polity, 2015); and Ann Cvetkovich, *An Archive of Feelings: Trauma, Sexuality, and Lesbian Public Cultures* (Durham, NC: Duke University Press, 2003). Finally, it is notable that the poet Terrance Hayes borrows the energetic compounding language—including the reference to poets and warriors—of the end of "Black Art" for the first sonnet sequence and then a later sonnet in *American Sonnets for My Past and Future Assassin* (New York: Penguin Books, 2018); see pp. 5, 22.

13   We might consider the poem's closing imperative through Wynter's arguments for upending genres of black nonbeing, her "re-enchantment of humanism," which, in David Scott's language, imagines "the emancipated ecumenical conception of the

human." Sylvia Wynter, "The Re-enchantment of Humanism: An Interview with Sylvia Wynter," by David Scott, *Small Axe* 8 (2000): 197. That is, one can read "the ecumenical" in Baraka's relatively open and abstract language at the end of "Black Art," language that contrasts with the excessively concrete diction earlier and that idiomizes a black world as a black poem. Baraka's closing also evokes Édouard Glissant's *tout-monde*, the all-world of relation as a universe of change and exchange: "Thus, I dream, since I am a writer, I dream of a new approach to literature in this excess that is the *Tout-Monde*." Quoted in Bernadette Cailler, "*Totality and Infinity*, Alterity, and Relation: From Levinas to Glissant," *Journal of French and Francophone Philosophy* 19, no. 1 (2011): 143–144; Cailler is translating and quoting from Glissant's *Introduction à une poetique du divers* (Montreal: Presses de l'Université de Montréal, 1995), 91–92. Glissant's thinking will become central to the arguments in chapters 1 and 2. Also see Eric Prieto, "Edouard Glissant, *Littérature-monde*, and *Tout-monde*," *Small Axe* 14, no. 3 (2010): 111–120; Kara Keeling on Glissant and imagination in *Queer Times, Black Futures* (New York: New York University Press, 2019); and Robin Kelley's *Freedom Dreams*. Finally, my thinking here acknowledges that worldmaking is all over Baraka's poetics, including in poems like "Black Dada Nihilismus" and "Return of the Native," both in *The Leroi Jones/Amiri Baraka Reader*, ed. William J. Harris (New York: Thunder's Mouth Press, 2000), 71–73, 217. I am also thinking with Essex Hemphill's "Heavy Breathing," an epic poem of blackness that invokes Négritude and that also rages through an expansive black collectivity, though this one is queer and feminist; Hemphill's poem is from his collection *Ceremonies: Poetry and Prose* (New York: Plume, 1992).

14 Harper describes this especially well in his argument about double-voicedness in *Are We Not Men? Masculine Anxiety and the Problem of African-American Identity* (New York: Oxford University Press, 1996):

Because of the way the poetry uses direct address and thus invites us to conflate addressee and audience, it appears that the material is meant to be *heard* by blacks, and *over*heard by whites, who would respond fearfully to the threat of mayhem it embodies. I think that this is appearance only, however, and it will be a secondary effect of my argument to demonstrate that, while Black Arts poetry very likely does depend for its power on the division of its audience along racial lines, it achieves its maximum impact in a context in which it is understood as being *heard* directly by whites, and *over*heard by blacks. (45–46; emphases in original)

Harper also uses Baraka's epigraphic poem, "SOS," and Sonia Sanchez's "blk/rhetoric" to explore the nature and limits of the call toward a black collective as such is conceptualized in the era.

15 Wynter, "Re-enchantment of Humanism" 197. I know that Wynter didn't mean this statement exclusively, but if its idealism is to work, it has to be of a black world too. Wynter's use of "form of life" resonates with Giorgio Agamben's grappling with the same phrase, sometimes hyphenated, in *Means without End: Notes on Politics* (Minneapolis: University of Minnesota Press, 2000). There is a striking parallel between Wynter's phrasing here and Baraka's "The World You're Talking About," his introduction to David Henderson's collection of poems *Felix of the Silent Forest* (New York: Poets,

1967), published under the name LeRoi Jones: "The Black Poetry is a sensitivity to the world total, to the American total. It is *about*, or *is* feeling(s). Even governmental structures are made the way people *feel* they should be made. The animating intelligence is a total of all existence. . . . Ways of making sense, of sensing. . . . Worlds. Spectrums. Galaxies. What the god knows" (n.p. [first page]; emphasis in original). Later, Jones (Baraka) concludes that "our content is literally about a world of humans and their paths and forms" (n.p. [first page]), which resonates, too, with his verse in and the ambition of *In Our Terribleness*. I am grateful to J. Peter Moore for pointing me to Henderson's collection and Jones's (Baraka's) introduction.

16   Another way to think of the poem's invocation is through Crawford's notion of "public interiority," especially the idea of the Black Arts movement as "the call for a black interior and the call for the *black* collection of blackness" (*Black Post-blackness* 167; emphasis in original). Crawford's work, like Harper's, frames the matter of audience in Black Arts literature; also see Rolland Murray, *Our Living Manhood: Literature, Black Power, and Masculine Ideology* (Philadelphia: University of Pennsylvania Press, 2007); Robert F. Reid-Pharr, *Conjugal Union: The Body, the House, and the Black American* (Baltimore: Johns Hopkins University Press, 2002); and Stephen Michael Best, *None like Us: Blackness, Belonging, Aesthetic Life* (Durham, NC: Duke University Press, 2018).

17   My reference in this paragraph is to Hartman's body of work, especially *Scenes of Subjection*; *Lose Your Mother: A Journey along the Atlantic Slave Route* (New York: Macmillan, 2008); "Venus in Two Acts," *Small Axe* 12, no. 2 (2008): 1–14; and her conversation with Frank B. Wilderson III, "The Position of the Unthought," *Qui Parle* 13, no. 2 (2003): 183–201.

18   Though there are ideological distinctions between black/Afro-pessimism and black optimism, I choose "black pessimism" as an encompassing term since I am not arguing the difference. And though Fred Moten does not identify with black pessimism, I am citing his ideas in this gloss precisely because Moten's exploration of black radical aesthetics and of fugitivity are often incorporated into the field. For more in this regard, see Jared Sexton, "The Social Life of Social Death: On Afro-pessimism and Black Optimism," *Intensions* 5 (2011), http://www.yorku.ca/intent/issue5/articles /jaredsexton.php; Sexton, "Afro-pessimism: The Unclear Word," *Rhizomes* 29 (2016), https://doi.org/10.20415/rhiz/029.e02; David Marriott, "Judging Fanon," *Rhizomes* 29 (2016), https://doi.org/10.20415/rhiz/029.e03; and Fred Moten, "The Case of Blackness," *Criticism* 50, no. 2 (2008): 177–218. Worldmaking is present conceptually in many works in the field, including in Stefano Harney and Fred Moten, *The Undercommons: Fugitive Planning and Black Study* (New York: Minor Compositions, 2013); in Hartman's refiguring of the archive via fabulation ("Venus in Two Acts"); in Sharpe's exposition of the wake (*In the Wake: On Blackness and Being* [Durham, NC: Duke University Press, 2016]); in Frank B. Wilderson III's conceptualization of the hold and his claim that there is no assumption of human equilibrium for the black (*Red, White and Black: Cinema and the Structure of U.S. Antagonisms* [Durham, NC: Duke University Press, 2010]); in Nahum Dimitri Chandler's exposition of the DuBoisian color line as a thought horizon (*X—The Problem of the Negro as a Problem for Thought* [New York: Fordham University Press, 2014]); and in Katherine McKittrick's assertion that "our

historically present black geographies . . . are from nowhere . . . inventions, just as we are" (*Demonic Grounds: Black Women and the Cartographies of Struggle* [Minneapolis: University of Minnesota Press, 2006], 97). Black pessimism's philosophical thinking allies with the black radical tradition that conceptualizes a black world totality, what Cedric Robinson calls "ontological totality" in *Black Marxism: The Making of the Black Radical Tradition* (Chapel Hill: University of North Carolina Press, 2000), 171. There is, too, a manner of worldmaking in the way black pessimism conceptualizes black study: all thinking is blackness, black thinking is black being (see especially Harney and Moten, *Undercommons*, as well as Jared Sexton, "Ante-Anti-Blackness: Afterthoughts," *Lateral* 1, no. 1 [2012]: n.p.).

19 I am gleaning this summation from studying Sylvia Wynter and Frank Wilderson, especially *Afropessimism* (New York: Liveright, 2020), though I imagine that Wilderson might disagree with my exact formulation in this summary.

20 See especially Jared Sexton, who offers a clear rejection of death in "Ante-Anti-Blackness." If we read for it, vitality is evident in Fred Moten's "scream" and his sustained interest in fugitivity (*In the Break: The Aesthetics of the Black Radical Tradition* [Minneapolis: University of Minnesota Press, 2003]) as well his attention to the "aesthetic sociology or a social poetics of nothingness" ("Blackness and Nothingness [Mysticism in the Flesh]," *South Atlantic Quarterly* 112, no. 4 (2013): 742); Glissant's opacity (*Poetics of Relation*, trans. Betsy Wing [Ann Arbor: University of Michigan Press, 1997]); the theoretical astuteness of the word "social" in Orlando Patterson's conceptualization of social death (*Slavery and Social Death: A Comparative Study* [Cambridge, MA: Harvard University Press, 2018]); Avery Gordon's sociological haunting (*Ghostly Matters: Haunting and the Sociological Imagination* [Minneapolis: University of Minnesota Press, 2008]); Lewis R. Gordon's revision of Sartre's bad faith ("Yet the slave is also simultaneously aware of not fully *being a slave*; he is, after all, *conscious of the beyond*" [*Bad Faith and Antiblack Racism* (Amherst, NY: Humanity Books, 1995), 16; emphasis in original]); Fanon's zone of nonbeing (*Black Skin, White Masks*); Vincent Brown's understanding of the dead as a social force in *The Reaper's Garden: Death and Power in the World of Atlantic Slavery* (Cambridge, MA: Harvard University Press, 2008). I could note, too, Frank Wilderson's use of the idioms "Slave" and "Savage," which surpass the terms of death (in *Red, White and Black*). My thinking is inspired by Alexander G. Weheliye, *Habeas Viscus: Racializing Assemblages, Biopolitics, and Black Feminist Theories of the Human* (Durham, NC: Duke University Press, 2014), particularly his warning about suffering as an overriding conceit in some biopolitical formations of blackness, as it is by Achille Mbembe ("Necropolitics," *Public Culture* 15, no. 1 [2003]: 11–40; and *Critique of Black Reason* [Durham, NC: Duke University Press, 2017]), Darieck Scott (*Extravagant Abjection: Blackness, Power, and Sexuality in the African American Literary Imagination* [New York: New York University Press, 2010]), Joshua Chambers-Letson (his revision of death and/as communism in *After the Party: A Manifesto for Queer of Color Life* [New York: New York University Press, 2018]), and Neil Roberts (*Freedom as Marronage* [Chicago: University of Chicago Press, 2015]). Surely death is endemic to the construction of the rational subject and the racialized subject, as Denise Ferreira da Silva argues in *Toward a Global Idea of Race* (Minneapolis: University of Minnesota Press, 2007), but the matter of black theory always theorizes

life. And again, I am cohering an array of thinkers under the rubric of black pessimism, though not all of them claim—or have had the chance to claim—the label.

21 I am borrowing the notion of opacity from Glissant's *Poetics of Relation*; the refer-
ence to "ontological terror" is from Calvin L. Warren, *Ontological Terror: Blackness,
Nihilism, and Emancipation* (Durham, NC: Duke University Press, 2018). Also, I read
Wilderson's iteration of the Savage/Slave dyad—explored in *Red, White and Black*
and in *Afropessimism*—in conjunction with Iyko Day's elision of such a binary in
"Being or Nothingness: Indigeneity, Antiblackness, and Settler Colonial Critique,"
Critical Ethnic Studies 1, no. 2 (2015): 102–121.

22 At stake here is thinking about the role that a history of the black past plays in how
we conceptualize terms in black studies. Again, this is not a dispute of the totality of antiblackness, which is past and now, which Sharpe conceptualizes via "the
weather [as] the totality of our environments . . . the total climate; and that climate is
antiblack" (*In the Wake* 104), a totality that leads Warren to assert that "Black freedom,
then, would constitute a form of *world destruction*, and this is precisely why humanism has failed to accomplish its romantic goals of equality, justice, and recognition"
(*Ontological Terror* 6; emphasis in original). Yes, and still I hear Jared Sexton's important query, "Must one always think blackness to think antiblackness?" ("Social Life of
Social Death"), which leads me to ask, Must one always and only think antiblackness
to think—or imagine—blackness? This question is asked directly in Best's *None like Us*,
which notes that "black studies [is] burdened by . . . the omnipresence of history in our
politics . . . [and] confronts the more difficult task of disarticulating itself . . . from the
historical accretions of slavery, race, and racism, or from a particular commitment to
the idea that the slave past provides a ready prism for understanding and apprehending the black political present" (2). The disarticulation is impossible and so too is the
balance between Sexton's question and mine. This complication of blackness and time
thrives in work by Sharon P. Holland, *Raising the Dead: Readings of Death and (Black)
Subjectivity* (Durham, NC: Duke University Press, 2000); Wright, *Physics of Blackness* (66); Nyong'o, *Afro-fabulations*; Robert F. Reid-Pharr, *Archives of the Flesh: African
America, Spain, and Post-humanist Critique* (New York: New York University Press, 2016);
as it does in post-soul studies (see, for example, Nelson George, *Post-soul Nation: The
Explosive, Contradictory, Triumphant, and Tragic 1980s as Experienced by African Americans
(Previously Known as Blacks and before That Negroes)* (New York: Penguin, 2004); Mark
Anthony Neal, *Soul Babies: Black Popular Culture and the Post-soul Aesthetic* (New York:
Routledge, 2001); and Paul C. Taylor, "Post-Black, Old Black," *African American Review*
41, no. 4 [2007]: 625–640). Also, my reference to "anti/ante" riffs on Sexton's "Ante-
Anti-Blackness." Finally, thanks to Daphne Lamothe for a conversation here.

23 Thanks to Nichole Calero, a former student, for the conversation that sparked the
insight about the expectation of blackness.

24 The word "being" consorts easily with naïve constructions of freedom, individuation, and even agency. In *Ontological Terror*, Warren asks, "What is black existence
without Being?" (14), a question that notices the ways that being/Being is already
sequestered by Enlightenment imagining. (Throughout the text, Warren uses the
term "being" with a strikethrough.) It is important, then, to be clear that I always
mean "becoming" when I say "being," since being is not static; being unfurls and

dissolves and accretes, each happening yielding another instantiation. In this
work, my thinking on being inclines toward the phenomenology of Audre Lorde
(a Lordean phenomenology—see chapters 1 and 2) rather than toward what Moten
describes as the exhausted language of ontology (in the preface to *Black and Blur*).
See also the case Carl Phillips makes in his essay "A Politics of Mere Being," *Poetry*,
December 2016, https://www.poetryfoundation.org/poetrymagazine/articles/91294
/a-politics-of-mere-being.

25 I am inspired here by the clarity of Christopher Freeburg's assertion, in his study of
black interiority, "that the powers of human identification never cause ontological
ambiguity between people—that is, one never really confuses another person for something else under normative conditions" (*Black Aesthetics and the Interior Life* [Charlot-
tesville: University of Virginia Press, 2017], 42). Wilderson's claim echoes what Nahum
Dimitri Chandler describes as the problem of exorbitance, that there is no outside—no
"free zone or quiet place"—for black writing and thinking (*X* 14). My invocation of a
black world is an attempt to argue that such a zone can be read in the world of the
text, not unlike the language Harney and Moten use for the aesthetics of the undercommons: "the sociopoetic force we wrap tightly round us" (*Undercommons* 19).

26 Thanks to Alexis Pauline Gumbs for the reminder about this essential line in the
Combahee statement, which helps me to signal my debt to the particular ways
black women thinkers have engaged blackness and worldmaking. Central in
this regard is bell hooks, *Sisters of the Yam: Black Women and Self-Recovery* (Boston:
South End Press, 1993), a book that holds singular meaning in my studying and
that opens, in invocation, "Sisters—and you who are our friends, loved ones, and
comrades" (1). Those words are like a spell, the kind of shapeshifting and embodied praxis that Aimee Meredith Cox writes about in *Shapeshifters: Black Girls and
the Choreography of Citizenship* (Durham, NC: Duke University Press, 2015) or the
worldmaking that black girls enact through the poetic in Ruth Nicole Brown's
work (see especially "Pleasure Verses: A Five Element Set," *American Quarterly* 71,
no. 1 [2019]: 179–189; and *Hear Our Truths: The Creative Potential of Black Girlhood* [Ur-
bana: University of Illinois Press, 2014]). In terms of thinking about blackness and
heterogeneity, see Roderick A. Ferguson, *Aberrations in Black: Toward a Queer of Color
Critique* (Minneapolis: University of Minnesota Press, 2003); C. Riley Snorton, *Black
on Both Sides: A Racial History of Trans Identity* (Minneapolis: University of Minnesota
Press, 2017); and Jennifer C. Nash, *Black Feminism Reimagined: After Intersectionality*
(Durham, NC: Duke University Press, 2019). And as with all my feminist black
doings, I learned much from and with Monique J. Savage.

27 Also see the argument that Robin D. G. Kelley makes in the opening of *Yo Mama's
Disfunktional! Fighting the Culture Wars in Urban America* (Boston: Beacon, 2008), particularly his reading of John L. Gwaltney's *Drylongso: A Self-Portrait of Black America*.
The phrase "calling all black people" repeats a line from Amiri Baraka's poem "SOS"
and invokes the argument Phillip Brian Harper makes about the poem in *Are We
Not Men?* Because my commitment is to be thoughtful about gender and gendering, I often use the singular third-person pronoun "their" to refer to speakers when
a gender designation is not clear; I also use the reflexive pronoun "themself" for

the same reason. These choices are repeated and become clearer in thinking about aliveness and oneness in chapter 2.

28 Gwendolyn Brooks, "The Second Sermon on the Warpland," in *Blacks* (Chicago: Third World Press, 1987), 453. I am grateful for conversation with Matt Ashby that sharpened my thinking here.

29 Wilderson explores the ethical limits of/within an antiblack world in *Red, White and Black* (see especially "Introduction: Unspeakable Ethics"). The matter of ethics is taken up in chapter 5.

30 Unsaid here is a larger conversation about citational practice as a matter of scholarly or disciplinary legibility. I am inspired first by Barbara Christian's iconic essay "The Race for Theory," then by Phillip Brian Harper's example in the introduction of *Abstractionist Aesthetics: Artistic Form and Social Critique in African American Culture* (New York: New York University Press, 2015), esp. 15.

31 Their names are, respectively, Christian Cooper and Skhylur Davis.

32 In thinking about catastrophe and the terms of the modern world, I am reading with Sylvia Wynter (especially "Unsettling the Coloniality of Being/Power/Truth/Freedom: Towards the Human, After Man, Its Overrepresentation—an Argument," *CR: The New Centennial Review* 3, no. 3 [2003]: 257–337; and "The Ceremony Must Be Found"), Hortense Spillers (especially "Mama's Baby, Papa's Maybe"), Maria Lugones (especially "Heterosexualism and the Colonial/Modern Gender System," *Hypatia* 22, no. 1 [2007]: 186–209; and "Toward a Decolonial Feminism," *Hypatia* 25, no. 4 [2010]: 742–759), Kara Keeling (*Queer Times, Black Futures* [New York: New York University Press, 2019]), Sean Gaston (*The Concept of World from Kant to Derrida* [Lanham, MD: Rowman and Littlefield, 2013]), Jacques Khalip (*Last Things: Disastrous Form from Kant to Hujar* [New York: Fordham University Press, 2018], esp. chap. 4), Massimo Livi Bacci (*Conquest: The Destruction of the American Indios* [Cambridge, UK: Polity, 2008]), Jason W. Moore (*Anthropocene or Capitalocene? Nature, History, and the Crisis of Capitalism* [Oakland: PM, 2016]), Jodi Byrd (*The Transit of Empire: Indigenous Critiques of Colonialism* [Minneapolis: University of Minnesota Press, 2011]), Mark Rifkin (*Beyond Settler Time: Temporal Sovereignty and Indigenous Self-Determination* [Durham, NC: Duke University Press, 2017], which argues against the logic of time and world imposed by colonial and imperial imagination), Kathryn Yusoff (*A Billion Black Anthropocenes or None* [Minneapolis: University of Minnesota Press, 2019]), and Achille Mbembe (especially *Critique of Black Reason*). Gratitude to Khalip for a conversation that extended my thinking here.

33 For a good engagement with matters of address, see Monique Roelofs, *Arts of Address: Being Alive to Language and the World* (New York: Columbia University Press, 2020).

Chapter 1. Aliveness and Relation

1 I am quoting here from Alexis De Veaux's indispensable *Warrior Poet: A Biography of Audre Lorde* (New York: W. W. Norton, 2004), 199.

2 I'll come to affect theory later, though I want to acknowledge Teresa Brennan's argument about the transmission of feeling in *The Transmission of Affect* (Ithaca,

NY: Cornell University Press, 2004). Thanks to John Casey, who encouraged me to highlight rather than embed Christian's statement.

3 The first quotation is from p. xvi, the second is the title of chapter 1 from Jane Bennett's *Vibrant Matter: A Political Ecology of Things* (Durham, NC: Duke University Press, 2010). My thinking about life and aliveness, especially the notion of force, is inspired by phenomenology, especially Maurice Merleau-Ponty and Michel Henry, as will be specified in subsequent notes.

4 First, in addition to Bennett's *Vibrant Matter*, my thinking on materiality is indebted to Fred Moten, "The Case of Blackness," *Criticism* 50, no. 2 (2008): 177–218; Moten, "Blackness and Nothingness (Mysticism in the Flesh)," *South Atlantic Quarterly* 112, no. 4 (2013): 737–780; Bill Brown, *A Sense of Things: The Object Matter of American Literature* (Chicago: University of Chicago Press, 2003); Mel Y. Chen, *Animacies: Biopolitics, Racial Mattering, and Queer Affect* (Durham, NC: Duke University Press, 2012); Dana Luciano and Mel Y. Chen, "Has the Queer Ever Been Human?," *GLQ* 21, no. 2–3 (2015): 183–207 (indeed, the entire discussion in that "Queer Inhumanisms" special issue of *GLQ*); Elizabeth Grosz, *The Incorporeal: Ontology, Ethics, and the Limits of Materialism* (New York: Columbia University Press, 2018); Grosz, *Volatile Bodies: Toward a Corporeal Feminism* (Bloomington: Indiana University Press, 1994); Tim Ingold, *Being Alive: Essays on Movement, Knowledge and Description* (London: Routledge, 2011); Nikolas Rose, *The Politics of Life Itself: Biomedicine, Power, and Subjectivity in the Twenty-First Century* (Princeton, NJ: Princeton University Press, 2006); Gilles Deleuze, *Pure Immanence: Essays on a Life* (New York: Zone Books, 2001); Rachel C. Lee, *The Exquisite Corpse of Asian America: Biopolitics, Biosociality, and Posthuman Ecologies* (New York: New York University Press, 2014); Donna V. Jones, *The Racial Discourses of Life Philosophy: Négritude, Vitalism, and Modernity* (New York: Columbia University Press, 2010); Zakiyyah Iman Jackson, *Becoming Human: Matter and Meaning in an Antiblack World* (New York: New York University Press, 2020); Katie Genel, "The Question of Biopower: Foucault and Agamben," *Rethinking Marxism* 18, no. 1 (2006): 43–62; Donna J. Haraway, *Primate Visions: Gender, Race, and Nature in the World of Modern Science* (London: Psychology Press, 1989); Haraway, "A Cyborg Manifesto: Science, Technology, and Socialist-Feminism in the Late Twentieth Century," in *Simians, Cyborgs and Women: The Reinvention of Nature* (New York: Routledge, 1991), 149–181; and Michel Henry, *Material Phenomenology* (New York: Fordham University Press, 2008), which extends the case he made in *The Essence of Manifestation* (New York: Springer, 1973). (I am grateful to Jeffrey Hanson and Michael R. Kelly, eds., *Michel Henry: The Affects of Thought* [London: Continuum, 2002], for help in thinking with Henry.)

On the question of life and the state, in addition to works listed earlier, see also Michel Foucault, *The History of Sexuality*, vol. 1, *An Introduction* (New York: Pantheon Books, 1978); Giorgio Agamben, *Homo Sacer: Sovereign Power and Bare Life* (Stanford, CA: Stanford University Press, 1998); Simone Brown, *Dark Matters: On the Surveillance of Blackness* (Durham, NC: Duke University Press, 2015); and Alexander Weheliye, *Habeas Viscus: Racializing Assemblages, Biopolitics, and Black Feminist Theories of the Human* (Durham, NC: Duke University Press, 2014), which makes a case for thinking of life that exists "alongside the violence, subjection, exploitation, and racialization that define the modern human being" (1). Though Agamben doesn't specifically take up blackness, Weheliye warns us of the limits of the notion of *homo sacer* as a framework for thinking about black vitality; in this regard see also Achille Mbembe, "Necropolitics," *Public Culture* 15, no. 1 (2003): 11–40; and Marcelo Svirsky and Simone Bignall, eds., *Agamben and Colonialism* (Edinburgh: Edinburgh University Press, 2012). Indeed, we could look to Agamben's articulation of "form-of-life," a hyphenated phrase distinct from the notion of "form of life," as an example of his appreciation of the limits of *homo sacer* to characterize human life at all; see "Form-of-Life," in *Means without End: Notes on Politics* (Minneapolis: University of Minnesota Press, 2000), 3–12. In this way, Weheliye's caution (and Agamben's) relates to my comment about blackness as a problem to conceits of life. In this comment, I am citing W. E. B. DuBois's question in the opening of *The Souls of Black Folk*, ed. Henry Louis Gates and Terri Hume Oliver (New York: W. W. Norton, 1999), "How does it feel to be a problem?" (9), as well as invoking Orlando Patterson's conceptualization of social death (*Slavery and Social Death* [Cambridge, MA: Harvard University Press, 2018]); Sharon Patricia Holland's engagement of Patterson in *Raising the Dead: Readings of Death and (Black) Subjectivity* (Durham, NC: Duke University Press, 2000); Achille Mbembe, *On the Postcolony* (Berkeley: University of California Press, 2001); Ronald A. T. Judy, "Fanon's Body of Black Experience," in *Fanon: A Critical Reader*, ed. Lewis R. Gordon et al. (Oxford: Blackwell, 1996), 53–73; and Nahum Dimitri Chandler, *X—The Problem of the Negro as a Problem for Thought* (New York: Fordham University Press, 2013), as well as Hartman, Moten, Sexton, and Sharpe, who are cited in the introduction.

On the question of hierarchy, value, and quantification, see Denise Ferreira da Silva, *Toward a Global Idea of Race* (Minneapolis: University of Minnesota Press, 2007); Silva, "1 (life) ÷ 0 (blackness) = ∞ − ∞ or ∞ / ∞: On Matter beyond the Equation of Value," *E-Flux* 79 (2017), https://www.e-flux.com/journal/79/94686/1 -life-o-blackness-or-on-matter-beyond-the-equation-of-value/; Katherine McKittrick, "Mathematics: Black Life," *Black Scholar* 44, no. 2 (2014): 16–28; Zakiyyah Iman Jackson, *Becoming Human* (especially the introduction); Ian Baucom, *Specters of the Atlantic: Finance Capital, Slavery, and the Philosophy of History* (Durham, NC: Duke University Press, 2005); Lindon W. Barrett, *Blackness and Value: Seeing Double* (Cambridge: Cambridge University Press, 2009); Edward E. Baptist, *The Half Has Never Been Told: Slavery and the Making of American Capitalism* (New York: Basic Books, 2016); Kyla Schuller's exploration of impression, impressibility, and racialized unimpressibility in *The Biopolitics of Feeling: Race, Sex, and Science in the Nineteenth Century* (Durham, NC: Duke University Press, 2018); and Victoria Pitts-Taylor, *The Brain's Body: Neuroscience and Corporeal Politics* (Durham, NC: Duke University Press, 2016). Relatedly, my thinking about aliveness and worthiness is informed by disability studies, in particular, Robert McRuer, *Crip Theory: Cultural Signs of Queerness and Disability* (New York: New York University Press, 2006); Alison Kafer, *Feminist, Queer, Crip* (Bloomington: Indiana University Press, 2013); Jonathan M. Metzl and Anna Kirkland, *Against Health: How Health Became the New Morality* (New York: New York University Press, 2010); Eli Claire, *Exile and Pride: Disability, Queerness, and Liberation* (Durham, NC: Duke University Press, 2015); and Rosemarie Garland Thomson's field-shaping *Extraordinary Bodies: Figuring Physical Disability in American Culture and*

Literature (New York: Columbia University Press, 1997), as well as Mel Chen's consideration of linguistic hierarchy in *Animacies*. Finally, by "inherence" I mean simply being inherent more than I mean to call on the Platonic philosophical notion.

5 I want to be clear that my term "aliveness" is not consistent with the fallacy of transparency or legibility or self-consciousness, as explored by Denise Ferreira da Silva in *Toward a Global Idea of Race*; nor is it commensurate with "personhood, sovereignty, and property" in Imani Perry's formulation of the terms of modern legal subjecthood in *Vexy Thing: On Gender and Liberation* (Durham, NC: Duke University Press, 2018), 9–10. Also, while iterations of excess can be useful in eliding biopolitical constructs, I am cautious of the ever-present idea of black excessiveness; I have learned much from the ways that scholars think with and against excess, including in Daphne A. Brooks, *Bodies in Dissent: Spectacular Performances of Race and Freedom, 1850–1910* (Durham, NC: Duke University Press, 2007) (especially her use of "sybaritic" to indicate that which is pleasurable beyond use [205]); Darieck Scott, *Extravagant Abjection: Blackness, Power, and Sexuality in the African American Literary Imagination* (New York: New York University Press, 2010); Omise'eke Natasha Tinsley, "Black Atlantic, Queer Atlantic: Queer Imaginings of the Middle Passage," *GLQ* 14, no. 2–3 (2008): 191–216 ("corporeal effluvia" [198]); J. Kameron Carter and Sarah Jane Cervenak, "Black Ether," *CR: The New Centennial Review* 16, no. 2 (2016): 203–224 (as "exorbitant life force" [209]); Joshua Chambers-Letson, *After the Party* (New York: New York University Press, 2018) (especially his thinking about death and "More Life"); Ashon T. Crawley, *Blackpentecostal Breath: The Aesthetics of Possibility* (New York: Fordham University Press, 2016); and especially Saidiya Hartman's thinking about the archive (in "Venus in Two Acts" [*Small Axe* 12, no. 2 (2008): 1–14]) and her method in *Wayward Lives, Beautiful Experiments* (New York: W. W. Norton, 2019). Also see Hartman's response essay "Intimate History, Radical Narrative," Black Perspectives, May 22, 2020, https://www.aaihs.org/intimate-history-radical-narrative/. For further consideration on the limits of excessiveness, see Sianne Ngai, *Ugly Feelings* (Cambridge, MA: Harvard University Press, 2007); Toni Morrison, *Playing in the Dark: Whiteness and the Literary Imagination* (New York: Vintage Books, 1993); Robin Bernstein, *Racial Innocence: Performing American Childhood from Slavery to Civil Rights* (New York: New York University Press, 2011); Eric Lott, *Love and Theft: Blackface Minstrelsy and the American Working Class* (Oxford: Oxford University Press, 2013); Achille Mbembe, *Critique of Black Reason* (Durham, NC: Duke University Press, 2017); and my discussion of the trouble of publicness in Kevin Quashie, *The Sovereignty of Quiet: Beyond Resistance in Black Culture* (New Brunswick, NJ: Rutgers University Press, 2012).

6 Following the case Lyndon K. Gill makes in "In the Realm of Our Lorde: Eros and the Poet Philosopher," *Feminist Studies* 40, no. 1 (2014): 169–189, I read Lorde as a theorist and philosopher, particularly in the ways that she resolves Kantian ambivalence about imagination. I think this especially about the way her argument mixes experience, the sublime, and the ideal (via imagination). For more on that ambivalence and its ideological implications, see Jane Kneller, *Kant and the Power of Imagination* (Cambridge: Cambridge University Press, 2009); Sarah Jane Cervenak, *Wandering: Philosophical Performances of Racial and Sexual Freedom*

(Durham, NC: Duke University Press, 2014) (especially her notion of philosophical kinesis); Charles W. Mills, *Blackness Visible: Essays on Philosophy and Race* (Ithaca, NY: Cornell University Press, 1998); Ronald Judy, "Kant and the Negro," *Surfaces* 1 (1991), https://doi.org/10.7202/1065256ar; and Silva, *Toward a Global Idea of Race* (her exploration of knowledge and the discursive meanings of experience and difference). Also see Paul C. Taylor's reading of Lorde via aesthetic philosophy in *Black Is Beautiful: A Philosophy of Black Aesthetics* (Hoboken, NJ: Wiley-Blackwell, 2016). I am grateful to Matt Ashby for conversations about the nature of knowing in Lorde's work.

7   My thinking about matter and the body is informed by phenomenology, materialism, affect theory, and especially Judith Butler's explication of the iterative term "matter" in *Bodies That Matter: On the Discursive Limits of Sex* (London: Routledge, 1993). In that regard, I read Lorde's theorization here to be about matter in at least three ways: about being of form (matter), about coming into form (matter), about being of consequence (matter). In *Zami: A New Spelling of My Name—a Biomythography* (Berkeley: Crossing, 1982) and in *The Cancer Journals* (San Francisco: Aunt Lute Books, 1980), Lorde engages the body more literally than in "Poetry" and "Uses," though throughout all four works, the body serves as a metaphor of phenomenological assemblage, similar to the case that Elizabeth Grosz makes for embodiment of consciousness in *Volatile Bodies*: "[Maurice] Merleau-Ponty begins with the negative claim that the body is not an object. It is the condition and context through which I am able to have a relation to objects. It is both immanent and transcendent. Insofar as I live the body, it is a phenomenon experienced by me and thus provides the very horizon and perspectival point that places me in the world and makes relation between me, other objects and other subjects possible. It is the body as I live it, as I experience it" (86). This is in keeping with the aims of new materialism (see, for example, Diana Coole and Samantha Frost's claims in the introduction to *New Materialisms: Ontology, Agency, and Politics*, ed. Diana Coole and Samantha Frost [Durham, NC: Duke University Press, 2010], that "materiality is always something more than 'mere' matter" [9]). For more on this, see Grosz's argument about the material and the ideal in *Incorporeal*; Judith Butler, "Performative Acts and Gender Constitution," *Theatre Journal* 20, no. 4 (1988): 519–531; Gayle Salamon's superb glossing of psychoanalysis and phenomenology in *Assuming a Body: Transgender and Rhetorics of Materiality* (New York: Columbia University Press, 2010); Amber Jamilla Musser's thinking about Lorde and materiality in *Sensational Flesh: Race, Power, and Masochism* (New York: New York University Press, 2014); Elizabeth Freeman's notion of erotohistoriography in *Time Binds: Queer Temporalities, Queer Histories* (Durham, NC: Duke University Press, 2010); Ann Cvetkovich's thinking about the relational embodiment of affect in *An Archive of Feelings: Trauma, Sexuality, and Lesbian Public Cultures* (Durham, NC: Duke University Press, 2003); Charles Johnson, "A Phenomenology of the Black Body," *Michigan Quarterly Review* 32, no. 4 (1993): 599–614, which cites embodied consciousness in reading Fanon; Brittney C. Cooper's explication of "embodied discourse" (3) in *Beyond Respectability: The Intellectual Thought of Race Women* (Urbana: University of Illinois Press, 2017); Robin D. G. Kelley's consideration of poetic knowledges in *Freedom Dreams: The Black Radical Imagination* (Boston: Beacon, 2002); and Elizabeth Alexander's reading

of Lorde's engagement with the body in "'Coming Out Blackened and Whole': Fragmentation and Reintegration in Audre Lorde's *Zami* and *The Cancer Journals*," *American Literary History* 6, no. 4 (1994): 695–715. Lorde's is a black feminism of feeling; see Jennifer C. Nash, *Black Feminism Reimagined: After Intersectionality* (Durham, NC: Duke University Press, 2019).

8 See Hortense Spillers, "Mama's Baby, Papa's Maybe: An American Grammar Book," in *Black, White, and in Color: Essays on American Literature and Culture* (Chicago: University of Chicago Press, 2003), 203–229; and Sylvia Wynter, "The Ceremony Must Be Found: After Humanism," *Boundary 2* 12, no. 3 (1984): 19–70; as well as Katherine McKittrick, ed., *Sylvia Wynter: On Being Human as Praxis* (Durham, NC: Duke University Press, 2015). Thanks to Quinn Anex-Ries for reminding me that this claim about the body is akin to Fanon's phenomenological encounter in *Black Skins, White Mask*, trans. Charles Lam Markmann (London: Pluto, 2008).

9 In the essay "In the Realm," Gill makes a compelling case that "we must read Lorde for the audience gathered and not presume that she would reject the proposition that eros as a principle be allowed to retain the widest possible applicability—without losing its necessary attention to the ground of lived experience (of women, men, trans people, heterosexuals, queers, and people of color, etc.)" (185). And in attending to the specificity of Lorde's language in this moment, I have opted to put the word "black" in parentheses so as to acknowledge the explicit general reference she makes to femaleness. Appreciating Lorde's interest in the theoretical capaciousness of embodiment is important to reading her use of "black mothers" in "Poetry": "The white fathers told us, I think therefore I am; and the black mothers in each of us—the poet—whispers in our dreams, I feel therefore I can be free" (38). On one hand, Lorde's use of "black mothers" invokes the specific identity of the essay's speaker; on the other hand, the iteration is idiomatic and conceptual à la the deployment of black motherhood in Spillers ("Mama's Baby"), Saidiya Hartman (*Lose Your Mother: A Journey along the Atlantic Slave Route* [New York: Macmillan, 2008]), and Jennifer L. Morgan (*Laboring Women: Reproduction and Gender in New World Slavery* [Philadelphia: University of Pennsylvania Press, 2004]). The challenge in thinking with Lorde is to navigate between the specificity of embodiment and the universality of her philosophical interest in questions of the human. For more on this declaration in "Poetry," see Lorde's conversation with Adrienne Rich, also in *Sister Outsider* (101–102) and Margaret Kissam Morris, "Textual Authority and the Embodied Self," *Frontiers* 23, no. 1 (2002): esp. 177–183. And in addition to Gill's essay, my studying of Lorde's conceptualization of the erotic, feeling, and being has learned from Sharon Patricia Holland, *The Erotic Life of Racism* (Durham, NC: Duke University Press, 2012); Farah Jasmine Griffin, "Textual Healing: Claiming Black Women's Bodies, the Erotic and Resistance in Contemporary Novels of Slavery," *Callaloo* 19, no. 2 (1996): 519–536; Sharon Marcus, "The State's Oversight: From Sexual Bodies to Erotic Selves," *Social Research* 78, no. 2 (2011): 509–532; Jafari S. Allen, *¡Venceremos? The Erotics of Black Self-Making in Cuba* (Durham, NC: Duke University Press, 2011); Kristie Dotson, "How Is This Paper Philosophy?," *Comparative Philosophy* 3, no. 1 (2012): 3–29; Amber Musser, *Sensational Flesh*; Keguro Macharia, *Frottage: Frictions of Intimacy across the Black Diaspora* (New York: New York University Press, 2019),

esp. 55–57; and Greg Thomas, *The Sexual Demon of Colonial Power: Pan-African Embodiment and Erotic Schemes of Empire* (Bloomington: Indiana University Press, 2007).

10   Notions of immanence and transcendence are relevant to Lorde's conceptualization of the erotic in "Uses of the Erotic": "The erotic is a measure between the beginnings of our sense of self and the chaos of our strongest feelings. It is an internal sense of satisfaction to which, once we have experienced it, we know we can aspire," and then, "To encourage excellence is to go beyond . . ." (*Sister Outsider* 54). Moreover, Lorde's merger of the ideal and the material is noted in "Poetry Is Not a Luxury": "At this point in time, I believe that women carry within ourselves the possibility for fusion of these two approaches so necessary for survival, and we come closest to this combination in our poetry" (*Sister Outsider* 37). (The two approaches she means are the ideas of the "european fathers [*sic*]" and the feelings of "ancient non-european consciousness.")

Though I say more about immanence and transcendence in the next chapter, I want to acknowledge here that the conceptualization of aliveness and relation (and, later, of oneness) harmonizes with some of the thinking in transcendentalism and Romanticism. That is, even as these two aesthetic traditions don't center black female subjects (nor, importantly, indigenous subjects), one can use their ideas to frame the ecstatic conceptualization of being, of what it means to be alive and to be of experience—a reclamation of human value against capitalist encroachment: "The ethics of Romanticism is impelled by a will to value in the face of a prevailing reduction of value," Laurence S. Lockridge tells us in *The Ethics of Romanticism* (Cambridge: Cambridge University Press, 1989), 43. Some citations here include Paul Outka, *Race and Nature from Transcendentalism to the Harlem Renaissance* (London: Palgrave, 2008); Peter Wirzbicki, "Black Transcendentalism: William Cooper Nell, the Adelphic Union, and the Black Abolitionist Intellectual Tradition," *Journal of the Civil War Era* 8, no. 2 (2018): 269–290; Charles Capper, "'A Little Beyond': The Problem of the Transcendentalist Movement in American History," *Journal of American History* 85, no. 2 (1998): 502–539; Christoph Bode, "Discursive Constructions of the Self in British Romanticism," *Romanticism and Victorianism on the Net* 51 (2008), https://doi.org/10.7202/019264ar; George Boas, "The Romantic Self: An Historical Sketch," *Studies in Romanticism* 4, no. 1 (1964): 1–16; and Jacques Khalip, *Anonymous Life: Romanticism and Dispossession* (Stanford, CA: Stanford University Press, 2009), as well as recent efforts to reconsider Romanticism through thinking about racial blackness, including Joel Pace, "Afterthoughts: Romanticism, the Black Atlantic, and Self-Mapping," *Studies in Romanticism* 56, no. 1 (2017): 113–123; Paul Youngquist, "Black Romanticism: A Manifesto," *Studies in Romanticism* 56, no. 1 (2017): 3–14; and Youngquist and Frances Botkin, "Introduction: Black Romanticism: Romantic Circulations," in *Circulations: Romanticism and the Black Atlantic*, ed. Paul Youngquist and Frances Botkin, Romantic Circles PRAXIS (October 2011), https://romantic-circles.org/praxis/circulations/HTML/praxis.2011.youngquist .html. Finally, as I will note later, I think of Lorde's philosophy in concert with American pragmatism, especially as described in V. Denise James, "Theorizing Black Feminist Pragmatism: Forethoughts on the Practice and Purpose of Philosophy as Envisioned by Black Feminists and John Dewey," *Journal of Speculative*

Philosophy 23, no. 2 (2009): 92–99. Also see Kristie Dotson, "'Thinking Familiar with the Interstitial': An Introduction," *Hypatia* 29, no. 1 (Winter 2014): 1–17; and Devonya N. Havis, "'Now, How You Sound': Considering a Different Philosophical Praxis," *Hypatia* 29, no. 1 (Winter 2014): 237–252.

11 In using *ars vitalia*, I am riffing on Michel Foucault's distinction between *ars erotica* and *scientia sexualis* in *The History of Sexuality* (New York: Pantheon Books, 1978).

12 Judith Butler, *Frames of War: When Is Life Grievable?* (London: Verso, 2009), 19.

13 My thinking through aliveness has been inspired by a cohort of black female characters: Walker's Celie as well as Sula (Toni Morrison, *Sula*), Maud Martha (Gwendolyn Brooks, *Maud Martha*), Clare (Nella Larsen, *Passing*), Beulah (Rita Dove, *Thomas and Beulah*), Janie (Hurston, *Their Eyes*), and the unnamed narrator of Morrison's *Jazz*. This theorizing is in keeping with Barbara Christian's enduring and enduringly clear authorization in "The Race for Theory," *Cultural Critique*, no. 6 (1987): 51–63, her declaration that the "variety, multiplicity, eroticism" of black women's writing characterizes a philosophy of dynamic black being (59). And in thinking about Celie's phrasing, I am reminded of Milkman's offering of himself to Guitar at the end of Morrison's *Song of Solomon* (New York: Vintage Books, 2004)—"Here I am," he says—and of Claudia Rankine's glossing of the word "here" in *Don't Let Me Be Lonely: An American Lyric* (Minneapolis: Graywolf, 2004), 130–131. Thanks to Mike King for reminding me of Rankine's doing. Finally, the notion of possessiveness is taken up further in chapter 3.

14 Quashie, *Sovereignty of Quiet* 21.

15 Throughout this chapter, my thinking has been inflected by phenomenology and affect theory; this inflection is sustained in the forthcoming chapters, though I want to acknowledge Michel Henry's explication of the interior of a phenomenological life in *Material Phenomenology* (New York: Fordham University Press, 2008) and this passage from Maurice Merleau-Ponty's *Phenomenology of Perception* (New York: Routledge, 2002), which resonates in kind with Lorde's thinking through embodiment:

> Even when involved in situations with other people, the subject, in so far as he has a body, retains every moment the power to withdraw from it. At the very moment when I live in the world, when I am given over to my plans, my occupations, my friends, my memories, I can close my eyes, lie down, listen to the blood pulsating in my ears, lose myself in some pleasure or pain, and shut myself up in this anonymous life which subtends my personal one. But precisely because my body can shut itself off from the world, it is also what opens me out upon the world and places me in a situation there. The momentum of existence towards others, towards the future, towards the world can be restored as a river unfreezes. . . . Even if I become absorbed in the experience of my body and in the solitude of sensations, I do not succeed in abolishing all reference of my life to a world. (191)

I have been influenced by Lewis R. Gordon (*Bad Faith and Antiblack Racism* [Amherst, NY: Humanity Books, 1995] and *Existentia Africana: Understanding Africana Existential Thought* [New York: Routledge, 2000]) and Paget Henry ("Africana Phenomenology: Its Philosophical Implications," *CLR James Journal* 11, no. 1 [2005]: 79–112) in studying phenomenology, though my interest is not in black subjection as a phenomenological condition but in phenomenology as a condition of the black world. In addition to Brian Massumi (*The Politics of Affect* [Cambridge, UK: Polity, 2015]), Sara Ahmed (*Queer Phenomenology: Orientations, Objects, Others* [Durham, NC: Duke University Press, 2006]), and other work cited earlier, also see M. Jacqui Alexander's thinking about feelings, embodiment, and the sacred in *Pedagogies of Crossing: Meditations on Feminism, Sexual Politics, Memory, and the Sacred* (Durham, NC: Duke University Press, 2006), esp. chap. 7; and more recently, Aliyyah Abdur-Rahman, "The Black Ecstatic," *GLQ* 24, no. 2–3 (2018): 343–365.

16 Walter Arnold Kaufmann translates the binary as I-You so as to reflect the inflection of mutuality in English pronouns. Except in one case noted shortly, I use Kaufman's translation here; see Martin Buber, *I and Thou*, trans. Walter Arnold Kaufmann (New York: Touchstone, 1996). Thanks to Sarah Bellows-Meister for conversations about Buber—and for the gift of a Kaufman edition.

17 In the second quotation here, I am citing from Martin Buber, *I and Thou*, trans. Ronald Gregor Smith (New York: Charles Scribner's Sons, 1958).

18 I read Buber's *I and Thou* with Buber, *Eclipse of God: Studies in the Relation between Religion and Philosophy* (Princeton, NJ: Princeton University Press, 2015), as well as with Maurice S. Freidman, *Martin Buber: The Life of Dialogue* (New York: Routledge, 2002). My study also gains from Emmanuel Levinas's philosophy of the other, especially *Totality and Infinity: An Essay on Exteriority* (Pittsburgh: Duquesne University Press, 1969); Alain Badiou, *In Praise of Love* (New York: New Press, 2012); Jacques Derrida, *Of Hospitality* (Stanford, CA: Stanford University Press, 2000); Derrida, *The Animal That Therefore I Am* (New York: Fordham University Press, 2008); Jean-Luc Nancy, *Being Singular Plural* (Stanford, CA: Stanford University Press, 2000); and Luce Irigaray, *To Be Two* (London: Psychology Press, 2001). On relation and intersubjectivity, see also M. Jacqui Alexander, *Pedagogies of Crossing*; Deborah Achtenberg, *Essential Vulnerabilities: Plato and Levinas on Relations to the Other* (Evanston, IL: Northwestern University Press, 2014); Robert R. Williams, *Hegel's Ethics of Recognition* (Berkeley: University of California Press, 2000); Stephen Hudson, "Intersubjectivity of Mutual Recognition and the I-Thou: A Comparative Analysis of Hegel and Buber," *Minerva—An Internet Journal of Philosophy* 14 (2010), http://www .minerva.mic.ul.ie/Vol14/Intersubjectivity.pdf; TreaAndrea Russworm, *Blackness Is Burning: Civil Rights, Popular Culture, and the Problem of Recognition* (Detroit: Wayne State University Press, 2016); Moten, "Blackness and Nothingness"; Judith Butler, *Notes toward a Performative Theory of Assembly* (Cambridge, MA: Harvard University Press, 2018); and Peter Sas, "A Relation to End All Relations: On Badiou's Scandalous Closeness to Levinas and Buber," *Critique of Pure Interest* (blog), May 7, 2012, http://critique-of-pure-interest.blogspot.com/2012/05/relation-to-end-all -relations-on_6111.html. I should say, too, that I use Buber's relationality—rather than Levinas's—because Buber imagines relation as possible in regard to the literary (a book, for example); this capacity will become important to thinking about the ethical via aesthetics later on. For extended consideration of this difference between Levinas and Buber, see Jill Robbins, "Aesthetic Totality and Ethical Infinity: Levinas on Art," *L'Esprit Créateur* 35, no. 3 (1995): 66–79; and Akos Krassoy, "The Transcendence of Words," *Levinas Studies* 10, no. 1 (2016): 1–42, as well as Achtenberg,

Essential Vulnerabilities; Williams, *Hegel's Ethics of Recognition*; and Hudson, "Intersubjectivity of Mutual Recognition."

19   Goldman is quoting Michel Foucault and is keen to focus on improvisation as a way of navigating "tight" or restricted social spaces: "To ignore the constraints that improvisers inevitably encounter is not only to deny the real conditions that shape daily life; it is also to deny improvisation's most significant power as a full-bodied critical engagement with the world, characterized by both flexibility and perpetual readiness. . . . Improvised dance involves literally giving shape to oneself by deciding how to move in relation to an unsteady landscape" (5). I am grateful to J. Kameron Carter, who recommended Goldman's book, and inspired also by reading Daphne Lamothe's work in progress on black thresholds.

20   I want to note Glissant's inattention to gender difference in *Poetics of Relation* (and in *Caribbean Discourse: Selected Essays* [Charlottesville: University of Virginia Press, 1991] and *Poetic Intention*, trans. Nathanaël with Anna Malena [Callicoon, NY: Nightboat Books, 2010]), even as his thinking about relation, abyss, and poetics relies on idioms (the womb, pregnancy, fluidity) that seem informed by conceptual femaleness. In this particular elision, Glissant's doing runs against the case I am making for aliveness that centers black feminist/women's thinking in pursuing a notion of black being. For more on Glissant and gender difference, see Max Hantel, "Toward a Sexual Difference Theory of Creolization," *Journal of French and Francophone Philosophy* 22, no. 1 (2014): 1–18; and Omise'eke Natasha Tinsley, *Thiefing Sugar: Eroticism between Women in Caribbean Literature* (Durham, NC: Duke University Press, 2010). Also, I am grateful to S. A. Smythe who suggested that the resonance between Glissant's and Lorde's mobilization of the poetic might be informed by their shared Caribbean subjectivities.

21   I read Glissant's *Poetics of Relation* in conjunction with Glissant, *Poetic Intention*, and his conversation with Manthia Diawara, "One World in Relation," *Nka: Journal of Contemporary African Art* 28 (2011): 4–19, as well as J. Michael Dash's critical biography *Edouard Glissant* (Cambridge: Cambridge University Press, 1995); John E. Drabinski and Marisa Parham, *Theorizing Glissant: Sites and Citations* (Lanham, MD: Rowman and Littlefield, 2015); Ronaldo Walcott, *Queer Returns: Essays on Multiculturalism, Diaspora, and Black Studies* (London, ON: Insomniac, 2016); Kara Keeling on Glissant and imagination in *Queer Times, Black Futures* (New York: New York University Press, 2019); and Bernadette Cailler's indispensable "*Totality and Infinity*, Alterity, and Relation," *Journal of French and Francophone Philosophy* 19, no. 1 (2011): 135–151. Traveling here, too, is the thinking about black life in two essays by J. Kameron Carter: "The Inglorious: With and Beyond Giorgio Agamben," *Political Theology* 14, no. 1 (2013): 77–87; and "Paratheological Blackness," *South Atlantic Quarterly* 112, no. 4 (2013): 589–612. I should note the distinction between Levinas's notion of totality and Glissant's; indeed, Levinas's infinity is more akin to what Glissant means by totality. For more on this, see Silvia Benso, "Joy beyond Boredom: *Totality and Infinity* as a Work of Wonder," and John E. Drabinksi, "Future Interval: On Levinas and Glissant," in *Totality and Infinity at 50* ed. Scott Davidson and Diane Perpich (Pittsburgh: Duquesne University Press, 2011), 11–28, 227–252; Williams, *Hegel's Ethics of Recognition*; and Fred Moten's critique of totality (*In the Break: The Aesthetics*

of the Black Radical Tradition [Minneapolis: University of Minnesota Press, 2003] and "The Case of Blackness," *Criticism* 50, no. 2 [2008]: 177–218), though Moten means "totality" as a synonym for Enlightenment transparency. As long as I am making distinctions, it is worth saying that Glissant's totality complements Cedric Robinson's notion of "ontological totality" in *Black Marxism: The Making of the Black Radical Tradition* (Chapel Hill: University of North Carolina Press, 2000), 171. And because assemblage is so relevant to Glissant's thinking, see also Gilles Deleuze and Felix Guattari, *A Thousand Plateaus: Capitalism and Schizophrenia* (Minneapolis: University of Minnesota Press, 1987); Jasbir Puar, *Terrorist Assemblages: Homonationalism in Queer Times* (Durham, NC: Duke University Press, 2017); Weheliye, *Habeas Viscus*; Manuel DeLanda, *A New Philosophy of Society: Assemblage Theory and Social Complexity* (London: Bloomsbury, 2006); and Erin Manning, *Always More Than One: Individuation's Dance* (Durham, NC: Duke University Press, 2013).

22 The invitation poem is a form that I find throughout Clifton's oeuvre, including the iconic "brothers," which will be discussed later. See Erik Gray's exploration of the form in English literary tradition in "Come Be My Love: The Song of Songs, *Paradise Lost*, and the Tradition of the Invitation Poem," *PMLA* 128, no. 2 (2013): 370–385. Also, in regard to the matter of address here, see Monique Roelofs's claim that "address orchestrates relational life" (8) in *Arts of Address: Being Alive to Language and the World* (New York: Columbia University Press, 2020).

23 We might note the prevalence of hands, as an idiom of relation, in Clifton's poem "wild blessings" (369).

24 In calling this poem "a poem of relation," I am highlighting something particular about the way the text engages voice through its speaking persona. "Voice" is a historically and theoretically complicated idiom in black literary studies; see, for example, Meta DuEwa Jones, *The Music Is Music: Jazz Poetry from the Harlem Renaissance to Spoken Word* (Urbana: University of Illinois Press, 2011), esp. the introduction and chaps. 1 and 2; Stephen Michael Best's caution about "the cult of voice" in *None like Us: Blackness, Belonging, Aesthetic Life.* (Durham, NC: Duke University Press, 2018), 132; Evie Shockley's provocation "voice held me hostage," which titles pt. 1 of *Renegade Poetics: Black Aesthetics and Formal Innovation in African American Poetry* (Iowa City: Iowa University Press, 2011); and Howard Ramsey II's exploration of voice and persona in "Catching Holy Ghosts: The Diverse Manifestations of Black Persona Poetry," *African American Review* 42, no. 3 (2008): 549–564. In specific regard to Clifton, see Hilary Holladay, *Wild Blessings: The Poetry of Lucille Clifton* (Baton Rouge: Louisiana State University Press, 2004), esp. chaps. 3 and 5, which consider Clifton's use of voice to construct a multitudinous speaking self. I come back to the matter of voice—via the lyric—in chapter 2. Thanks to Mike King for a conversation about that "starshine and clay" line.

25 The idea of the poetic as force, resonant in Glissant and Lorde, recalls Aimé Césaire's argument in "Poetry and Knowledge," in *Refusal of the Shadow: Surrealism and the Caribbean*, ed. Michael Richardson, trans. Michael Richardson and Krysztof Fijalkowski (London: Verso, 1996), 134–146; and Imanu Amiri Baraka's in "Poetry and Karma," in *Raise, Race, Rays, Raze: Essays since 1965* (New York: Random House, 1969), 17–26. This notion of force is vital to black poetic studies, including Evie Shockley, *Renegade*

Poetics; Rowan Ricardo Phillips, *When Blackness Rhymes with Blackness* (Champaign: Dalkey Archive Press, 2010); Aldon Lynn Nielsen, *Black Chant: Languages of African-American Postmodernism* (Cambridge: Cambridge University Press, 1997); Meta DuEwa Jones, *The Muse Is Music*; Lorenzo Thomas, *Extraordinary Measures: Afrocentric Modernism and Twentieth-Century American Poetry* (Tuscaloosa: University of Alabama Press, 2000); Fahamisha Patricia Brown, *Performing the Word: African American Poetry as Vernacular Culture* (New Brunswick, NJ: Rutgers University Press, 1999); Tony Bolden, *Afro-blue: Improvisations in African American Poetry and Culture* (Urbana: University of Illinois Press, 2003); Keith D. Leonard, *Fettered Genius: The African American Bardic Poet from Slavery to Civil Rights* (Charlottesville: University of Virginia Press, 2005); Adam Bradley, *Book of Rhymes: The Poetics of Hip Hop* (New York: Civitas Books, 2017); Alexs Pate, *In the Heart of the Beat: The Poetry of Rap* (Lanham, MD: Scarecrow, 2009); and Eugene B. Redmond's enduringly important *Drum Voices: The Mission of Afro-American Poetry: A Critical History* (New York: Anchor/Doubleday, 1976). I am indebted, forever, to Joanne V. Gabbin's work with Furious Flower and Maryemma Graham's 2015 National Endowment for the Humanities seminar Black Poetry after Black Arts, since both have organized my studying of poetics. In addition to the works noted, I could also cite Michael Thurston's exploration of poetic doing in *Making Something Happen: American Political Poetry between the World Wars* (Chapel Hill: University of North Carolina Press, 2001); Kevin McLaughlin's consideration of the aesthetics of Kantian sublime in *Poetic Force: Poetry after Kant* (Stanford, CA: Stanford University Press, 2014); Jacques Derrida's idiom of witnessing and surrender in "'A Self-Unsealing Poetic Text': Poetics and Politics of Witnessing," in *Revenge of the Aesthetic: The Place of Literature in Theory Today*, ed. Michael P. Clark (Berkeley: University of California Press, 2000), 180–207; and Julia Kristeva's conceptualization of the Symbolic and the Semiotic in *Revolution in Poetic Language* (New York: Columbia University Press, 1985).

26   I cite the poem from Jordan's collected works. My use of the idiom "made and unmade" riffs on the florid end of Morrison's *Jazz*. Indeed, Morrison's novel opens with an epigraph from the Nag Hammadi gnostic gospels, which speak in a voice that claims itself to be both self and other; this doing is akin to June Jordan's speaker in "Fragments from a Parable," who speaks spiritual transformation in a language that mirrors that of the gnostic gospel; see Jordan, *Directed by Desire: The Collected Poems of June Jordan*, ed. Jan Heller Levi and Sara Miles (Port Townsend, WA: Copper Canyon, 2005), 155–164. Moreover, my reference to the subject as both I and you echoes two references: one is Glissant's notion of relationality, where "it is possible to be one and multiple at the same time; that you can be yourself and the other; that you can be the same and different" ("One World in Relation" 6); the other is the case of being in Arthur Rimbaud, *Illuminations* (New York: W. W. Norton, 2012). For the latter, see Adrianna M. Paliyenko, "The Dialogic *Je* in Rimbaud's *Illuminations*," *French Forum* 19, no. 3 (1994): 261–277, which argues that Rimbaud's syntax "construct[s] the poetic self in relation to its otherness" (262). I am grateful to John Casey for reminding me of this instance. For further discussion of Jordan's poetics, see Kevin Quashie and Amy Fish, "A Subjunctive Imagining: June Jordan's *Who Look at Me* and the Conditions of Black Agency," in

Literary Cultures and Twentieth-Century Childhoods, ed. Rachel Conrad and Brown Kennedy (London: Palgrave, forthcoming). Finally, in thinking about the poetic as a "form-of-life," I am borrowing the phrase from Agamben's essay of the same name from *Means without End*, 3–12. Here, Agamben distinguishes between the unhyphenated phrase, "form of life," which is synonymous with an idea or a definition of life, and the hyphenated term, which he intends to refer to life that is indescribable, that resides in possibility, that is in process and "can never be separated from its form" (3). I am invoking also the case that philosopher Monique Roelofs makes that "racial formations are aesthetic phenomena and aesthetic practices are racialized structures" (83); see "Racialization as an Aesthetic Production," in *White on White/ Black on Black*, ed. George Yancy (New York: Rowman and Littlefield, 2005), 83–124. This point about aesthetics will be given further attention in chapter 3.

27　The stranger shows up in the relational thinking of Buber, Glissant, and Levinas.

28　The second person is a vital case in black letters; in addition to Phillip Brian Harper's engagement of the second person in *Are We Not Men? Masculine Anxiety and the Problem of African-American Identity* (New York: Oxford University Press, 1996), which I cited in the introduction, see my discussion of the pronoun case in chapter 2 of *Sovereignty of Quiet*. My reading here of Clifton's and Jordan's use of the second person could inform how we read instances of the second person in other contemporary poetry collections, including Terrance Hayes, *American Sonnets to My Past and Future Assassin* (London: Penguin Books, 2018); Claudia Rankine, *Citizen: An American Lyric* (Minneapolis: Graywolf, 2014); and Evie Shockley, *The New Black* (Middletown, CT: Wesleyan University Press, 2011).

29　Glissant makes this point in his distinction between relation and cosmopolitanism: "Cosmopolitanism is a sort of upheaval that lacks direction" (*Poetics of Relation* 10).

30　This elegant definition of poiesis comes from Donald E. Polkinghorne, *Practice and the Human Science: The Case for a Judgment-Based Practice of Care* (New York: State University of New York Press, 2004), 115. Thanks to an anonymous reader who suggested that I emphasize poiesis.

Chapter 2. Aliveness and Oneness

This chapter is an expansion of my essay "To Be (a) One: Notes on Coupling and Black Female Audacity," *differences* 29, no. 2 (2018): 68–95, and it also extends my brief exploration of oneness in *The Sovereignty of Quiet: Beyond Resistance in Black Culture* (New Brunswick, NJ: Rutgers University Press, 2012) (see 119–120).

1　The term "oneness" is used varyingly in religion and philosophy. Though it is often noted as a concept in Eastern religions (see Philip J. Ivanhoe, *Oneness: East Asian Conceptions of Virtue, Happiness, and How We Are All Connected* [Oxford: Oxford University Press, 2017]), I am interested here in philosophical, relational inflections of the term, including the notion of "soul" in the history of body-mind dualism.

2　This comment on individuality is foundational to my understanding of black pessimism. For more here, see especially Frank B. Wilderson III, *Afropessimism* (New York: Liveright, 2020), as well as endnotes on black pessimism in the introduction; also see Denise Ferreira da Silva, *Toward a Global Idea of Race* (Minneapolis: University of

Minnesota Press, 2007), as well as endnotes on the terms of life at the beginning of chapter 1.

3   In "Mama's Baby, Papa's Maybe: An American Grammar Book," in *Black, White, and in Color: Essays on American Literature and Culture* (Chicago: University of Chicago Press, 2003), 203-229, Spillers writes that "as a category of 'otherness,' the captive body . . . embodies sheer physical powerlessness that slides into a more general 'powerlessness,' resonating through various centers of human and social meaning" (206). And throughout her work, including "Interstices: A Small Drama of Words," Spillers sustains an argument about black femaleness—about blackness and femaleness—as an exception to the figuring of the human. See also Zakiyyah Iman Jackson, *Becoming Human: Matter and Meaning in an Antiblack World* (New York: New York University Press, 2020).

4   The anthology's title phrase seems to have originated in the book, though Farah Jasmine Griffin notes that Toni Cade Bambara's introduction to *The Black Woman* anthology anticipates the title; see "Conflict and Chorus: Reconsidering Toni Cade's *The Black Woman: An Anthology*," in *Is It Nation Time? Contemporary Essays on Black Power and Black Nationalism*, ed. Eddie S. Glaude (Chicago: University of Chicago Press, 2002), 113-129. Thanks to Nora Daniels for research assistance here.

5   I think of this exemption as similar to Emmanuel Levinas's asymmetry described in *Totality and Infinity: An Essay on Exteriority* (Pittsburgh: Duquesne University Press, 1969), or in regard to Spillers's articulation of "*being* for the captor" in "Mama's Baby" (206). For more on difference, especially in regard to Audre Lorde's relationality, see Quashie, "To Be (a) One."

6   The importance of cancer in Lorde's life is reflected in the structure of Alexis De Veaux's biography *Warrior Poet: A Biography of Audre Lorde* (New York: W. W. Norton, 2004), which is divided into two sections, with cancer marking Lorde's second life. Notable, too, is that nearly all of the *Sister Outsider* essays and all of *Zami: A New Spelling of My Name* (Berkeley: Crossing, 1982) were written in this period after her diagnosis. Furthermore, De Veaux links Lorde's ideological investment in being an outsider to cancer (230); of *The Cancer Journals*, she writes, "If the publication of *The Black Unicorn* expressed a poetic embracing of African mythologies, for spiritual sustenance, then *The Cancer Journals* signaled Lorde's self-styled transfiguration as Seboulisa incarnate. She became a living version of the one-breasted warrior goddess, central to her spiritual links to be a reimagined, mythic Africa. . . . It was not simply that Lorde had breast cancer or a mastectomy; it was what she did with those facts" (271). And what Lorde did with those facts, one could argue, was to construct an ontological idiom.

7   The conceptual uses of the black autobiographical are considered in Barbara Christian, "The Race for Theory," *Cultural Critique*, no. 6 (1987): 51-63; Kimberly Nichele Brown, *Writing the Black Revolutionary Diva: Women's Subjectivity and the Decolonizing Text* (Bloomington: Indiana University Press, 2010); William Andrews, *African-American Autobiography* (London: Pearson, 1992); Patricia Hill Collins, "Learning from the Outsider Within: The Sociological Significance of Black Feminist Thought," *Social Problems* 33, no. 6 (1986): S14-S32; and Farah Jasmine Griffin, "An Interview with Farah Jasmine Griffin," by Charles H. Rowell, *Callaloo* 22, no. 4

(1999): 872–892. Also see Nahum Dimitri Chandler's reading of the autobiographical in DuBois's philosophical imagining in *X—The Problem of the Negro as a Problem
for Thought* (New York: Fordham University Press, 2014), chap. 2; and Sarah J.
Cervenak's explication of the first-person wandering evident in classical philosophy
in *Wandering: Philosophical Performances of Racial and Sexual Freedom* (Durham, NC:
Duke University Press, 2014).

8   The full passage reads, "There is no desire more natural than the desire for knowledge. We try all the ways that can lead us to it. When reason fails us, we use experi-
ence . . . which is a weaker and less dignified means. But truth is so great a thing
that we must not disdain any medium that will lead us to it" (407), from Michel de
Montaigne, *Essays and Selected Writings*, trans. and ed. Donald M. Frame (New York:
St. Martin's, 1963). Montaigne also exclaims experience in "Of Practice." See also
Andrea Frisch, "Cannibalizing Experience in the Essais," in *Montaigne after Theory,
Theory after Montaigne*, ed. Zahi Zalloua (Seattle: University of Washington Press,
2009), 180–201, which considers Montaigne's ambivalences in "Of Experience."

9   I am riffing here on Saidiya Hartman's interview by Frank B. Wilderson, titled "The
Position of the Unthought," *Qui Parle* 13, no. 2 (2003): 183–201, as well as Chandler, *X*.
The first quotation is from the title of Jean-Luc Nancy's book; the second is from
Glissant's conversation with Manthia Diawara ("One World in Relation," *Nka:
Journal of Contemporary African Art* 28 [2011]: 5). These appeals to multiplicity recall
for me Rinaldo Walcott's call for a "community of singularities" (93) in "Outside
in Black Studies," in *Black Queer Studies: A Critical Anthology*, ed. E. Patrick Johnson
and Mae G. Henderson (Durham, NC: Duke University Press, 2005), 90–105. It is
also useful to think about Lorde's investment in mythos—for example, her adoption of the name Afrekete, her stylization as Zami, her embrace of a Caribbean
subjectivity—as a manifestation of a transcendent multiplicity of being everything
and nothing; see De Veaux, *Warrior Poet* 261, 271. For further consideration of black
femaleness as an idiom of exception/exemption, see Kai M. Green and Marquis
Bey, "Where Black Feminist Thought and Trans* Feminism Meet," *Souls: A Critical
Journal of Black Politics, Culture, and Society* 19, no. 4 (2017): 438–454; C. Riley Snorton,
Black on Both Sides: A Racial History of Trans Identity (Minneapolis: University of
Minnesota Press, 2017); L. H. Stallings, *Mutha' Is Half a Word: Intersections of Folklore,
Vernacular, Myth, and Queerness in Black Female Culture* (Columbus: Ohio State
University Press, 2007); Omise'eke Natasha Tinsley, *Thiefing Sugar: Eroticism between
Women in Caribbean Literature* (Durham, NC: Duke University Press, 2010); Sarah
Haley's explication of carceral gendering in *No Mercy Here: Gender, Punishment, and
the Making of Jim Crow Modernity* (Chapel Hill: University of North Carolina Press,
2016); and Farah Jasmine Griffin, "That the Mothers May Soar and the Daughters
Know Their Names: A Retrospective of Black Feminist Literary Criticism," *Signs* 32,
no. 2 (2007): 483–507.

10 The quotation is from Sarah Bakewell, *At the Existentialist Café: Freedom, Being,
and Apricot Cocktails* (New York: Other Press, 2016), 20. This commitment to the
quotidian is informed by ordinary language philosophy, including Stanley Cavell,
Must We Mean What We Say? (Cambridge: Cambridge University Press, 2002); Toril
Moi, *Revolution of the Ordinary: Literary Studies after Wittgenstein, Austin, and Cavell*

(Chicago: University of Chicago Press, 2017); and Iris Murdoch's notion of inhabited philosophy in *The Sovereignty of Good* (New York: Routledge, 2001), 30. Also see Maria Antonaccio, *Picturing the Human: The Moral Thought of Iris Murdoch* (Oxford: Oxford University Press, 2003), esp. chap. 1; and the case Kristie Dotson makes in "How Is This Paper Philosophy?," *Comparative Philosophy* 3, no. 1 (2012): 3–29.

11 See Lucille Clifton, "won't you celebrate with me" (427); June Jordan, "Poem for South African Women" (*Directed by Desire* 278–279); Ntozake Shange, *For Colored Girls Who Have Considered Suicide When the Rainbow Is Enuf: A Choreopoem* (New York: Scribner, 1997), 63; Alice Walker, "Womanist" (*In Search of Our Mothers' Gardens* xi–xii); Maya Angelou, "Phenomenal Woman" (*Phenomenal Woman: Four Poems Celebrating Women* [New York: Random House, 1995], 3–6); and Nikki Giovanni, "Ego Tripping (there may be a reason why)," 125–126. Also see my argument for girlfriend selfhood in Kevin Quashie, *Black Women, Identity, and Cultural Theory: (Un)Becoming the Subject* (New Brunswick, NJ: Rutgers University Press, 2004), esp. chaps. 1–3. Finally, as I note at the beginning and conclusion of this book, my debt to black women/feminist scholars is enduring.

12 The phrase "monumental first person" is from Claudia Rankine, *Citizen: An American Lyric* (Minneapolis: Graywolf, 2014), 73, which explores the fractures and alliances between the second- and first-person vocative. For a consideration of Rankine's pronouns, see Andrew Gorin, "Lyric Noise: Lisa Robertson, Claudia Rankine, and the Phatic Subject of Poetry in the Mass Public Sphere," *Criticism* 61, no. 1 (2019): 97–131; also see Rankine's essay "The First Person in the Twenty-First Century," in *After Confession: Poetry as Autobiography* (Minneapolis: Graywolf, 2001), 132–136. On the specificity of indigeneity as a critical idiom, see Iyko Day's incisive essay "Being or Nothingness: Indigeneity, Antiblackness, and Settler Colonial Critique," *Critical Ethnic Studies* 1, no. 2 (2015): 102–121, as well as Mark Rifkin, Daniel Heath Justice, Daniel Heath, and Bethany Schneider, eds., "Sexuality, Nationality, and Indigeneity," special issue, *GLQ* 16, no. 1–2 (2010). Relevant here is the extended argument Rifkin makes in *Fictions of Land and Flesh: Blackness, Indigeneity, Speculation* (Durham, NC: Duke University Press, 2019), which invites us to struggle with the distinctions between the terms of Indigenous struggles and black ones. In agreement with Rifkin, I want to be clear that my use of "first person" generates from the grammar of English syntax and a Western cultural discourse. Also see Brittney Cooper's explication of black women's theorizing of "American peculiarity" and exceptionalism (49) in *Beyond Respectability: The Intellectual Thought of Race Women* (Urbana: University of Illinois Press, 2017).

13 I am drawing here on Jonathan Culler, *Theory of the Lyric* (Cambridge, MA: Harvard University Press, 2015), as well as Reed's argument in *Freedom Time: The Poetics and Politics of Black Experimental Writing* (Baltimore: Johns Hopkins University Press, 2014) for a black postlyric in which the self is "extinguished of person," where voice is inflected with saturation, maximality, even avant-garde or experimental complexity (100). In addition to Reed, also see Evie Shockley, *Renegade Poetics: Black Aesthetics and Formal Innovation in African American Poetry* (Iowa City: University of Iowa Press, 2011), esp. pt. 1; and the case Gillian White makes about the debate between lyric and antilyric in *Lyric Shame: The "Lyric" Subject of Contemporary American Poetry*

(Cambridge, MA: Harvard University Press, 2014). I am deploying the terms of lyric in a manner consistent with Virginia Jackson's query, "Can a text not intended as a lyric become one?" (24), in *Dickinson's Misery: A Theory of Lyric Reading* (Princeton, NJ: Princeton University Press, 2005). Here, Jackson leans on the case that Yopie Prins makes for "lyrical reading, or reading lyrical" (27). Finally, in thinking about the elisions and illusions of voice and authenticity, see the superb arguments ethnomusicologist Nina Sun Eidsheim makes in *Sensing Sound: Singing and Listening as Vibrational Practice* (Durham, NC: Duke University Press, 2015) and especially *The Race of Sound: Listening, Timbre and Vocality in African American Music* (Durham, NC: Duke University Press, 2019), particularly the idea of voice as a "thick event" (5).

14   See Tavia Nyong'o, *Afro-fabulations: The Queer Drama of Black Life* (New York: New York University Press, 2018). In terms of the black experimental, see Reed, *Freedom Time*; J. Kameron Carter and Sarah Jane Cervenak, "Black Ether," *New Centennial Review* 16, no. 2 (2016): 203–224; Fred Moten, *In the Break: The Aesthetics of the Black Radical Tradition* (Minneapolis: University of Minnesota Press, 2003); and Saidiya Hartman, *Wayward Lives, Beautiful Experiments: Intimate Histories of Social Upheaval* (New York: W. W. Norton, 2019), as some examples.

15   See Glissant, who asserts that the "poem is the poetic tool of the One" in *Poetic Intention*, trans. Nathanaël with Anna Malena (Callicoon, NY: Nightboat Books, 2010), 200. In *Poetic Intention*, Glissant makes regular, elusive references to oneness.

16   We can see Sula's subjectivity-in-formation in crucial moments from her childhood, especially her exchange with Shadrack after the death of Chicken Little. Other moments of this discernment include when Ajax and his friends yell "pig meat" at her and Nel; when Sula cuts off the tip of her finger to protect Nel against the young white bullies; and when she overhears Hannah, her mother, in a moment of confession with a couple of other women about children, saying, "You love her, like I love Sula. I just don't like her," which sets Sula off in "bewilderment" (57).

17   This moment recalls Shadrack's reading "a command to fuck himself" on the wall of the jail cell, moments before he has his moment of reckoning and self-awareness by looking in a toilet bowl (13).

18   I have previously interpreted this moment as a regression for Sula (see *Black Women, Identity, and Cultural Theory* 58–59), and therefore I offer this reading as a clarification in my sustained study of the novel. Indeed, we can appreciate Sula's surrender to domesticity as "the embracing dream . . . [that] provides an image of an expanded self" (Lauren Berlant, *Desire/Love* [New York: Punctum, 2012], 6), such that Sula's hallucination creates a romantic scene in which she, Sula, can revel through wanting to feel dependency. (Berlant's insight about the essential fantasy in the love narrative mirrors the case that Ann duCille makes about the marriage plot in *The Coupling Convention: Sex, Text, and Tradition in Black Women's Fiction* [Oxford: Oxford University Press, 1993]). As such, Sula's sex reveries are material and immaterial, following the case Naana Banyiwa-Horne makes for immateriality in the novel ("The Scary Face of the Self: An Analysis of the Character of Sula in Toni Morrison's *Sula*," *Sage* 2, n. 1 [1985]: 28–31).

19   Spillers's essay "A Hateful Passion, a Lost Love: Three Women's Fiction" (originally published in *Feminist Studies* 9, no. 2 [1983]: 293–323) was really the first to centralize

thinking about the ideology of black femaleness in the book. Also see Deborah McDowell's similarly formative argument in "The Self and the Other: Reading Toni Morrison's *Sula* and the Black Female Text," in *Critical Essays on Toni Morrison*, ed. Nellie Y. McKay (Boston: G. K. Hall, 1998), 77–89; and Diane Gillespie and Missy Dehn Kubitschek, "Who Cares? Women-Centered Psychology in *Sula*," *Black American Literature Forum* 24, no. 1 (1990): 21–48, which takes up relational being.

20   The matter of respectability is part of thinking about Sula and ethics; in that regard, see Candace Jenkins's essential *Private Lives, Proper Relations: Regulating Black Intimacy* (Minneapolis: University of Minnesota Press, 2007); Roderick A. Ferguson, *Aberrations in Black: Toward a Queer of Color Critique* (Minneapolis: University of Minnesota Press, 2003); and Terrion L. Williamson's use of "scandalize" as a way to notice "the black woman who both is and causes a scandal within the field of representation[,] . . . to contemplate a black female subjectivity that attains meaning by way of an *amoral* social order that exists beyond the dichotomous regulatory regimes that structure so much of representational discourse" (*Scandalize My Name* [New York: Fordham University Press, 2016], 19; emphasis in original). We could think more about the ethical possibility in oneness via the case Alan H. Goldman makes in *Reasons from Within: Desires and Values* (Oxford: Oxford University Press, 2009). Also see the discussion of ethics in chapter 5.

21   The question is from Ta-Nehisi Coates, *Between the World and Me* (New York: Spiegel and Grau, 2015), 12.

22   In *Poetics of Relation*, trans. Betsy Wing (Ann Arbor: University of Michigan Press, 1997), Édouard Glissant writes, "'Being is relation': but Relations is safe from the idea of Being. . . . The idea of relation does not preexist (Relation)" (185). His stance against abstraction mirrors that of Levinas and Martin Buber, though in Glissant's specificity about universality, I read a caution about the collectivity of blackness. On immanence and transcendence, see especially chap. 4 of Lewis R. Gordon, *Bad Faith and Antiblack Racism* (Amherst, NY: Humanity Books, 1995). I know that we might be reluctant to embrace immanence and transcendence because of racist logics that conceptualize blackness either as exceptionally material (immanence) or as needing to overcome its excessive materiality (transcendence). Such conceptualizations are of an antiblack world, where blackness exists as the mark of otherness rather than as a human herself. For more on immanence and transcendence as terms in philosophy, see Patrice Haynes, *Immanent Transcendence* (New York: Bloomsbury, 2012); Daniel W. Smith, "Deleuze and Derrida, Immanence and Transcendence: Two Directions in Recent French Thought," *Contemporary Philosophy* 11 (2007): 123–130; Gilles Deleuze, *Pure Immanence: Essays on a Life* (New York: Zone Books, 2001); and Marc Rölli, *Gilles Deleuze's Transcendental Empiricism* (Edinburgh: Edinburgh University Press, 2016), as well as Alain Badiou's reading of the One in *Deleuze: The Clamor of Being* (Minneapolis: University of Minnesota Press, 1999); Daniel Barber, *Deleuze and the Naming of God* (Edinburgh: Edinburgh University Press, 2014); and Christoph Bode, "Discursive Constructions of the Self in British Romanticism," *Romanticism and Victorianism on the Net* 51 (2008), https://doi.org/10.7202/019264ar. I also read Stephen Best's *None like Us* as an exploration of immanence and transcendence, especially in his claim for obliteration as a stay against the communitarian impulse.

Indeed, the case for black phenomenological being in Frantz Fanon, *Black Skins, White Masks*, trans. Charles Lam Markmann (New York: Grove, 2008), toggles between immanence (being) and transcendence (becoming); see David Marriott's excellent "Judging Fanon," *Rhizomes* 29 (2016), https://doi.org/10.20415/rhiz/029.e03.

23 I am signifying here on the end of Lucille Clifton's "poem in praise of menstruation."

24 Buber, indeed, would say we should approach the poem as a Thou.

25 See chap. 3 of *Sovereignty of Quiet* for further consideration of this scene and *Maud Martha* as a whole. My thinking about the pronoun "one" is inspired by reading James Baldwin's navigation of pronouns, especially in the essay "Nothing Personal," in *The Price of the Ticket: Collected Nonfiction, 1948–1985* (New York: St. Martin's, 1985), 381–395.

26 See Reed, *Freedom Time* 31, 99. In thinking of voice, the lyric "I," and oneness, I am leaning on Reed's expansion of lyric universality and singularity (see esp. chaps. 2 and 3) as I am on Evie Shockley's consideration of the lyric "I" as a renegade black poetic (see esp. chap. 3 of *Renegade Poetics*). I also find useful Helen Vendler's claim that the lyric "requires not a character but a voice, one engaged in solitary meditation [. . . , which] may of course include direct address" (*The Given and the Made: Strategies of Poetic Redefinition* [Cambridge, MA: Harvard University Press, 1995], x). Also see the title essay of Carl Phillips, *Coin of the Realm: Essays on the Life and Art of Poetry* (Minneapolis: Graywolf, 2004), esp. 239, for more on the lyric and ecstasy.

27 The DuBois reference is from the opening chapter of *The Souls of Black Folk*, ed. Henry Louis Gates and Terri Hume Oliver (New York: W. W. Norton, 1999), 9; the Moten reference is to the opening of *In the Break: The Aesthetics of the Black Radical Tradition* (Minneapolis: University of Minnesota Press, 2003); the Fanon reference is from *Black Skin, White Masks*, 82; the Crawford reference is from *Black Post-blackness* (Urbana: University of Illinois Press, 2017), 42. I could add here Frank Wilderson's *Afropessimism*, which characterizes abstraction as part of the project of antiblackness (esp. 12–17). I know that Glissant, in a passage cited earlier, collates abstraction with universality, though I want to think about abstraction as a possibility of the self-in-relation and even akin to the larger argument that Philip Brian Harper makes in *Abstractionist Aesthetics: Artistic Form and Social Critique in African American Culture* (New York: New York University Press, 2015). Also see abstraction as considered in Christopher Freeburg, *Black Aesthetics and the Interior Life* (Charlottesville: University of Virginia Press, 2017); and Michael Boyce Gillespie, *Film Blackness: American Cinema and the Idea of Black Film* (Durham, NC: Duke University Press, 2016). My thinking here is informed by Moten's work, which has done much to explore blackness via subject, object, thing (especially *The Universal Machine* [Durham, NC: Duke University Press, 2018]); studies of phenomenology that, as a philosophy, refuse a subject-object dualism (for example, Sara Ahmed, *Queer Phenomenology: Orientations, Objects, Others* [Durham, NC: Duke University Press, 2006]); and studies in black feminism that grapple with states of being object. This latter group includes Ann DuCille, "The Occult of True Black Womanhood," in *Skin Trade* (Cambridge, MA: Harvard University Press, 1996), 81–119; Patricia J. Williams, *The Alchemy of Race and Rights: Diary of a Law Professor* (Cambridge, MA: Harvard University Press, 1992), especially her exploration of being the object of property; and Evelyn Higginbotham, "African American Women's History and the

Metalanguage of Race," *Signs* 17, no. 2 (1992): 251–274, on the "metaphoric and metonymic" language of racialization (254). Related here is the exploration of a poetics of nothing in J. Kameron Carter and Sarah Jane Cervenak, "Black Ether," *CR: The New Centennial Review* 16, no. 2 (2016): 203–224; Denise Ferreira da Silva, "Toward a Black Feminist Poethics: The Quest(ion) of Blackness toward the End of the World," *Black Scholar* 44, no. 2 (2014): 81–97; Dawn Lundy Martin, "A Black Poetics: Against Mastery," *boundary 2* 44, no. 3 (2017): 159–163; and Fred Moten, "Blackness and Nothingness (Mysticism in the Flesh)," *South Atlantic Quarterly* 112, no. 4 (2013): 737–780. I am indebted to Quinn Anex-Ries for a series of conversations about phenomenology, objectness, and black feminist studies.

28 For more on colons, especially their capacity to cleave, see Jennifer DeVere Brody, *Punctuation* (Durham, NC: Duke University Press, 2008), 148.

29 In thinking about the ambivalence of force and willfulness, see Sara Ahmed, *Willful Subjects* (Durham, NC: Duke University, 2014). Also, Shockley's use of syllepsis and objectification recalls for me Camille Rankine's poem "We," in *Incorrect Merciful Impulses* (Port Townsend, WA: Copper Canyon, 2015), 77–78.

30 I am evoking Moten on possession as an unsettled inhabitance, a disturbed, thrilling thing "troubled by a dispossessive force objects exert such that the subject seems to be possessed—infused, deformed—by the object it possesses" (*In the Break* 1). One could also read Shockley's poem in tandem with Rita Dove, "The Oriental Ballerina," in *Thomas and Beulah* (Pittsburgh: Carnegie Mellon University Press, 1986), 75–77; see my essay "The Black Woman as Artist: The Queer Erotics of Rita Dove's Beulah," *Tulsa Studies in Women's Literature* 37, no. 2 (2018): esp. 410–412. Finally, we might consider syllogism, a conclusion made based on the assumption of two premises, as another doubleness running through Shockley's poem.

31 Awkward-Rich's question is a riff on Fanon's comment on the object. And in reading Awkward-Rich's consideration of femaleness and gendering through a transgender male speaker, I am reminded of the argument C. Riley Snorton makes about black femaleness as a defining trope of the terms of both blackness and transness; see *Black on Both Sides: A Racial History of Trans Identity* (Minneapolis: University of Minnesota Press, 2017). I have chosen to use the singular pronoun "themself" as a way to circumvent the inherent binary in singular pronouns in English. I do this here and elsewhere in instances where the speaker's gender is not explicitly identifiable via the terms of the poem, so as to avoid narrowing the terms of black world imagining that I am exploring in the book.

32 This poetic moment is characteristic of how Awkward-Rich uses pronouns (especially the first and second person) to do nuanced gender work. For example, in "Essay on the Awkward/Black/Object," the speaker says, "Now, when the thing is made to do / dangerous work, he flings its body from the / low rungs of a ladder" (19). In this clause, the subject moves from being "thing" to being "he" to being "its," in a terrific articulation of suspension.

33 I am grateful to have studied this collection in four classes: Readings in Black and Queer (spring 2019), Blackness and Being (spring 2019), Black Poetics (fall 2019), and Fanon and Spillers (spring 2020); these occasions sharpened my appreciation of the work. This attention to "splits" and refraction gestures also to the matter

of gendered violence: "splits" coheres with "slit" and "hole," as well as with the slashes that punctuate the poems; all of these reflect the threat of violation to the young person who is gendered female, who is navigating gendered being. See other poems in the collection, including "The Little Girl Is Busy Asking Questions about Desire" (Awkward-Rich 26), "Tonight" (29–31), "Essay on Crying in Public" (36–38), "Theory of Motion (3): Another Middle-Class Black Kid Tries to Name It" (46–47), "The Child Formerly Known as _____" (50–51), "Ars Poetica" (56), and "Theory of Motion (4), Nocturne" (57–58)." Finally, I want to acknowledge my student Lyle Cherneff's observation that the treble repetition of "splits" acts as an ellipsis.

34 My reference to authority here invokes Ann duCille's binary of authority and authenticity in "The Occult of True Black Womanhood," in *Skin Trade*, 81–119.

35 The Awkward-Rich quotation is from the poem "Essay Amending the Nature of My Mother's Tears"; the uncited quotation is from Quashie, *Black Women, Identity, and Cultural Theory* 17.

36 Again, in making this claim about black women's intellectual contributions, I work in company with scholars like Kimberly Nichele Brown, Brittney Cooper, Kristie Dotson, Lyndon Gill, Farah Jasmine Griffin, V. Denise James, Saidiya Hartman, and L. H. Stallings, as well as a whole generation of scholars from the 1980s and 1990s, including Barbara Christian, Patricia Hill Collins, Ann duCille, Trudier Harris, bell hooks, Hortense Spillers . . . and many, many others.

Chapter 3. Aliveness and Aesthetics

1 My reference to performance studies here is indebted to the field's arguments about ideation, aesthetics, and performativity in the being of blackness. In this regard, I am drawing especially on E. Patrick Johnson's idiom of appropriation (see *Appropriating Blackness: Performance and the Politics of Authenticity* [Durham, NC: Duke University Press, 2003]), as well as on Thomas F. DeFrantz and Anita Gonzalez, *Black Performance Theory* (Durham, NC: Duke University Press, 2014); Robert Reid-Pharr's thinking about blackness in the opening of *Once You Go Black: Choice, Desire, and the Black American Intellectual* (New York: New York University Press, 2007); and Harvey Young, *Embodying Black Experience: Stillness, Critical Memory, and the Black Body* (Ann Arbor: University of Michigan Press, 2010), especially his exploration of how ideation creates the black social body in chap. 1. Here I am not interested in nonblack performances of blackness, though these exist as part of the circuit of ideation. In terms of thinking about aesthetics and blackness, see Paul C. Taylor, *Black Is Beautiful: A Philosophy of Black Aesthetics* (Hoboken, NJ: Wiley-Blackwell, 2016), particularly the race-aesthetic nexus that he develops in conjunction with Roelofs's argument. Taylor writes that "black aesthetics is an unavoidably political subject. It exists as a cultural phenomenon and as a subject of philosophical study because of political conditions" (79). Taylor does well to surpass the "racial regimes" of aesthetic theory that David Lloyd notes in *Under Representation: The Racial Regime of Aesthetics* (New York: Fordham University Press, 2018). Also see the subfield of existential aesthetics, including Galen Johnson, *The Retrieval of the Beautiful: Thinking*

through *Merleau-Ponty's Aesthetics* (Evanston, IL: Northwestern University Press, 2009); Eugene Kaelin, *An Existentialist Aesthetic: the Theories of Sartre and Merleau-Ponty* (Madison: University of Wisconsin Press, 1962); Richard Kearney, *Poetics of Imagining: From Modern to Postmodern* (Edinburgh: Edinburgh University Press, 1998); Jerrold Levinson, *The Pleasures of Aesthetics: Philosophical Essays* (Ithaca, NY: Cornell University Press, 1996); Richard Wollheim, *Art and Its Objects* (Cambridge: Cambridge University Press, 1980); and Amie Thomasson, "The Ontology of Art," in *The Blackwell Guide to Aesthetics*, ed. Peter Kivy (Oxford: Blackwell, 2004), 78–92. And to cite more broadly, my study of aesthetics draws from the following works: Jacques Rancière, *The Politics of Aesthetics* (New York: Bloomsbury, 2006); Sara Ahmed, *The Cultural Politics of Emotions* (Edinburgh: Edinburgh University Press, 2004); Mikhail Bakhtin, *Art and Answerability: Early Philosophical Essays* (Austin: University of Texas Press, 1990); José Muñoz, *Cruising Utopia: The Then and There of Queer Futurity* (New York: New York University Press, 2009); Phillip Brian Harper, *Abstractionist Aesthetics: Artistic Form and Social Critique in African American Culture* (New York: New York University Press, 2015); Jared Sexton, "All Black Everything," *e-flux* 79 (2017), https://www.e-flux.com/journal/79/94158/all-black-everything; Yuriko Saito, *Aesthetics of the Familiar: Everyday Life and World-Making* (Oxford: Oxford University Press, 2017); Martha C. Nussbaum, *Love's Knowledge: Essays on Philosophy and Literature* (New York: Oxford University Press, 1992); Marc Redfield, *The Politics of Aesthetics: Nationalism, Gender, Romanticism* (Stanford, CA: Stanford University Press, 2003); Russ Castronovo, *Beautiful Democracy: Aesthetics and Anarchy in a Global Era* (Chicago: University of Chicago Press, 2007); Roland Barthes, *S/Z* (New York: Hill and Wang, 1975); Barthes, *Pleasure of the Text* (New York: Hill and Wang, 1975); Jacques Derrida, "'A Self-Unsealing Poetic Text': Poetics and Politics of Witnessing," in *Revenge of the Aesthetic: The Place of Literature in Theory Today*, trans. Rachel Bowlby, ed. Michael P. Clark (Berkeley: University of California Press, 2000), 180–207; and Samantha Pinto, *Difficult Diasporas: The Transnational Feminist Aesthetic of the Black Atlantic* (New York: New York University Press, 2013), especially her consideration of aesthetics and black experimentalism.

2 In thinking with Morrison's declaration about language—and writing as a specific creative genre—I am engaging Mel Y. Chen's work in *Animacies: Biopolitics, Racial Mattering, and Queer Affect* (Durham, NC: Duke University Press, 2012), especially her consideration of materiality and vitality (51–53). Other works relevant to my engagement of aesthetics and representation include Lauren Berlant, *Cruel Optimism* (Durham, NC: Duke University Press, 2011): "Aesthetics is not only the place where we rehabituate our sensorium by taking in new material and becoming more refined in relation to it. But it provides metrics for understanding how we pace and space our encounters with things, how we manage the too closeness of the world and also the desire to have an impact on it that has some relation to its impact on us" (12); Gayatri Gopinath, *Unruly Visions: The Aesthetic Practices of Queer Diaspora* (Durham, NC: Duke University Press, 2018): "The aesthetic *enacts, produces, and performs*," which is why she writes of "aesthetic *practices*, not just aesthetic forms, because they do things in the world" (16; emphases in original); and Kandice

Chuh's argument for aesthetics, relation, and a notion of "illiberal humanism" in *The Difference Aesthetics Makes: On the Humanities "After Man"* (Durham, NC: Duke University Press, 2019). And again, I am using the phrase "form-of-life" from Giorgio Agamben, "Form-of-Life," in *Means without End: Notes on Politics* (Minneapolis: University of Minnesota Press, 2000), 3–12, though it also occurs in Ludwig Wittgenstein (*Philosophical Investigations* [London: Pearson, 1973]).

3 See Amit S. Rai, "Race Racing: Four Theses on Race and Intensity," *WSQ: Women's Studies Quarterly* 40, no. 1 (2012): 64–75, which I came to via Tavia Nyong'o's compelling "Unburdening Representation," *Black Scholar* 44, no. 2 (2014): 70–80.

4 Jones's essay serves as the introduction to David Henderson's poetry collection *Felix of the Silent Forest*. Thanks to J. Pete Moore for pointing me to Henderson's collection. As I've noted in the introduction, aesthetics and worldmaking are central features of the work in the Black Arts/Aesthetics movement. For more here, see Margo Natalie Crawford, *Black Post-blackness: The Black Arts Movement and Twenty-First-Century Aesthetics* (Urbana: University of Illinois, 2017), as well as the range of works mentioned in the endnotes in the introduction. Also see the case Farah Jasmine Griffin makes for textuality and materiality in "Textual Healing: Claiming Black Women's Bodies, the Erotic and Resistance in Contemporary Novels of Slavery," *Callaloo* 19, no. 2 (1996): 519–536.

5 Geoffrey Pullum, in "Being a Subjunctive," says that subjunctive clauses are "finite and tenseless" (*Chronicle of Higher Education*, March 29, 2016), which follows the case that Rodney Huddleston makes in "Content Clauses and Reported Speech," in *The Cambridge Grammar of the English Language*, ed. Rodney Huddleston and Geoffrey K. Pullum (Cambridge: Cambridge University Press, 2002), 947–1031 (but see esp. 993–1000). For a brief consideration of the tense of imperatives and subjunctives, see Frank Parker, Charles Mayer, and Kathryn Riley, "Here Us Go Again," *American Speech* 69, no. 4 (1994): 435–439. Also see Charles D. Cannon, "A Survey of the Subjunctive Mood in English," *American Speech* 34, no. 1 (1959): 11–19; F. R. Palmer, *Mood and Modality* (Cambridge: Cambridge University Press, 2001); and Paul Portner, *Mood* (Oxford: Oxford University Press, 2018). The subjunctive matters to blackness; indeed, Saidiya V. Hartman has made the case for the subjunctive as an aesthetic of black being in regard to reading historical archives (see "Venus in Two Acts," *Small Axe* 12, no. 2 [2008]: 1–14). Also see Tavia Nyong'o, *Afro-fabulations: The Queer Drama of Black Life* (New York: New York University Press, 2018); Tina Campt's engagement of tense in *Listening to Images* (Durham, NC: Duke University Press, 2017); and Muñoz's attention to the "here and now" of any utopia or call for futurity (in *Cruising Utopia*). Especially in reading Muñoz, I came to think of the subjunctive as a structure of feeling à la Raymond Williams. Finally, the poet Lyrae Van Clief-Stefanon, in a presentation at the Callaloo conference "The Legacy of 1619" at the University of Pennsylvania, October 19, 2019, advances the idea of "adynaton," the impractical and impossible as rendered in a hyperbolic figure of speech, in a manner that echoes my consideration of the subjunctive.

6 In regard to black maleness as a poetic (and bardic) ontology, Hayes makes early reference to the caged-bird metaphor, in an allusion to Paul Laurence Dunbar

("Sympathy") and Countee Cullen ("Yet Do I Marvel"); as well as to Orpheus, Sylvia Plath, Emily Dickinson, Prince, Ginuwine, and Gucci Mane, among others.

7   See Farah Jasmine Griffin, "When Malindy Sings: A Meditation on Black Women's Vocality," in *Uptown Conversation: The New Jazz Studies*, ed. Robert G. O'Meally, Brent Hayes Edwards, and Farah Jasmine Griffin (New York: Columbia University Press, 2004), 102–125.

8   An excellent example of subjunctivity's if-then logic is Lucille Clifton, "poem in praise of menstruation" (in *The Collected Poems of Lucille Clifton, 1965–2010*, ed. Kevin Young and Michael S. Glaser [Rochester, NY: BOA Editions, 2012], 357), where poetic force resides in the compounding of the subjunctive phrasing, "if there is a river," a phrase that is intensified by repetition and varied enjambment, such that with each iteration the clause becomes more dramatic. Clifton's staggered declaration generates suspension as we wait for the phrase that will append each iteration of "if." Another well-known example of subjunctive-into-imperative is Claude McKay's poem "If We Must Die" (*The Complete Poems of Claude McKay* [Urbana: University of Illinois Press, 2004], 177).

9   These syntactical dynamics include the compounded adjectives "tree-loving / gun-hating" and the lovely "about-to-do deed." Notice, also, how the work of "imagine" surpasses the subjunctive possibility of "could" and "maybe," which are articulated in the epigraphic paragraph that opens the poem.

10 Part of the sublime is that "imagine" mixes syntax that is both interior (which is the normative habitat of the subjunctive, as a mood) and exterior (the habitat of the imperative command). Here I am borrowing from Elizabeth Povinelli, who, in *The Cunning of Recognition: Indigenous Alterities and the Making of Australian Multiculturalism* (Durham, NC: Duke University Press, 2002), cites the subjunctive as interior (72).

11 This quotation, which is explored considerably in chapter 1, is from a letter Barbara Christian wrote to Audre Lorde; see Alexis DeVeaux, *Warrior Poet: A Biography of Audre Lorde* (New York: W. W. Norton, 2004), 199.

12 I mean "timelessness" here to emphasize the fact that the subjunctive and the imperative, as moods, don't really indicate time on their own and are therefore not overtly tensed. We tend to read the subjunctive as future-oriented because of its signifying possibility, and perhaps we read the imperative through the present, but these time sentiments are not inherent in either syntax.

13 See Fred Moten, *Black and Blur* (Durham, NC: Duke University Press, 2017), especially the first paragraph, where he notes that "our resistant, relentlessly impossible object is subjectless predication, subjectless escape, escape from subjection, in and through the paralegal flaw that animates and exhausts the language of ontology" (vii), which describes his undertaking in *In the Break* and "The Case of Blackness," *Criticism* 50, no. 2 (2008): 177–218. Also see Stephen Best (*The Fugitive's Properties: Laws and the Poetics of Possession* [Chicago: University of Chicago Press, 2004]), Saidiya Hartman (*Scenes of Subjection: Terror, Slavery, and Self-Making in Nineteenth-Century America* [New York: Oxford University Press, 1997]), Hortense Spillers (especially "Mama's Baby, Papa's Maybe: An American Grammar Book," in *Black, White, and in Color: Essays on American Literature and Culture* [Chicago: University of Chicago Press, 2003], 203–229), and Alexander Weheliye (*Habeas Viscus: Racializing Assemblages, Biopolitics, and Black Feminist*

Theories of the Human [Durham, NC: Duke University Press, 2014]). I also want to recall the discussion of Toni Morrison's characters Sula and Ajax (in chapter 2) and to cite two other works that engage the terms of possession in ways I find compelling: Natasha Trethewey's poetry collection *Thrall* (Boston: Houghton Mifflin Harcourt, 2012), including the title poem's use of "as if" and the way that a sensibility of imagine radiates through the book's poetics; and Stephanie L. Batiste, "Dunham Possessed: Ethnographic Bodies, Movement, and Transnational Constructions of Blackness," *Journal of Haitian Studies* 13, no. 2 (2007): 8–22.

14 I thank John Casey for helping me achieve the clarity of this reading. In considering these dialectics of being, one could look toward Lauren Berlant's description of intersubjectivity in *Cruel Optimism*, where, thinking about Barbara Johnson's conceptualizing of apostrophe, Berlant explicates "the reaching out to a you" that is "actually a turning back, an animating of a receiver on behalf of the desire to make something happen *now* that realizes something in *the speaker*, makes the speaker more or differently possible, because she has admitted, in a sense, the importance of speaking for, as, and to, two—but only under the condition, and illusion, that the two are really (in) one" (25–26; emphasis in the original).

15 My quick reference to smallness here evidences my debt to affect studies as it intersects with thinking about materiality, aesthetics, the ordinary, and phenomenology. This confluence of ideas informs and is cited in the discussion of aliveness in chapter 1.

16 Michel de Certeau, *The Practice of Everyday Life*, trans. Steven Rendall (Berkeley: University of California Press, 1988), 115.

17 The quotation is from *Encyclopaedia Britannica Online*, Academic ed., s.v. "essay," accessed June 14, 2020, britannica.com/search?query=essay.

18 See Carl H. Klaus, "Toward a Collective Poetics of the Essay," in *Essayists on the Essay: Montaigne to Our Time*, ed. Carl H. Klaus and Ned Stuckey-French (Iowa City: University of Iowa Press, 2012), xv–xxvii, esp. xxiii–xxiv. Cheryl B. Butler makes a similar claim in *The Art of the Black Essay: from Meditation to Transcendence* (New York: Routledge, 2003): "In the African American essay, the uncanny moment happens upon the reader as it happens upon the essayist and upon the character the essayist constructs" (11).

19 The matter of audience and the biographical is taken up in chapter 4. In regard to thinking about the author function, see Michael Boyce Gillespie, *Film Blackness: American Cinema and the Idea of Black Film* (Durham, NC: Duke University Press, 2016); and Patrick Colm Hogan, *Narrative Discourse: Authors and Narrators in Literature, Film, and Art* (Columbus: Ohio State University Press, 2013). In regard to the genre more broadly, see Ned Stuckey-French, *The American Essay in the American Century* (Columbia: University of Missouri Press, 2011); and Terence Cave, *How to Read Montaigne* (London: Granta Books, 2013).

20 We might do well to think of the personal essay in the genre of memoir, as a text of memory, unreliability, and indeterminacy, where the dialectic is between writer and speaker, not speaker and reader. Or we might consider the way Robert McRuer puts pressure on the word "composition"—a text of failing and willful disorder; see "Composing Bodies; or, De-composition: Queer Theory, Disability Studies, and Alternative Corporealities," *JAC* 24, no. 1 (2004): 47–78. That is, I want to be clear that

the conventional matter of voice and authority is not read flatly in regard to the essay's dynamism. As Stefano Harney and Fred Moten ask, "What if authoritative speech is detached from the notion of a univocal speaker" and from a "possessive individualism"? (*Undercommons* 135, 140). As an extension of comments made earlier about voice (see chapter 2), I would add that not only is voice in the essay not engaged with audience, but the voice represents a commitment to becoming, perhaps even "dissensus" in the way Jacques Rancière means that term to characterize that "gap in the sensible itself" ("Ten Theses on Politics," in *Dissensus: On Politics and Aesthetics*, trans. Steven Corcoran [London: Continuum, 2010], 38). We might recall also heteroglossia as explored in Mae G. Henderson, "Speaking in Tongues: Dialogics, Dialectics, and the Black Woman Writer's Literary Tradition," in *Changing Our Own Words*, ed. Cheryl Wall (New Brunswick, NJ: Rutgers University Press, 1989), 16–37. Related here is Gerard Genette's arguments in *Narrative Discourse: An Essay in Method* (Ithaca, NY: Cornell University Press, 1983), particularly the claim that there is no "third-person" narrator; also see Mieke Bal and Jane E. Lewin, "The Narrating and the Focalizing: A Theory of the Agents in Narrative," *Style* 17, no. 2 (1983): 234–269.

21 The matter of abstraction is addressed in chapter 2.

22 From John D'Agata, "2003," in Klaus and Stuckey-French, *Essayists on the Essay*, 172–173.

23 William Hazlitt calls this "familiar style" ("On Familiar Style," in *Table-Talk: Essays on Men and Manners* [Charleston, SC: BiblioBazaar, 2007], 113–114); also see Gerald Early's discussion of the essay's conversational tone in the introduction to *Tuxedo Junction: Essays on American Culture* (New York: Ecco, 1989).

24 I mean poetic here in accord with the discussion of lyric voice in the previous chapter.

25 Vinson Cunningham, in "What Makes the Essay American," *New Yorker*, May 13, 2016, argues with D'Agata's attempt to reenvision the essay as "neutral attempt" in the vein of Montaigne and argues that "most of us Americans are Emersons: artful sermonizers, pathological point-makers." I'll address Cunningham's argument for the essay as a site of "conflict [that] is elemental to America" in the next chapter. And in regard to experience and Hall's argument, I am recalling Joan W. Scott's iconic essay, "The Evidence of Experience," *Critical Inquiry* 17, no. 4 (1991): 773–794, particularly her notion of "the discursive character of experience" (787). Scott's argument ignited a debate in feminist studies, especially in women-of-color feminism; see Linda Alcoff's response to Scott, "Phenomenology, Post-structuralism, and Feminist Theory on the Concept of Experience," in *Feminist Phenomenology*, ed. Linda Fisher and Lester Embree (Berlin: Spinger, 2000), 39–56; and Johanna Oksala's more recent "In Defense of Experience," *Hypatia* 29, no. 2 (2014): 388–403. My interest in Scott's exploration of experience generates from a black world orientation, where the calculus of experience, evidence, and value is not at stake; indeed, this is how I have read Audre Lorde's claim for experience in chapters 1 and 2. Unrelated to the discourse about Scott's essay, see Harvey Young's thinking about black embodiment and misrecognition in *Embodying Black Experience*.

26 Bigé's comment is from a personal conversation; see also Patrizia Pallaro, ed., *Authentic Movement: Essays by Mary Starks Whitehouse, Janet Adler and Joan Chodorow*, 2 vols. (London: Jessica Kingsley, 1999); D. Soyini Madison, foreword to *Black Performance*

Theory, ed. Thomas F. DeFrantz and Anita Gonzalez (Durham, NC: Duke University Press, 2014), vii–ix; and Thomas F. DeFrantz and Anita Gonzalez, "Introduction: From 'Negro Experiment' to 'Black Performance,'" in DeFrantz and Gonzalez, *Black Performance Theory*, 1–15.The phrase "autonomous passage" is from conversation with Matt Ashby. I think of this consideration of inauthenticity as akin to Derek Walcott's idiom of feasting in the poem "Love after Love," in *The Poetry of Derek Walcott, 1948-2013*, ed. Glyn Maxwell (New York: Farrar, Straus and Giroux, 2014), 227.

27 See José Esteban Muñoz on disidentification (*Disidentifications* [Minneapolis: University of Minnesota Press, 1999]), Daphne Brooks on distanciation ("Nina Simone's Triple Play," *Callaloo* 34, no. 1 [2011]: 176–197), and Phillip Brian Harper on abstraction (*Abstractionist Aesthetics*).

28 The essay embodies thingness. As such, we could think of it as a kind of fetish that Monique Allewaert theorizes in *Ariel's Ecology: Plantations, Personhood, and Colonialism in the American Tropics* (Minneapolis: University of Minnesota Press, 2013): "Diasporic Africans' production of fetishes recognized that objects, far from being wordless or mute, could be conceived as dense interiorities or constellations of force that could store, process, and actualize information and that were also crucial to the production of the collectivities, or assemblages, through which personhood was articulated" (118–119). I am compelled by Allewaert's notice of "dense interiorities or constellations of force" since it evokes my claim of the essay's worldness through its small, fierce partiality. Furthermore, her attention to the aesthetics of the object collates with the Black Aesthetic movement's engagement and "critique of the text as object and monument" (Crawford, *Black Post-blackness*, 17), its investment in a textual force of aliveness that resides in the inanimate. Writers like Amiri Baraka and Larry Neal knew that even in the face of treacherous discourses of black objectification, the art object in a black world imaginary could instantiate being. Or, as Allewaert describes it, "Here, subjects and objects are recalibrated as assemblages that are animate and entangling. It then follows that personhood is neither an a priori category nor a mode of being oppositional to objects, but a composition produced through the relation of (para)humans, artifacts, and ecological forces" (119). My consideration of the broad and complicated discourse of thingness includes Moten, "The Case of Blackness"; Bill Brown, *A Sense of Things* (Chicago: University of Chicago Press, 2003); Sara Ahmed, *Queer Phenomenology: Orientations, Objects, Others* (Durham, NC: Duke University Press, 2006); Jane Bennett, *Vibrant Matter: A Political Ecology of Things* (Durham, NC: Duke University Press, 2010); Robin Bernstein, *Racial Innocence: Performing American Childhood from Slavery to Civil Rights* (New York: New York University Press, 2011); Zakiyyah Jackson, "Outer Worlds: The Persistence of Race in Movement 'Beyond the Human,'" *GLQ* 21, no. 2–3 (2015): 215–218; Jackson, "Losing Manhood: Animality and Plasticity in the (Neo)Slave Narrative," *Qui Parle* 25, no. 1–2 (2016): 95–136; Jayna Brown, "Being Cellular: Race, the Inhuman, and the Plasticity of Life," *GLQ* 21, no. 2–3 (2015): 321–341; and Aime Cesaire's notion of "Thingification," from *Discourse on Colonialism*, trans. Joan Pinkham (New York: Monthly Review Press, 2000), 42.

29 The idiom "aesthetics of existence" comes from Michel Foucault's essay "An Aesthetics of Existence," in *Philosophy, Politics, Culture: Interviews and Other Writings*, ed.

Lawrence D. Kritzman (New York: Routledge, 1988), 47–53. And in thinking of the essay's volatility, I am leaning on Elizabeth Grosz's conceit of *Volatile Bodies: Toward a Corporeal Feminism* (Bloomington: Indiana University Press, 1994), as I am also recalling Adorno's claim that "the essay's innermost formal law is heresy. Through violations of the orthodoxy of thought, something in the object becomes visible which it is orthodoxy's secret and objective aim to keep invisible" ("The Essay as Form," trans. Bob Hullot-Kentor and Frederic Will, *New German Critique* 32 (1984): 151–171, 171).

30 My conceptualization of aliveness is phenomenological, which my engagement of the essay-as-genre bears out. And I should note here Moten's critique of "phenomenology's assumption of thingly individuation [that] renders no-thingness unavoidable and unavowable" (*The Universal Machine* [Durham, NC: Duke University Press, 2018], ix), where no-thingness is blackness. I am aware that phenomenology proper often excludes blackness, but I think that its ideas can be used for blackness in a black world, which indeed seems to be the point of Moten's discussion of Fanon in *Universal Machine*, chap. 3.

31 See *Seneca Review*'s fall 1997 issue on the lyric essay, though I retain the term "first-person essay" because I am speaking of works here that are less intentionally hybrid in form than the canonical examples of lyric essays (for example, Maggie Nelson, *The Argonauts* [Minneapolis: Graywolf, 2015]).

32 In *Film Blackness*, Michael Gillespie describes this collapsing as characteristic of the problem of black representations and cultural criticism. Moira Ferguson, in *Jamaica Kincaid: Where the Land Meets the Body* (Charlottesville: University of Virginia Press, 1994), argues that "in *A Small Place* the speaker is concerned for her native land, not herself" (78), which is one way to read Kincaid's work though different from my attention to the singularity of the speaker. Also see J. Brooks Bouson's reading in *Jamaica Kincaid: Writing Memory, Writing Back to the Mother* (Albany: State University of New York Press, 2005).

33 See Julieta Singh's argument about Kincaid's engagement of ambivalence in *Unthinking Mastery: Dehumanism and Decolonial Entanglements* (Durham, NC: Duke University Press, 2018). For scholarly considerations of the second person in *A Small Place* (New York: Farrar, Straus and Giroux, 1988), see Claudia Marquis, "'Making a Spectacle of Yourself': The Art of Anger in Jamaica Kincaid's *A Small Place*," *Journal of Postcolonial Writing* 54, no. 2 (2018): 147–160; and Suzanne Gauch, "A Small Place: Some Perspectives on the Ordinary," *Callaloo* 25, no. 3 (2002): 910–919. Finally, Kincaid uses direct address superbly in her well-known short story (or is it an essay?) "Girl," *New Yorker*, June 26, 1978, https://www.newyorker.com/magazine/1978/06/26/girl.

34 In the first section, there are only two references where "I" is the subject of the sentence, though I am not including here this sentence where the singular first person operates as an exclamation: "I mean, in a way; I mean, your dismay and puzzlement are natural to you" (15).

35 See Harper, *Abstractionist Aesthetics*, esp. chap. 3, as well as his discussion of the second person in *Are We Not Men? Masculine Anxiety and the Problem of African-American Identity* (New York: Oxford University Press, 1996), chap. 2.

36 See David Wills, "Passionate Secrets and Democratic Dissidence," *Diacritics* 38, no. 1–2 (2008): 17–29. On virtuals, see Gilles Deleuze, *Difference and Repetition*, trans.

Paul Patton (New York: Columbia University Press, 1994) and *Pure Immanence: Essays on a Life* (New York: Zone Books, 2005). I am also inspired here by Brian Massumi's conceptualization of affect (the use of "pure" and "raw" echoes him from *The Politics of Affect* [Cambridge, UK: Polity, 2015], 207) and Ashon Crawley's notion of otherwise in *Blackpentecostal Breath: The Aesthetics of Possibility* (New York: Fordham University Press, 2016). This tension between explicitness and furtiveness fuels the performative aspect of the anecdote, its quality of discursive unfolding, which Wills goes on to track via the secrecy embedded in the etymology of the word:

> The anecdote, *anekdota*, is etymologically the unedited (*inédit*). One should hear that in two senses: in the first place as that which hasn't yet been published, or prepared for publication, that which remains out of the light, in secret, but simply waiting for the inquisitive or all-seeing gaze of an editor; and in the second place as that which appears without the benefit of an editor's red pen, what is spoken of in excess of what needs to be written, that which appears unexpurgated, *unsecreted*. Thus the anecdote as *inédit* has, between its two senses, the paradoxical structure of the "patent secret": it can both give and withhold. (22–23)

See also Jane Gallop, *Anecdotal Theory* (Durham, NC: Duke University, 2002), especially for its suggestion that the anecdote merges the literary and the real; and Joel Fineman's essay "The History of the Anecdote," in *The Subjectivity Effect in Western Literary Tradition: Essays toward the Release of Shakespeare's Will* (Cambridge, MA: MIT Press, 1991), esp. 61–62. Wills's thinking about the anecdote parallels Foucault's theorizing in "Lives of Infamous Men," which considers the power to be had in the characterization of ordinary happenings, what he calls "nameless misfortunes and adventures gathered into a handful of words" and later, "those flash existences, those poem-lives" (in *Power: The Essential Works of Foucault, 1954–1984*, ed. James D. Faubion [New York: New Press, 2001], 3:157, 159). I find this compelling even though Foucault is describing accounts made *of* rather than *by* subjects. Thanks to Tamar Katz for pointing me to Wills's article and John Casey for the Gallop reference.

37 Indeed, it is an anxiety of audience that inspires much of the harsh criticism of Kincaid's writing; see, for example, Derik Smith and Cliff Beumel, "My Other: Imperialism and Subjectivity in Jamaica Kincaid's *My Brother*," in *Jamaica Kincaid and Caribbean Double Crossings*, ed. Linda Lang-Peralta (Newark: University of Delaware Press, 2006), 96–112. In addition to Greg Thomas's arguments in *The Sexual Demon of Colonial Power: Pan-African Embodiment and Erotic Schemes of Empire* (Bloomington: Indiana University Press, 2007), see also Jane King, "A Small Place Writes Back," *Callaloo* 25, no. 3 (2002): 885–909.

38 See Ahmed, *Queer Phenomenology*. Bouson notes that shame is central to Kincaid's conceptualization of diasporic subjectivity. On the aesthetics of bad/ugly/difficult feelings, see José Esteban Muñoz, "Feeling Brown: Ethnicity and Affect in Ricardo Bracho's *The Sweetest Hangover (and Other STDs)*," *Theatre Journal* 52, no. 1 (2000): 67–71; Muñoz, "Feeling Brown, Feeling Down: Latina Affect, the Performativity of Race, and the Depressive Position," *Signs* 31, no. 3 (2006): 675–688; Sianne Ngai, *Ugly Feelings* (Cambridge, MA: Harvard University Press, 2007); and Darieck Scott, *Extravagant Abjection: Blackness, Power, and Sexuality in the African American Literary*

Imagination (New York: New York University Press, 2010). This speaking of one's self through the object case coheres with the inclination of affect theory in these works. Also see Shaundra Myers, "Black Anaesthetics: The New Yorker and Andrea Lee's *Russian Journal*," *American Literary History* 31, no. 1 (2019): 47–73, on black aesthetics and the pronoun case.

39 That is, this closing abstraction reprises the subjunctive ambivalence of Kincaid's speaker, her aesthetic of "Caribbean impossibility," a phrase that is the title of Thomas W. Sheehan's useful study "Caribbean Impossibility: The Lack of Jamaica Kincaid," in Lang-Peralta, *Jamaica Kincaid and Caribbean Double Crossings*, 79–95. In using "ordinary language" here, I am making reference to the school of ordinary language philosophy; see Stanley Cavell, *Must We Mean What We Say?* (Cambridge: Cambridge University Press, 2002), especially the title essay; and *Themes Out of School: Effects and Causes* (Chicago: University of Chicago Press, 1984), especially the opening essay, as well as Toril Moi, *Revolution of the Ordinary: Literary Studies after Wittgenstein, Austin, and Cavell* (Chicago: University of Chicago Press, 2017). Finally, it is notable that Kincaid's final passage uses an equation that is strikingly similar to both Édouard Glissant's near the end of *Poetics of Relation* (trans. Betsy Wing [Ann Arbor: University of Michigan Press, 1997]) ("There would be something great and noble about initiating such a movement, referring not to Humanity but to the exultant divergence of humanities. Thought of self and thought of other here become obsolete in their duality. Every Other is a citizen and no longer a barbarian" [190]) and Frantz Fanon's near the end of *Black Skin, White Masks* (trans. Charles Lam Markmann [London: Pluto, 2008]): "There is no Negro mission; there is no white burden" (178).

40 This doing reminds me of Saidiya Hartman's undertaking in *Lose Your Mother: A Journey along the Atlantic Slave Route* (New York: Macmillan, 2008). That is, the imperative in Hartman's title, "lose your mother," is an ambivalence that infers an act of colonial imposition, a loss made inevitable and irrecuperable via the horrors of modernity, as well as a call to relinquish the meager practices of recovery. (Think, for example, about the speaker's journey through the trouble and fictions of kinship.) For a scholarly exploration of such losing, see Stephen Michael Best, *None like Us: Blackness, Belonging, Aesthetic Life* (Durham, NC: Duke University Press, 2018), especially his consideration of elimination and his engagement of Toni Morrison's *Beloved* and *A Mercy*.

41 The case for this making resonates with Jana Evans Braziel's argument about autofiction in "'Another Line Was Born . . .': Genesis, Genealogy, and Genre in Jamaica Kincaid's *Mr. Potter*,'" in Lang-Peralta, *Jamaica Kincaid and Caribbean Double Crossings*, 127–150.

42 See Ahmed, *Cultural Politics of Emotions* 12.

43 The quotation comes from Gilles Deleuze and Félix Guattari, *What Is Philosophy?*, trans. Hugh Tomlinson and Graham Burchell (New York: Columbia University Press, 1994): "Percepts are no longer perceptions; they are independent of a state of those who experience them. Affects are no longer feelings or affections; they go beyond the strength of those who undergo them. Sensations, percepts, and affects are *beings* whose validity lies in themselves and exceeds any lived. They could be said to exist in the absence of man because man, as he is caught in stone, on the canvas, or

by words, is himself a compound of percepts and affects. The work of art is a being of sensation and nothing else: it exists in itself" (164; emphasis in original).

44 The quotation is the title of William Irwin's book, which was inspired by a moment in Kamel Daoud, *The Meursault Investigation* (New York: Other Press, 2015).

Chapter 4. Aliveness in Two Essays

1 Its mantra could be "We cannot represent ourselves. We can't be represented" (Stefano Harney and Fred Moten, *The Undercommons: Fugitive Planning and Black Study* [New York: Minor Compositions, 2013], 20). And though Harney and Moten use the plural first person to make the case for the undercommons, I am inspired by their commitment to a collectivity that is not indexed to institutionality and that is relational. I consider the matter of the commons, collectivity, and oneness in the conclusion.

2 Shepherd explores some of this terrain in his poetry, especially the first section of *Some Are Drowning* (Pittsburgh: University of Pittsburgh Press, 1995); and his particular use of the lyric direct address in "Slaves" seems resonant with his use of the second person in the essay. Also see Reginald Shepherd, "An Interview with Reginald Shepherd," by Charles H. Rowell, *Callaloo* 21, no. 2 (1998): 290–307. In regard to thinking about literary expressions of black queer interracial desire, see Darieck Scott, "Jungle Fever? Black Gay Identity Politics, White Dick, and the Utopian Bedroom," GLQ 1, no. 3 (1994): 299–321; Scott, *Extravagant Abjection: Blackness, Power, and Sexuality in the African American Literary Imagination* (New York: New York University Press, 2010); Robert Reid-Pharr, *Black. Gay. Man: Essays* (New York: New York University Press, 2001); Kendall Thomas, "'Ain't Nothing like the Real Thing': Black Masculinity, Gay Sexuality, and the Jargon of Authenticity," in *The House That Race Built: Black Americans, U.S. Terrain*, ed. Wahneema Lubiano (New York: Vintage, 1998), 116–135; Stefanie Dunning, *Queer in Black and White: Interraciality, Same Sex Desire, and Contemporary African American Culture* (Bloomington: Indiana University Press, 2009); and David A. Gerstner, *Queer Pollen: White Seduction, Black Male Homosexuality, and the Cinematic* (Urbana: University of Illinois Press, 2012). And in citing Scott, I want to recall his notion of a politics without defense noted at the end of the previous chapter. Finally, the territory Shepherd explores here, especially the specificity of thinking about the black queer male subject as a negative inflection of (white) masculinity, reminds me of James Baldwin, *Giovanni's Room* (New York: Vintage Books, 2013), as well as the mix of abjection and the negative in Hilton Als, *The Women* (New York: Farrar, Straus and Giroux, 1996).

3 See Dagmawi Woubshet, *The Calendar of Loss: Race, Sexuality, and Mourning in the Early Era of AIDS* (Baltimore: Johns Hopkins University Press, 2015), especially the introduction, and Brad McCoy, "Chiasmus: An Important Structural Device Commonly Found in Biblical Literature," *CTS Journal* 9 (2003): 18–34. Perhaps the most iconic chiasmus in the black literary canon is what Frederick Douglass writes after his fight with Edward Covey: "You have seen how a man was made a slave; you shall see how a slave was made a man" (*Narrative of the Life of Frederick Douglass*, ed. Philip Smith [New York: Dover, 1995], 39).

4 The reference to Eliot is oblique, through the phrase "objective correlative" in the essay's opening paragraph.

5 See Anne Anlin Cheng, *Ornamentalism* (New York: Oxford University Press, 2019), xii; emphasis in the original. I am implying a relationship between aesthetics, pleasure, and innovation, an implication that is informed by my study of Harryette Mullen, "Incessant Elusives: The Oppositional Poetics of Erica Hunt and Will Alexander," in *The Cracks between What We Are and What We Are Supposed to Be: Essays and Interviews* (Tuscaloosa: University of Alabama Press, 2012), 173–182; and Daphne Brooks's idiom of troubling style in "Afro-sonic Feminist Praxis," in *Black Performance Theory*, ed. Thomas F. DeFrantz and Anita Gonzalez (Durham, NC: Duke University Press, 2014), 204–222. My reference to the "fantastic" borrows from Tzvetan Todorov, *The Fantastic: A Structural Approach to a Literary Genre* (Ithaca, NY: Cornell University Press, 1975). Indeed, my use of "fantastic" rather than "futuristic" reflects my sense that the suspending aesthetic quality originates in the specificity of smallness, in the phenomenological tendering in the body, such that time and space are remade not out there but in here (see esp. 24–40 of Todorov, *Fantastic*). As Lee Edelman argues in *Homographesis: Essays in Gay Literary and Cultural Theory* (New York: Routledge, 1994), "Language, syntax, the appurtenances of 'style,' *perform* more truly than they *register* an erotic cathexis, a condensation or dilation of pleasure" (25; emphases in the original).

I am also thinking with Aliyyah I. Abdur-Rahman, "The Black Ecstatic," *GLQ* 24, no. 2–3 (2018): 343–365, which explores pleasure via José Esteban Muñoz's work, not as a futurity but as "a beyond that is not temporal . . . but that reaches in and reckons with the ruinous now as the site of regenerative capacity and of renewed political agency" (344). Relevant to studying through this question are works by Audre Lorde ("Uses of the Erotic: The Erotic as Power," in *Sister Outsider: Essays and Speeches* [New York: Crossing, 1984], 53–59), Jennifer C. Nash (*The Black Body in Ecstasy: Reading Race, Reading Pornography* [Durham, NC: Duke University Press, 2014]), Ashon T. Crawley (*Blackpentecostal Breath: The Aesthetics of Possibility* [New York: Fordham University Press, 2016]), Roland Barthes (*Pleasure of the Text* [New York: Hill and Wang, 1975]), and especially Toril Moi, whose consideration of attention, reading, and pleasure in *Revolution of the Ordinary: Literary Studies after Wittgenstein, Austin, and Cavell* (Chicago: University of Chicago Press, 2017), chap. 10, is a useful way to imagine the speaker's inhabitance in the essay.

6 The reprisal and its language recall Cameron Awkward-Rich's poems discussed in chapter 2.

7 For more, see Barry Stampfl, "Hans Vaihinger's Ghostly Presence in Contemporary Literary Studies," *Criticism* 40, no. 3 (1998): 437–454; and Kwame Anthony Appiah, *As If: Idealizations and Ideals* (Cambridge, MA: Harvard University Press, 2017), the latter of which uses Vaihinger to extend a philosophical appeal for multiplicity.

8 My use of "floating signifier" here is a direct allusion to Patricia J. Williams's explication of polar bears throughout *The Alchemy of Race and Rights: Diary of a Law Professor* (Cambridge, MA: Harvard University Press, 1991), esp. 6, 7.

9 This suspension is phenomenological, in the way Sara Ahmed describes the idea of reaching: "Even when things are within reach, we still have to reach for those

things for them to be reached. The work of inhabiting space involves a dynamic negotiation between what is familiar and unfamiliar, such that it is possible for the world to create new impressions" (*Queer Phenomenology: Orientations, Objects, Others* [Durham, NC: Duke University Press, 2006], 7–8).

10   I am making direct reference to Sianne Ngai, *Ugly Feelings* (Cambridge, MA: Harvard University Press, 2007), which is one frame for beholding Shepherd's ideas. That is, I think about Shepherd's essaying abjection as a magic that operates through the negative. And my cohering of chiasmus, exchange, and terrible feelings is inspired, in part, by Chela Sandoval's reading of Frantz Fanon's title phrase "black skin, white masks" as a "chiasmic metaphor," a "location, which is neither inside nor outside, neither good nor evil, . . . an interstitial site out of which new, undecidable forms of being and original theories and practices for emancipation, are produced" (*Methodology of the Oppressed* [Minneapolis: University of Minnesota Press, 2000], 84–85). In regard to abjection, I could cite again Scott, *Extravagant Abjection*; Stephen Michael Best's idiom of "beautiful elimination" in *None like Us: Blackness, Belonging, Aesthetic Life* (Durham, NC: Duke University Press, 2018), chap. 1; Ahmed's consideration of shame in *The Promise of Happiness* (Durham, NC: Duke University Press, 2010) ("a refusal to be shamed by witnessing the other as being ashamed of you" [116]); José Esteban Muñoz, "Feeling Brown: Ethnicity and Affect in Ricardo Bracho's *The Sweetest Hangover (and Other STDs)*," *Theatre Journal* 52, no. 1 (2000): 67–71; Muñoz, "Feeling Brown, Feeling Down: Latina Affect, the Performativity of Race, and the Depressive Position," *Signs* 31, no. 3 (2006): 675–688; Ann Cvetkovich, *An Archive of Feelings* (Durham, NC: Duke University Press, 2003); Cvetkovich, *Depression: A Public Feeling* (Durham, NC: Duke University Press, 2012); Aida Levy-Hussen, *How to Read African-American Literature* (New York: New York University Press, 2016), particularly chap. 3, "The Missing Archive [on Depression]"; Nash's discussion of injury and wounding in *The Black Body in Ecstasy*; John Paul Ricco, *The Logic of the Lure* (Chicago: University of Chicago Press, 2002), particularly his thinking about shame in chap. 1; Alexander Weheliye's overall argument about suffering and the project of black studies in *Habeas Viscus: Racializing Assemblages, Biopolitics, and Black Feminist Theories of the Human* (Durham, NC: Duke University Press, 2014); and Kathryn Bond Stockton, *Beautiful Bottom, Beautiful Shame* (Durham, NC: Duke University Press, 2006). Shepherd explores negation and otherness in other essays too; see *Orpheus in the Bronx: Essays on Identity, Politics, and the Freedom of Poetry* (Ann Arbor: University of Michigan Press, 2008), where he makes "a resolute defense of poetry's autonomy" (1) and which includes the argumentative essay "The Other's Other: Against Identity Poetry, for Possibility."

11   See the discussion of individualism and oneness in chapter 2.

12   The distinction between grief and grievance is Robert Frost's, and it is taken up in affect studies, especially in Anne Anlin Cheng, *The Melancholy of Race: Psychoanalysis, Assimilation, and Hidden Grief* (Oxford: Oxford University Press, 2001), where Cheng argues that grief "speaks in a different language—a language that may seem inchoate because it is not fully reconcilable to the vocabulary of social formulation or ideology" (x). Moreover, Cheng argues that "how a racially impugned person processes the experience of denigration exposes a continuous interaction between sociality

and privacy, history and presence, politics and ontology" (x). On melancholia, also see Sharon P. Holland, *Raising the Dead: Readings of Death and (Black) Subjectivity* (Durham, NC: Duke University Press, 2000); Woubshet, *Calendar of Loss*; and Fred Moten, *In the Break: The Aesthetics of the Black Radical Tradition* (Minneapolis: University of Minnesota Press, 2003).

13 See Christina Sharpe, *Monstrous Intimacies: Making Post-slavery Subjects* (Durham, NC: Duke University Press, 2010). I think of this ambivalence as an "existential surprise," in the phrase poet and scholar Ed Pavlić uses to describe a poetics of "selfhood that claims a fluid, durable, and authoritative kind of presence in the world" ("How to 'Heal a Mouth Shut This Way,'" *Black Scholar* 43 [2013]: 103). Such surprise looms, for example, in the speaker's hesitancies and diversions as he moves through oblique anecdotes of rejection, talking wanderingly—that is, without conclusion—about being. And I must cite here Nasir (Nandi) Marumo for conversations about monstrosity and Shepherd's aesthetics.

14 Beth Loffreda and Claudia Rankine, introduction to *The Racial Imaginary: Writers on Race in the Life of the Mind*, ed. Claudia Rankine, Beth Loffreda, and Max King Cap (New York: Fence Books, 2015), 20.

15 My use of "exploit" is inspired partly by Anna Holmes's meditation on the distinction between empathy and exploitation in the "Bookends" section of the *New York Times* Book Review, though my use incorporates one into the other: "Here's how I see it: Empathy is the ability to respect and maybe even understand another's point of view, revealing larger truths about ourselves and others. Exploitation is the use of another's experience for personal gain. Empathy requires self-awareness. Exploitation is marked by self-interest. Empathy is about deepening connections. Exploitation, about filling one's pockets, literal or figurative" (May 29, 2016, 29).

16 In using "optimism" here, I am in conversation with Lauren Berlant's *Cruel Optimism* (Durham, NC: Duke University Press, 2011), though Berlant argues that "agency and urgency . . . extend from imperiled bodies" (101). I don't think of the essay as a body of urgency that generates from (and in response to) the political peril of being alive.

17 I am invoking Judith Butler's argument in *Excitable Speech: A Politics of the Performative* (New York: Routledge, 1997), particularly the idea that speech is always already beyond the control of the speaker.

18 Wall hedges in considering how Ralph Ellison "turns to the essay to answer personal questions" about collective black agency (3). I want to note, again, my appreciation for the breadth of Wall's scholarship in *On Freedom and the Will to Adorn: The Art of the African American Essay* (Chapel Hill: University of North Carolina Press, 2018), which makes clear the matter of the essay and public intellectualism. My difference from Wall (and Early) is that I think of the personal essay as a poetic and, as such, I am interested in its capacity to work beyond the political imperative of an antiblack world logic. For more on the particular history of the African American essay, see Cheryl B. Butler, *The Art of the Black Essay: From Meditation to Transcendence* (New York: Routledge, 2003), which, in thinking about the essay as a meditative form, falls much closer to my own interest in the genre. Indeed, Butler acknowledges the dissonance between the essay's wandering and conceptualizations of black public intellectualism (see the introduction, esp. 7–16).

19 I am borrowing the notion of surrogacy in keeping with Morrison's argument in *Playing in the Dark*. These matters of audience inform my reading of Jamaica Kincaid's diasporic wandering in *A Small Place* (New York: Farrar, Straus and Giroux, 1988); see the previous chapter. See also Chinua Achebe, "English and the African Writer," *Transition* 18 (1965): 27–30; Ngũgĩ wa Thiong'o, *Decolonising the Mind: The Politics of Language in African Literature* (Portsmouth, NH: Heinemann, 1986); Marlene Nourbese Philip, *She Tries Her Tongue, Her Silence Softly Breaks* (Charlottetown, Prince Edward Island: Ragweed, 1989); and, more recently, Binyavanga Wainaina, "How to Write about Africa," *Granta* 92, Winter 2005.

20 See, for example, James Baldwin, *Notes on a Native Son* (Boston: Beacon, 2012); Marita Bonner, "On Being Young, a Woman, and Colored," in *Frye Street and Other Environs: The Collected Works of Marita Bonner*, ed. Joyce Flynn and Joyce Occomy Sticklin (Boston: Beacon, 1987), 3–8; Ta-Nehisi Coates, "The Black Journalist and the Racial Mountain," *Atlantic*, June 2, 2016 (which revises Langston Hughes's iconic "The Negro Artist and the Racial Mountain," *Nation*, June 23, 1926); Ralph Ellison, "Little Man at Chehaw Station," *American Scholar* 47, no. 1 (1978): 25–48, and "The World and the Jug," in *Shadow and Act* (New York: Vintage, 1995), 107–143; Roxane Gay, *Bad Feminist* (New York: Harper Perennial, 2014); Zadie Smith, "*Their Eyes Were Watching God*: What Does *Soulful* Mean?," in *Changing My Mind: Occasional Essays* (New York: Penguin, 2009), 3–13; and Williams, *Alchemy of Race and Rights*. I could say, too, that the notion of the essay's prerogative might be a way to navigate pronouns and audience in Claudia Rankine's *Citizen: An American Lyric* (Minneapolis: Graywolf, 2014).

21 The Eady quotation is from Toi Derricotte, *The Black Notebooks: An Interior Journey* (New York: W. W. Norton, 1997), 121–122. This consideration of audience echoes my explication of the watcherlessness of quiet in *The Sovereignty of Quiet: Beyond Resistance in Black Culture* (New Brunswick, NJ: Rutgers University Press, 2012), 22, and also acknowledges the particular work that scholars have done to explore the question in regard to the Black Arts/Aesthetic movement and to black nationalism in general; see especially Phillip Brian Harper, *Are We Not Men? Masculine Anxiety and the Problem of African-American Identity* (New York: Oxford University Press, 1996); Evie Shockley, *Renegade Poetics: Black Aesthetics and Formal Innovation in African American Poetry* (Iowa City: Iowa University Press, 2011); Margo Crawford, *Black Post-blackness: The Black Arts Movement and Twenty-First-Century Aesthetics* (Urbana: University of Illinois Press, 2017), especially the idiom of "public interiority" on 167; and GerShun Avilez, *Radical Aesthetics and Modern Black Nationalism* (Urbana: University of Illinois Press, 2016). Further consideration of (and caution about) racialized publicness can be found in Hortense J. Spillers, "*The Crisis of the Negro Intellectual*: A Post-date," in *Black, White, and in Color: Essays on American Literature and Culture* (Chicago: University of Chicago Press, 2003), 428–470; Mae G. Henderson, "Speaking in Tongues: Dialogics, Dialectics, and the Black Woman Writer's Literary Tradition," in *Changing Our Own Words*, ed. Cheryl Wall (New Brunswick, NJ: Rutgers University Press, 1989), particularly her argument about expressive ways that are "outside the realm of public discourse and foreign to the known tongues of humankind" (122); Patricia J. Williams's thinking about privacy and dispossession in *The Alchemy of Race and Rights*; and Simone Browne's explication of publicness

and surveilling terror in *Dark Matters: On the Surveillance of Blackness* (Durham, NC: Duke University Press, 2015). Finally, in regard to the essay genre, Gerald Early's "Gnostic or Gnomic?" (in *Speech and Power: The African American Essay and Its Cultural Content from Polemics to Pulpit*, ed. Gerald Early, 2 vols. [New York: Ecco, 1992], 1:vii–xv) considers how class inflects the matter of audience—as in for whom and to whom is the black essayist, as a public intellectual, writing. For more on thinking about the idiom of the public intellectual, also see Hazel Carby, *Race Men* (Cambridge, MA: Harvard University Press, 1998); Eric Lott, *The Disappearing Liberal Intellectual* (New York: Basic Books, 2006); Brittney C. Cooper, *Beyond Respectability: The Intellectual Thought of Race Women* (Urbana, IL: University of Illinois Press, 2017); and Robert Reid-Pharr, "Cosmopolitan Afrocentric Mulatto Intellectual," in *Black. Gay. Man*, 44–61.

22   In this way, the idiom of reading does not import the mess of racialized audience, but instead luxuriates in the relationality of the black one. Not reading for comprehension or translation, but reading as the thrall of being in relationality, where the speaker makes himself the subject and gives back to himself the right to be ontologically of—rather than before—the act of reading. My thinking about reading here is informed first by Moi's *Revolution of the Ordinary*, where she theorizes "reading as a practice of acknowledgement" (196), as well as by Guglielmo Cavallo and Roger Chartier, *A History of Reading in the West* (Amherst: University of Massachusetts Press, 2003), especially its introduction; Heather Williams, *Self-Taught* (Chapel Hill: University of North Carolina Press, 2007); Elizabeth McHenry, *Forgotten Readers* (Durham, NC: Duke University Press, 2002); Alan Jacob, *The Pleasures of Reading in an Age of Distraction* (Oxford: Oxford University Press, 2011); Tara Bynum, "Phillis Wheatley's Pleasures," *Boston University World of Ideas*, October 22, 2017 (and her thinking about pleasure in "Phillis Wheatley on Friendship," *Legacy* 31, no. 1 [2014]: 42–51); and even works with which I disagree, like Robert Alter, *The Pleasures of Reading in an Ideological Age* (New York: W. W. Norton, 1996). I am also inspired by a cohort of black writers' thinking about the dynamics of writing: Jamaica Kincaid's characterization of the "perfect reader" in *My Brother* (New York: Farrar, Straus and Giroux, 1998); Patricia J. Williams's extended thinking about writing as "sacrifice, not denial" (92) in *The Alchemy of Race and Rights*; Marlene Nourbese Philip's still-compelling thesis on writing as spy-like in *She Tries Her Tongue*; James Baldwin's specific exploration of writing and being in "Everybody's Protest Novel" (in *Notes of a Native Son*, 13–23); and Harryette Mullen, "Imagining the Unimagined Reader: Writing to the Unborn and Including the Excluded," *boundary 2* 26, no. 1 (1999): 198–203. On witnessing, see James Baldwin's work, especially his articulation of the term in the preface to *Evidence of Things Not Seen* (New York: Henry Holt, 1995), xiii–xvi; Joshua Miller, "The Discovery of What It Means to Be a Witness," in *James Baldwin Now*, ed. Dwight McBride (New York: New York University Press, 1999), 331–359, and Ed Pavlić, "Open the Unusual Door: Visions from the Dark Window in Yusef Komunyakaa's Early Poems," *Callaloo* 28, no. 3 (2005): 780–796 (even as both essays explore witnessing by focusing on what Baldwin does for his readers); Naisargi Dave's caution about the limits of witnessing in "Witness: Humans, Animals, and the Politics of Becoming," *Cultural Anthropology* 29, no. 3 (2014): 433–456; and Giorgio Agamben's formulation in *Remnants of Auschwitz*:

The Witness and the Archive (New York: Zone Books, 2002), esp. 25–40. Finally, the consideration of reading here includes aspects of the arguments about criticism and critique, including those made by Eve K. Sedgwick, Stephen Best, Heather Love, Sharon Marcus, and Rita Felski; see Moi, *Revolution of the Ordinary*, chap. 8, for a crisp summary.

23 Trethewey's comment is from her brief introduction to the Poem column in the *New York Times* Sunday Magazine, July 5, 2015.

24 The essay is a text of relation, and relation is a poetic habitat according to Glissant ("poetics of relation") and Martin Buber (relation's surprises are "queer lyric dramatic episodes" [*I and Thou*, trans. Walter Arnold Kaufmann [New York: Touchstone, 1996], 84). In making this point, I want to acknowledge that I am focusing on essays from the late twentieth century, especially in light of the historical argument Cheryl Wall makes about the difference that social/political time makes in essaying (see *On Freedom and the Will to Adorn*). And still, my larger claim about the essay and aliveness—about the philosophical value of the personal—is not specific to era. Publishing and appraisal are matters of temporality and of history, but I don't believe they overdetermine what lives in the human or how the human comes to understand and engage their being alive.

25 Though I am not reading closely any essay by James Baldwin, this sense of openness and terror is explicated superbly in "Nothing Personal," which is cited briefly in the next chapter.

26 Benjamin Demott, "Passing," review of *The Black Notebooks: An Interior Journey*, by Toi Derricotte, *New York Times*, November 2, 1997.

27 The Kafka quotation is from *Wedding Preparations in the Country and Other Posthumous Prose Writings* (London: Secker and Warburg, 1954), 324. French feminist theorist Hélène Cixous famously cites this passage in describing writing as descent; see Cixous, *Three Steps on the Ladder of Writing* (New York: Columbia University Press, 1994), 5–6.

28 In thinking about the creative potency of the speaker, I am drawing especially on the ways Philip imagines the black woman as an artist in "The Absence of Writing or How I Almost Became a Spy," in *She Tries Her Tongue*, 10–25. Indeed, in "The Black Woman as Artist: The Queer Erotics of Rita Dove's Beulah," *Tulsa Studies in Women's Literature* 37, no. 2 (2018): 397–418, I argue that black women's criticism in the 1980s "make[s] the philosophical case that negotiations of black femaleness are akin to the making of art—that black femaleness is ontology and that ontology is creativity" (403). (There are striking parallels between the threats that domestic family dynamics make to black female girlhood in Dove's collection and in Derricotte's essay.) Also, Derricotte describes distance and pain as a function in her lived relationship with her father: "My father encouraged me to have an emotional distance between myself and things that other people would call *gruesome*. . . . My father could also make people suffer so much. He would put my mom down for crying, and when he beat me, he wouldn't let me cry. This was a very powerful form of control, and it cut me off from my emotions" (Toi Derricotte, "Toi Derricotte and the Psychology of the Sublime: An Interview," by Jessica M. Brophy, *African American Review* 50, no. 3 [2017]: 252).

29 In *Animacies: Biopolitics, Racial Mattering, and Queer Affect* (Durham, NC: Duke University Press, 2012), Mel Y. Chen posits that "first- and second-person animacies,

all else being equal, tend to value higher in animacy than third-person ones" (26), though I think the case for third-personness is different in a black world context. Derricotte describes childhood abuse—though not necessarily sexual abuse—in various entries in *The Black Notebooks*.

30 My use of "opulence" is inspired by the MC in Jennie Livingston, *Paris Is Burning* (Burbank, CA: Miramax, 1990), and echoes Cheryl Wall's adoption of Zora Neale Hurston's phrase "the will to adorn" as part of the title for her book on the art of the essay, the aesthetic overture of the genre; see *On Freedom and the Will to Adorn*. (Also note Wall's attention to "the [essay] form [as a] window . . . into the writer's mind" [7].) The comment about thought and quotation marks borrows from Edward St. Aubyn's review of Javier Marías, *The Infatuations*, which claims that Marías blurs "the distinction between what is said and what is only thought" by using quotation marks for both (*New York Times*, August 11, 2013, 8).

31 This discussion of the archive, time, fabulation, and incompleteness recalls the discussion of time and subjunctivity in chapter 3 (see the endnote there) and also invokes Saidiya Hartman's explication of the intersection between fabulation and archives in "Venus in Two Acts," *Small Axe* 12, no. 2 (2008): 1–14; and Aimee Bahng's formulation of fabulation and fabrication in "Specters of the Pacific: Salt Fish Drag and Atomic Hauntologies in the Era of Genetic Modification," *Journal of American Studies* 49, no. 4 (2015): 663–683. Also see Cvetkovich, *Archive of Feelings*; Achille Mbembe, "The Power of the Archive and Its Limits," in *Refiguring the Archive*, ed. Carolyn Hamilton et al. (Berlin: Springer, 2002), 19–26; and David Scott, "Introduction: On the Archaeologies of Black Memory," *Small Axe* 12, no. 2 (2008): v–xvi. We might think of Derricotte's— and Shepherd's—aesthetic praxis as one of "inquiry and assembly" in the way that Paul C. Taylor uses that term (drawing from Stuart Hall); see Paul C. Taylor, *Black Is Beautiful: A Philosophy of Black Aesthetics* (Hoboken, NJ: Wiley-Blackwell, 2016), 3. Or as the phenomenology of incoherent being from Lauren Berlant's formulation in talking about sex, such that the speaker is "not . . . shocked to discover their incoherence or the incoherence of the world; they find it comic, feel a little ashamed of it, or are interested in it, excited by it, and exhausted by it too" (Berlant and Edelman, *Sex, or the Unbearable* 6). Finally, in Derricotte's passage, one can't help but hear echoes of Immanuel Kant, Jacques Lacan, Emmanuel Levinas, and Audre Lorde.

32 Here I am thinking especially in the context Muñoz's articulates in *Cruising Utopia*: "The present must be known in relation to the alternative temporal and spatial maps provided by a perception of past and future affective worlds" (27). I read Muñoz's caution against the present not as a rejection of feeling and aesthetics—he makes a case for the quotidian, after all, a case that resonates with the everyday matter of the personal essay—but as a commitment to a queer politics of pleasure. I am also thinking in regard to Sara Ahmed's thinking about the present in *Queer Phenomenology*.

33 Carl H. Klaus, in "Toward a Collective Poetics of the Essay" (in *Essayists on the Essay: Montaigne to Our Time*, ed. Carl H. Klaus and Ned Stuckey-French [Iowa City: University of Iowa Press, 2012]), asserts that the speaker seems to "speak methodically unmethodically" (xx), which is a way to project the "quality of the author's mind" (xxiii). The reference to "after" engages the case that Theodor Adorno makes for the time of the essay; see the discussion in chapter 3.

34 See Giorgio Agamben, *Means without End: Notes on Politics* (Minneapolis: University of Minnesota Press, 2000).

35 Thanks to John Casey for helping me clarify this claim. See Koritha Mitchell's explication of the vagaries of evidence in her introduction to *Living with Lynching: African American Lynching Plays, Performance, and Citizenship, 1890–1930* (Urbana: University of Illinois Press, 2012).

36 I had intended to write about Als's *The Women*, though the arc of this chapter made more sense with Shepherd's and Derricotte's shorter essays. But Als's prose practice is superb, since even his argumentative essays tremble with the wiliness of a free-minded speaker. For an excellent recent example, see his stunning personal history essay "My Mother's Dreams for Her Son, and All Black Children," *New Yorker*, June 29, 2020. Thanks, also, to Devon Clifton for thinking about free black being.

Chapter 5. Aliveness and Ethics

1 Toni Morrison, "A Conversation with Toni Morrison," by Bill Moyers, in *Conversations with Toni Morrison*, ed. Danille K. Taylor-Guthrie (Jackson: University Press of Mississippi, 1994), 272. Thanks to Mike King for company in revising this chapter.

2 See James Phelan, "Sethe's Choice: *Beloved* and the Ethics of Reading," *Style* 32, no. 2 (1998): 318–333; Mariangela Palladino, *Ethics and Aesthetics in Toni Morrison's Fiction* (Leiden, Netherlands: Brill, 2018); and Yvette Christiansë, *Toni Morrison: An Ethical Poetics* (New York: Fordham University Press, 2012), though all three works focus on the ethics of Morrison's narrative choices. Also see Shatema Threadcraft's reading of Margaret Garner's case in *Intimate Justice: The Black Female Body and the Body Politic* (Oxford: Oxford University Press, 2016). One of the hallmarks of *Beloved* is that Morrison leaves the question of rightness open: "She [Baby Suggs] could not approve or condemn Sethe's rough choice" (180). Frank B. Wilderson III, in *Afropessimism* (New York: Liveright, 2020), reads Morrison's comment in regard to death as sanctuary (92)—that is, he focuses on one half of Morrison's statement as I choose to focus on the other. Finally, I am inspired by Farah Jasmine Griffin's study of the literary ethical in her new work, as reflected in her talk "In Pursuit of Justice and Grace: Reflections on the African-American Literary Tradition," delivered April 17, 2018, at the University of Massachusetts Amherst.

3 James Baldwin, "An Open Letter to My Sister Angela Y. Davis," in *The Cross of Redemption: Uncollected Writings* (New York: Vintage Books, 2011), 257.

4 Questions about the racial limits of ethics run through much of black critical studies, including the field of black pessimism. See a number of authors cited earlier (especially in the introduction), including Lewis R. Gordon, Nahum Dmitri Chandler, Denise Ferriera da Silva, Frank B. Wilderson III, David Ross Fryer, Achille Mbembe (*Critique of Black Reason* [Durham, NC: Duke University Press, 2017], esp. chap. 1), Lindon W. Barrett, Ashon T. Crawley, Terrion L. Williamson, Calvin Warren, Shatema Threadcraft, Paul C. Taylor, and Fred Moten (especially "The Case of Blackness," *Criticism* 50, no. 2 (2008): 177–218). Also see the case that Debra Walker King makes about the utility of black pain in *African Americans and the Culture of Pain* (Charlottesville: University of Virginia Press, 2008). Central in my thinking about

ethics is the notion of care articulated in Christina Sharpe, *In the Wake: On Blackness and Being* (Durham, NC: Duke University Press, 2016).

5 In *Toward a Global Idea of Race* (Minneapolis: University of Minnesota Press, 2007), Silva argues that there is no axiology for blackness in a racist world; she extends this argument in "Toward a Black Feminist Poethics: The Quest(ion) of Blackness toward the End of the World," *Black Scholar* 44, no. 2 (2014): 81–97. Also see Lindon W. Barrett's extensive consideration of black (non)value as a function of modern coloniality (*Blackness and Value: Seeing Double* [Cambridge: Cambridge University Press, 1998]). My own interest is in an idiom of value that could be imagined as inherent in human life, even if the terms of inherency get distorted by the ideologies of modernity. As such, I mostly use pronouns that avoid imposing a gender binary—"themself" and "their" in the singular case, or "they" to speak of the singular one. This doing, though sometimes ungrammatical, is in keeping with the open quality of a black world imaginary I am exploring in the book.

6 James Baldwin, *Notes of a Native Son* (Boston: Beacon, 2012), 23.

7 I am thinking here in the tradition of ordinary language philosophy; see Toril Moi, *Revolution of the Ordinary: Literary Studies after Wittgenstein, Austin, and Cavell* (Chicago: University of Chicago Press, 2017), especially her thinking with Simone Weil, Iris Murdoch, and Cora Diamond in chap. 10; Stanley Cavell, *Must We Mean What We Say?* (Cambridge: Cambridge University Press, 2002); and Cavell, *Themes Out of School: Effects and Causes* (Chicago: University of Chicago Press, 1984). Also see Kristie Dotson's argument about black women and livable philosophy in "How Is This Paper Philosophy?," *Comparative Philosophy* 3, no. 1 (2012): 3–29; Dotson, "'Thinking Familiar with the Interstitial': An Introduction," *Hypatia* 29, no. 1 (2014): 1–17; V. Denise James, "Musing: A Black Feminist Philosopher: Is That Possible?," *Hypatia* 29, no. 1 (2014): 189–195; Devonya N. Havis, "'Now, How You Sound': Considering a Different Philosophical Praxis," *Hypatia* 29, no. 1 (2014): 237–252; and the case for "ordinary ethics" in Michael Lambek, ed., *Ordinary Ethics: Anthropology, Language, and Action* (New York: Fordham University Press, 2010) and in Veena Das's essay "Ordinary Ethics" in *A Companion to Moral Anthropology*, ed. Didier Fassin (Hoboken, NJ: Wiley-Blackwell, 2012), 133–149.

8 There is a parallel question shaped by "why"—as in "Why do I live?"—but the impulse of such a question leans toward causation, a dangerous inclination as Morrison's narrator Claudia tells us in *The Bluest Eye* (New York: Vintage, 2007). My study of these ideas has been shaped by Sarah Bakewell's terrific *At the Existentialist Café: Freedom, Being, and Apricot Cocktails with Jean-Paul Sartre, Simone de Beauvoir, Albert Camus, Martin Heidegger, Maurice Merleau-Ponty and Others* (New York: Other Press, 2016), existentialism being important to questions about human life. Also see Todd May, *Gilles Deleuze: An Introduction* (Cambridge: Cambridge University Press, 2005), which explores the role that "How might one live?" plays in Continental philosophy and in Deleuzean thinking; Daniel W. Smith, "Deleuze and Derrida, Immanence and Transcendence: Two Directions in Recent French Thought," *Contemporary Philosophy* 11 (2007): 123–130, which distinguishes between the ethical as a transcendent imperative ("What must I do?") as well as a political specificity ("What can I do?"); Michel Foucault, "On the Genealogy of Ethics: An Overview of Work in Prog-

ress," in *The Foucault Reader*, ed. Paul Rabinow (New York: Pantheon Books, 1984), 340–372; Deleuze's reading of Spinoza's *Ethics* in *Spinoza: Practical Philosophy* (San Francisco: City Lights, 2001), chap. 2; and Gayatri Chakravorty Spivak's engagement of Derrida in "Responsibility," *boundary 2* 21, no. 3 (1994): 19–64.

9   Sula's awareness of her life as a force is related to her accounting of the moment of Chicken Little's death.

10 See the engagement of Sula's moral agency in chapter 2. And in regard to the ethic of full living in Morrison's works, see David Z. Wehner, "'To Live This Life Intensely and Well': The Rebirth of Milkman Dead in Toni Morrison's *Song of Solomon*," in *Toni Morrison and the Bible: Contested Intertextualities*, ed. Shirley A. Stave (Bern, Switzerland: Peter Lang, 2006), 71–93.

11 I am grateful to Lubabah Chowdhury, whose question and email (April 2017) helped me clarify this point, as I am to Diego Millan for a sustained conversation about care and regard.

12 See Jane Bennett's arguments about the ethical and the affective in *Vibrant Matter: A Political Ecology of Things* (Durham, NC: Duke University Press, 2010) and *The Enchantment of Modern Life: Attachments, Crossings, and Ethics* (Princeton, NJ: Princeton University Press, 2001), as well as the cases that Sara Ahmed (*The Cultural Politics of Emotions* [Edinburgh: Edinburgh University Press, 2004]) and Anne Cvetkovich (*An Archive of Feelings: Trauma, Sexuality, and Lesbian Public Cultures* [Durham, NC: Duke University Press, 2003]) make for studying emotions.

13 As sometimes translated, Socrates is recorded in Plato's *Apology of Socrates* (line 38a) as saying, "The unexamined life is not worth living," an idea that broadly characterizes the work of philosophy. In addition to the works cited earlier in the body and in succeeding endnotes, my thinking on study is informed by Stefano Harney and Fred Moten in *The Undercommons: Fugitive Planning and Black Study* (New York: Minor Compositions, 2013), especially their distinction between critique and study. I am also drawing on poet Mary Oliver's invitations to pay attention, especially in the poems "The Summer Day" and "Wild Geese," in *New and Selected Poems* (Boston: Beacon, 2004), 94, 110; and on my thinking about the nature of prayer in Kevin Quashie, *The Sovereignty of Quiet: Beyond Resistance in Black Culture* (New Brunswick, NJ: Rutgers University Press, 2012). I also come to this notion of studying through reading bell hooks, especially *Sisters of the Yam: Black Women and Self-Recovery* (Boston: South End, 1993) and *Teaching to Transgress: Education as the Practice of Freedom* (New York: Routledge, 1994).

14 Nikky Finney, *Head Off and Split* (Evanston, IL: TriQuarterly Books / Northwestern University Press, 2011), unpaginated final page.

15 See *Head Off and Split*, especially the poems "Resurrection of the Errand Girl: An Introduction" and "Instruction, Final: To Brown Poets from Black Girl with Silver Leica," 3–4, 97.

16 While I keep in mind the incisive critiques of work—see, for example, Jackie Wang, *Carceral Capitalism* (South Pasadena: Semiotext(e), 2018)—my own interest in recovering the term draws on Giorgio Agamben's notion of inoperativity as explored in Sergie Prozorov's reading in *Agamben and Politics: A Critical Introduction* (London: Edinburgh University Press, 2014). Also see Joshua Chambers-Letson's terrific explication of Nina Simone's minoritarian work performance in *After the Party: A Manifesto for*

Queer of Color Life (New York: New York University Press, 2018), 37–80; and Kathi Weeks, *The Problem with Work: Feminism, Marxism, Antiwork Politics, and Postwork Imaginaries* (Durham, NC: Duke University Press, 2011), especially her thinking about the terms "work" and "labor" in the introduction (1–36). Echoed here, too, is my thinking with Saidiya Hartman's brief prose-poem "Manual for General Housework" (in *Wayward Lives, Beautiful Experiments: Intimate Histories of Social Upheaval* [New York: W. W. Norton, 2019], 77–79), which conceptualizes black female labor via terms of subjection, even as the histories characterized in the book suggest other—richer— possibilities for thinking about what black women do with their hands.

17 Vinson Cunningham calls Baldwin's clauses "Jamesian," though he means this in a different sense from my attention to Baldwin's syntax. Writing in the essay "Why Ta-Nehisi Coates Isn't Our James Baldwin," Cunningham claims that "Baldwin's Jamesian sentences are long, but long because they are almost legal in intent: Each dependent clause hedges, qualifies, clarifies, and eliminates room for specious readings. (Coates recently tweeted his admiration of these rhetorical feats.) When Baldwin finally hits the period, his meaning is bare, and the only option left to the reader is to decide whether to agree" (*New York*, August 5, 2015). For more on the relationship between Baldwin's aesthetic and that of Henry James, see Robert J. Corber, *Homosexuality in Cold War America: Resistance and the Crisis of Masculinity* (Durham, NC: Duke University Press, 1997), chap. 6; as well as James Baldwin, "An Interview with James Baldwin on Henry James," by David Adam Leeming, *Henry James Review* 8, no. 1 (1986): 47–56.

18 Thanks to a student in my undergraduate Black Poetics class, Semi Oloko, for suggesting the Judas inference.

19 For more on Clifton's use of Lucifer, see Mandolin Brassaw, "The Light That Came to Lucille Clifton: Beyond Lucille and Lucifer," *MELUS* 37, no. 3 (2012): 43–70. Satan, in book 5 of John Milton's *Paradise Lost*, declaims God's authority by disavowing that he, Satan, originated from God. "No one before us," Satan advances. Scholars see this as Satan's hubris, arrogance, and failing, but Clifton, in imagining Lucifer, embraces this notion of automony, a self-authoring that doesn't preclude relation to the world. Also see Hilary Holladay, *Wild Blessings: The Poetry of Lucille Clifton* (Baton Rouge: Louisiana State University Press, 2004), esp. chaps. 5, 6; and Rachel Elizabeth Harding, "Authority, History, and Everyday Mysticism in the Poetry of Lucille Clifton: A Womanist View," *Meridians* 12, no. 1 (2014): 36–57. Thanks to Marney Rathbun for a shared love of Clifton's Lucifer poems in her undergraduate thesis work (and in classes)—and for casting Lucifer's illumination in a gift I will remember forever.

20 The quotation is from Moi, *Revolution of the Ordinary*, 91; Moi also refers to such inhabitance as being lost (89). For more on loneliness as a feature of creative and philosophical doing, see Denise Riley, "The Right to Be Lonely," in *Impersonal Passion: Language as Affect* (Durham, NC: Duke University Press, 2005), 49–58, the last paragraph of which mirrors the two iterations of loneliness in the coda of Morrison's *Beloved*; Wynton Marsalis, "Premature Autopsies (Sermon)," which includes the phrase "the loneliness that mastery demands" (track 4 on *The Majesty of the Blues* [Columbia Records, 1989]); and Jean-Jacques Rousseau, *Reveries of the Solitary Walker* (London:

Penguin Classics, 1980). Also see Darius Bost's exploration of "loneliness as black gay longing" (23) in *Evidence of Being: The Black Gay Cultural Renaissance and the Politics of Violence* (Chicago: University of Chicago Press, 2019). I am grateful to Andre C. Willis and Jacques Khalip for conversations that amplified my thinking here.

21   Thanks to Quinn Anex-Ries for reminding me of this passage.

22   My engagement of loneliness gestures, in part, to the question of community and collectivity in black study/studies. Though the distinction between community and collectivity is addressed in the conclusion, I want to acknowledge here some scholarly thinking about collectivity and black studies. For example, Hortense J. Spillers, in *"The Crisis of the Negro Intellectual*: A Post-date" (*Black, White, and in Color: Essays on American Literature and Culture* [Chicago: University of Chicago Press, 2003], 428–470), reminds us that Harold Cruse's call for black studies was toward many blacknesses, not blackness as singular legible value—black study as a praxis of black being, rather than black study intended to produce a recuperative idea of blackness. A similar claim toward multiplicity runs through Harney and Moten, *Undercommons*, and is amplified in Moten's critique of Hannah Arendt's *Of Violence*: *"Black study, in its turning over of the very ground of the distinction between intelligence and its Other*; which is to say black presence, in its continual displacement and deferral of here, now, and the subject which they determine and by which they are determined; which is to say blackness, which in its communicability is not reducible to the black people" (*The Universal Machine* [Durham, NC: Duke University Press, 2018], 67; emphasis added). Also see Christina Sharpe, "Black Studies: In the Wake," *Black Scholar* 44, no. 2 (2014): 59–69; Jared Sexton's description of black studies in "The Social Life of Social Death: On Afro-pessimism and Black Optimism," *Intensions* 5 (2011), http://www.yorku.ca/intent/issue5/articles/jaredsexton.php; and Stephen Michael Best's caution about the cult of voice and cult of death (*None like Us: Blackness, Belonging, Aesthetic Life* [Durham, NC: Duke University Press, 2018]).

23   See James Deetz, *In Small Things Forgotten: An Archaeology of Early American Life* (New York: Anchor Books, 1996); David K. Wiggins, "The Play of Slave Children in the Plantation Communities of the Old South, 1820–1860," *Journal of Sport History* 7, no. 2 (1980): 21–39; Wilma King, *Stolen Childhood: Slave Youth in Nineteenth-Century America* (Bloomington: Indiana University Press, 1995); and Kym S. Rice, *World of a Slave: Encyclopedia of the Material Life of Slaves in the United States* (Santa Barbara: ABC-CLIO, 2011), esp. 187–188. In my estimation, "regardless" is not akin to the term "unapologetic" that circulates in contemporary popular culture. As Wesley Morris concludes in his First Words essay "Guilt Free" (from the *New York Times* Sunday Magazine, July 30, 2017), "There's something celebratory in the phrase ["unapologetic"], *but it's also defensive and defiant*. Nearly all of this work has white patronage. So a great deal of the astonishment over the proud detail of its blackness comes with an awareness of a white gaze. Blackness was never forced to owe black people an apology for anything" (13; emphasis added). My argument for "regardless" imagines a black world. In a way, one could say that "regardless" is distinct from the term "despite" and could draw a parallel with Reginald Shepherd's reference, in the previous chapter, to the philosophical condition of "as if" being distinct from the phrase "if only."

24 Baby Suggs could be read here and elsewhere as a practitioner of Aristotelean virtue ethics, particularly when she claims, "Everything depends on knowing how much," and "Good is knowing when to stop" (87). For a recent exploration of Baby Suggs as a source of ethical consideration, see Pamela M. Hall, "The 'Desolated Center': Baby Suggs, Holy, in Toni Morrison's Beloved," in *Sainthood and Race: Marked Flesh, Holy Flesh*, ed. Molly H. Bassett and Vincent W. Lloyd [New York: Routledge, 2014], 164–181). On virtue ethics in general, see Roger Crisp and Michael Slote, eds., *Virtue Ethics* (Oxford: Oxford University Press, 1997); Lawrence Blum, "Racial Virtues," in *Working Virtue: Virtue Ethics and Contemporary Moral Problems*, ed. Rebecca L. Walker and Philip J. Ivanhoe (Oxford: Clarendon, 2007), 225–250; and Andre C. Willis, *Toward a Humean True Religion: Genuine Theism, Moderate Hope, and Practical Morality* (University Park: Pennsylvania State University Press, 2016), esp. chap. 4. One problem in the discourse of ethics is that blackness (or race, racialization, racism) is rarely considered, and when such happens, blackness amplifies the question of virtue for an unmarked white subject rather than in regard to a black subject (as is the case with Blum's otherwise compelling essay).

25 See Katie Cannon's iconic *Black Womanist Ethics* (Eugene, OR: Wipf and Stock, 2006), as well as Katie Cannon, Emilie M. Townes, and Angela D. Simms, eds., *Womanist Theological Ethics: A Reader* (Louisville, KY: Westminster John Knox, 2011). My argument here is cautious about the terms of respectability, not unlike the caution in Evelyn Brooks Higginbotham, *Righteous Discontent: The Women's Movement in the Black Baptist Church, 1880–1920* (Cambridge, MA: Harvard University Press, 1994). In the final chapter of that work, Higginbotham is attentive to the conservative impulses of the "politics of respectability," though sometimes readers miss this complexity. For other considerations of respectability, see Brittney Cooper, *Beyond Respectability: The Intellectual Thought of Race Women* (Urbana: University of Illinois Press, 2017); Brando Simeo Starkey, "Respectability Politics: How a Flawed Conversation Sabotages Black Lives," Undefeated, December 12, 2016, https://theundefeated.com/features/respectability-politics-how-a-flawed-conversation-sabotages-black-lives/; Cathy J. Cohen, "Deviance as Resistance: A New Research Agenda for the Study of Black Politics," *Du Bois Review* 1, no. 1 (2004): 27–45; and especially Aimee Meredith Cox, *Shapeshifters* (Durham, NC: Duke University Press, 2015). This matter of dignity is one that Imani Perry explores well via the notion of black formalism in *May We Forever Stand: A History of the Black National Anthem* (Chapel Hill: University of North Carolina Press, 2018) and that my colleague Aliyyah Abdur-Rahman explores in her current work on black feminism and regard. And though I have made overtures to ordinary language philosophy in this work, I am also compelled by American pragmatism; see especially V. Denise James, "Theorizing Black Feminist Pragmatism," *Journal of Speculative Philosophy* 23, no. 2 (2009): 92–99; Havis, "'Now, How You Sound'"; and Eddie S. Glaude Jr., *In a Shade of Blue: Pragmatism and the Politics of Black America* (Chicago: University of Chicago Press, 2008). In thinking about temporality and phenomenology, see Michelle M. Wright, *Physics of Blackness: Beyond the Middle Passage Epistemology* (Minneapolis: University of Minnesota Press, 2015), especially her notion of Epiphenomenal time and her explication of blackness through performance theory; José Esteban Muñoz, *Cruis-*

ing Utopia: The Then and There of Queer Futurity (New York: New York University Press, 2009); John Manoussakis, *The Ethics of Time* (New York: Bloomsbury, 2017); Heather Dyke, ed., *Time and Ethics: Essays at the Intersection* (Berlin: Springer, 2003); Michael R. Kelly, *Phenomenology and the Problem of Time* (London: Palgrave, 2016); Matthew Clemente, "Introduction: On *the Ethics of Time,*" *Journal of Theoretical and Philosophical Psychology* 38, no. 2 (2018): 92–95; and Robin Le Poidevin, "The Experience and Perception of Time," *The Stanford Encyclopedia of Philosophy* (Summer 2015), ed. Edward N. Zalta, https://plato.stanford.edu/archives/sum2015/entries/time -experience. In asserting the pronoun "one," I am thinking about Stephen Best's critique of "we" in *None like Us*, as I am also thinking about the way Stefano Harney and Fred Moten deploy "we" in a relational commons in *Undercommons*. (This is discussed further in the conclusion.) Finally, I am grateful to John Casey, Kristen Maye, and Hilary Rasch for conversations that helped my thinking here, and to Mike King for his engagement with the idea of regard, which, though different from my own, is companionate.

26   Toni Cade Bambara, "An Interview with Toni Cade Bambara," by Kay Bonetti, in *Conversations with Toni Cade Bambara*, ed. Thabiti Lewis (Jackson: University Press of Mississippi, 2012), 35.

27   Sylvia Wynter, "Unparalleled Catastrophe for Our Species? Or, to Give Humanness a Different Future: Conversations," by Katherine McKittrick, in *Sylvia Wynter: On Being Human as Praxis*, ed. Katherine McKittrick (Durham, NC: Duke University Press, 2015), 23. I know that Wynter talks about the structures of the modern world, but I also find her work compelling for its commitment to the enchanting idea of the human.

28   My citation of "measure" invokes uses of the term by Audre Lorde ("Uses of the Erotic," in *Sister Outsider: Essays and Speeches* [New York: Crossing, 1984], 57) and Toni Morrison ("The Nobel Lecture in Literature," in *What Moves at the Margin: Selected Nonfiction*, ed. Carolyn C. Denard [Jackson: University Press of Mississippi, 2008], 203).

29   The letter is addressed, "Dear God. Dear stars, dear trees, dear sky, dear peoples. Dear Everything. Dear God" (242).

30   On elliptical sentences, see Richard Gunter, "Elliptical Sentences in American English," *Lingua* 12, no. 2 (1963): 137–150; and Richard J. Stainton, *Words and Thoughts: Subsentences, Ellipsis, and the Philosophy of Language* (Oxford: Oxford University Press, 2009), esp. chaps. 5, 6.

31   For another beautiful understanding of work, see Philip Levine's iconic poem "What Work Is," in *What Work Is* (New York: Alfred A. Knopf, 2004), 18–19.

32   See, for example, Ruth Franklin, "Tracy K. Smith, America's Poet Laureate, Is a Woman with a Mission," *New York Times* Sunday Magazine, April 10, 2018.

33   See Robert Frost, "Mowing," in *The Poetry of Robert Frost: The Collected Poems*, ed. Edward Connery Lathem (New York: Henry Holt, 1969), 17.

34   Neal's statement is a riff off of Wittgenstein's equation from *Tractatus Logico-Philosophicus*. Also see Leonard Harris's discussion of Alain Locke's articulation of art, work, and transformation in *The Philosophy of Alain Locke: Harlem Renaissance and Beyond* (Philadelphia: Temple University Press, 1989).

35 I am borrowing the unattributed phrase from Cora Diamond, "Having a Rough Story about What Moral Philosophy Is," *New Literary History* 15, no. 1 (1983): 162, an idiom Diamond gleans from Iris Murdoch's work, particularly R. W. Hepburn and Iris Murdoch, "Symposium: Vision and Choice in Morality," *Proceedings of the Aristotelian Society* 30 (1956): 14–58. Also see Anthony Reed, *Freedom Time: The Poetics and Politics of Black Experimental Writing* (Baltimore: Johns Hopkins University Press, 2014), which argues that "for Black Arts theorists the poem relies on the transcendental facticity of words to achieve its reconstructive work: the encounter with the poem reactivates and participates in the inner lives of words and those who use them" (30–31). Later, Reed echoes Diamond's phrase in describing black lyric poetics as "textural and textual . . . worldliness and wordliness" (31). On narrative and ethics, see the special issue "Literature and/as Moral Philosophy," *New Literary History* 15, no. 1 (1983); Adam Zachary Newton, *Narrative Ethics* (Cambridge, MA: Harvard University Press, 1997), as well as Daniel R. Schwarz's extended review essay "Performative Saying and the Ethics of Reading," *Narrative* 5, no. 2 (1997): 188–206, which considers Newton's work; and Candace Vogler, "The Moral of the Story," *Critical Inquiry* 34, no. 1 (2007): 5–35. More classically and in regard to aesthetics, see Yuriko Saiko, *Aesthetics of the Familiar: Everyday Life and World-Making* (Oxford: Oxford University Press, 2017); Muñoz, *Cruising Utopia*; Wayne C. Booth, *The Company We Keep* (Berkeley: University of California Press, 1989); Booth, *The Rhetoric of Fiction* (Chicago: University of Chicago Press, 1983); Gayatri Chakravorty Spivak, *An Aesthetic Education in an Era of Globalization* (Cambridge, MA: Harvard University Press, 2013); J. Hillis Miller, *The Ethics of Reading: Kant, De Man, Eliot, Trollope, James, and Benjamin* (New York: Columbia University Press, 1989); and Suzanne Keen, *Empathy and the Novel* (Oxford: Oxford University Press, 2010). My thinking on ethics is also informed by Stephen Darwall, *The Second-Person Standpoint* (Cambridge, MA: Harvard University Press, 2009); Alan H. Goldman, *Reasons from Within: Desires and Values* (Oxford: Oxford University Press, 2009); Thomas E. Hill Jr., *Autonomy and Self-Respect* (Cambridge: Cambridge University Press, 1991); Tommie Shelby, "The Ethics of Uncle Tom's Children," *Critical Inquiry* 38, no. 3 (2012): 513–532; Iris Young, *Justice and the Politics of Difference* (Princeton, NJ: Princeton University Press, 2011); Jeffrey Alexander, "Theorizing the Good Society: Hermeneutic, Normative and Empirical Discourses," *Canadian Journal of Sociology* 25, no. 3 (2000): 271–310; Jeanne Randolph, *Ethics of Luxury: Materialism and Imagination* (Toronto: YYZ Books, 2007), especially the discussion of "ethical imagining" on 65–83; and Rosi Braidotti, *Transpositions: On Nomadic Ethics* (Cambridge, UK: Polity, 2006). Thanks to Lorne Falk for the Randolph and Braidotti suggestions and John Casey for research assistance.

36 I am inspired here by Paul C. Taylor's work in *Black Is Beautiful: A Philosophy of Black Aesthetics* (Hoboken, NJ: Wiley-Blackwell, 2016), especially his discussion of W. E. B. DuBois's argument for art as propaganda. In part, Taylor makes the case for black aesthetics as an ethical encounter with freedom, "self-legislation in the face of, and in recognition of, the wider resources for seeking the truth and pursuing the good" (97). The Spillers citation is from her essay "*The Crisis of the Negro Intellectual*: A Postdate" (in *Black, White, and in Color*), where she wards against being misread as naïvely individualistic by arguing that intellectual doing is part of "an *ensemble* of efforts"

(456; emphasis in the original). Overall, in this chapter, I am collating aesthetics, ethics, and relation through the figure of the black reader as a one; see the endnote about reading in the previous chapter. In addition to Taylor's book, I am inspired by Édouard Glissant, who, in *Poetics of Relation*, trans. Betsy Wing (Ann Arbor: University of Michigan Press, 1997), notes that "[relation] is an aesthetics of turbulence whose corresponding ethics is not provided in advance" (155); and by the sustained implicit argument Phillip Brian Harper makes about the reader/viewer and critical capacity in *Abstractionist Aesthetics: Artistic Form and Social Critique in African American Culture* (New York: New York University Press, 2015), esp. chap. 1. I am grateful to Kiran Saili and Marah Nagelhout for conversations about Taylor's book.

37   I would be remiss if I didn't mention again bell hooks's *Sisters of the Yam*, which helped me understand the role literature could play in imagining black oneness. I cite hooks's work more fully in the conclusion.

38   I am reading the openness of this prayer in conjunction with the ambivalent "blessing" Clifton describes in the poem "wild blessings." One way to think of Clifton's engagement with ethics is through an ideology of hope, as Tiffany Eberle Kriner does in "Conjuring Hope in a Body: Lucille Clifton's Eschatology," *Christianity and Literature* 54, no. 2 (2005): 185–208. The use of water here is akin to the abyss in Glissant's opening of *Poetics of Relation*, as well as water as a scene of blackness in Omise'eke Natasha Tinsley, "Black Atlantic, Queer Atlantic: Queer Imaginings of the Middle Passage," *GLQ* 14, no. 2–3 (2008): 191–215.

39   This characterization is epitomized by her persistent use of the first person uncapitalized.

40   In making this statement, I am leaning on Toni Morrison's Nobel lecture ("It is in your hands" is what the old woman says to the children [199]) and the closing lines of her novel *Jazz*: "Look, look. Look where your hands are. Now" (New York: Plume, 1993), 229.

41   In addition to *Maud Martha*, which I discuss in *The Sovereignty of Quiet*, I am thinking here of the iconic opening of Toni Cade Bambara, *The Salt Eaters* (New York: Vintage, 1992), which dramatizes the question of being and its weight, where Minnie asks Velma, "Are you sure, sweetheart, that you want to be well," and then "A lot of weight when you're well" (3, 5); I discuss the latter in Kevin Quashie, *Black Women, Identity, and Cultural Theory: (Un)Becoming the Subject* (New Brunswick, NJ: Rutgers University Press, 2004). Finally, my reference to "weight" calls me to distinguish that term from what Katherine McKittrick has called "mathematics of black life" ("Mathematics Black Life," *Black Scholar* 44, no. 2 [2014]: 16–28), those terms of black quantification that are well considered in Stephanie E. Smallwood, *Saltwater Slavery: A Middle Passage from Africa to American Diaspora* (Cambridge, MA: Harvard University Press, 2008); and Ian Baucom, *Specters of the Atlantic: Finance Capital, Slavery, and the Philosophy of History* (Durham, NC: Duke University Press, 2005).

42   The first quotation is from Amiri Baraka, "Black Art" (in *The LeRoi Jones/Amiri Baraka Reader*, ed. William J. Harris [New York: Thunder's Mouth, 2000], 220); the second is from the conclusion of Larry Neal's essay "Any Day Now: Black Art and Black Liberation," in *Black Poets and Prophets: The Theory, Practice, and Esthetics of the Pan-Africanist Revolution*, ed. Woodie King and Earl Anthony (New York: Mentor

Books, 1972), 148–165, and riffs on Baraka's poem (163; emphasis in the original). Oddly, my thinking about existentialism and the poetic found some harmony with Sylvia Walsh, *Living Poetically: Kierkegaard's Existential Aesthetics* (University Park: Pennsylvania State University Press, 2005); indeed, it was compelling to see how Walsh used the poetic as a manner for thinking through Kierkegaard's seeming hierarchy of the ethical and religious superseding the aesthetic.

Conclusion

1 It is worth saying that I have deliberately avoided extended consideration of incidents involving people.

2 The first essay in James Baldwin's *The Fire Next Time* (New York: Vintage International, 1993) speaks specifically to a black us through the idiom of the letter to his nephew.

3 It is clear that I have a debt to the language of common/commons in Stefano Harney and Fred Moten, *The Undercommons: Fugitive Planning and Black Study* (New York: Minor Compositions, 2013). I know that terms like "community" and "collectivity" aren't inherently oppositional, and in some everyday use they are synonyms. My intention here is to sustain the idea, from the introduction, that a black world is heterogeneous and nonnormative, akin to conversations about the uses and limits of black nationalism. See, for example, Eddie S. Glaude Jr., ed., *Is It Nation Time? Contemporary Essays on Black Power and Black Nationalism*, (Chicago: University of Chicago Press, 2002), especially the essays by Farah Jasmine Griffin and Cornel West. Other references that inform my thinking about community and collectivity include Hortense Spillers, "'All the Things You Could Be by Now, If Sigmund Freud's Wife Was Your Mother': Psychoanalysis and Race," in *Black, White, and in Color: Essays on American Literature and Culture* (Chicago: University of Chicago Press, 2003), 376–427; José Esteban Muñoz, *Cruising Utopia: The Then and There of Queer Futurity* (New York: New York University Press, 2009), especially the idea of a gathering or "field of utopian possibility . . . [where] multiple forms of belonging in difference adhere to a belonging in collective" (20); Robin D. G. Kelley, *Race Rebels* (New York: Free Press, 1996); Kelley, *Yo Mama's Disfunktional: Fighting the Culture Wars in Urban America* (Boston: Beacon, 1997); Joshua Chambers-Letson, *After the Party: A Manifesto for Queer of Color Life* (New York: New York University Press, 2018); and Jane Bennett, *Vibrant Matter: A Political Ecology of Things* (Durham, NC: Duke University Press, 2010), especially the exploration of demos and public in chap. 7. See also my consideration of publicness, quiet, and collectivity in Kevin Quashie, *The Sovereignty of Quiet: Beyond Resistance in Black Culture* (New Brunswick, NJ: Rutgers University Press, 2012). Finally, thanks to Britt Threat for a useful conversation about Spillers and community, and to Mike King and Daphne Lamothe, whose exquisite company helped me ride through this saying.

4 The quotation is from Toni Morrison's essay "Goodness: Altruism and the Literary Imagination," in *Toni Morrison: Goodness and the Literary Imagination*, ed. Davíd Carrasco, Stephanie Paulsell, and Maria Willard (Charlottesville: University of

Virginia Press, 2019), 19; also see Josslyn Luckett, "Quiet, as It's Kept and Lovingly Disrupted by Baby Suggs, Holy: On the Volume of Goodness in Beloved," in the same volume (216–225). I am inspired here by "Freedom: Soon," the final chapter of Alexander Weheliye, *Habeas Viscus: Racializing Assemblages, Biopolitics, and Black Feminist Theories of the Human* (Durham, NC: Duke University Press, 2014).

5   This is how Sharon P. Holland explores death in her formative *Raising the Dead: Readings of Death and (Black) Subjectivity* (Durham, NC: Duke University Press, 2000), how Sula and Shadrack behold death in Toni Morrison's *Sula*. See my engagement of death and black pessimism in the introduction. I have long been struck by a specific claim Douglas Crimp makes in his iconic essay "Mourning and Militancy," *October* 51 (1989): "I am saying that by ignoring the death drive, that is, by making all violence external, we fail to confront ourselves, to acknowledge our ambivalence, to comprehend that our misery is also self-inflicted" (17). Here Crimp tries to advance a deepening of what we prioritize of gay experience in the midst of responding to the political and material horror of the AIDS epidemic in the 1980s. This claim facilitates the beautiful ending of his essay—and gives rise to its title: "The fact that our militancy may be a means of dangerous denial in no way suggests that activism is unwarranted. There is no question but that we must fight the unspeakable violence we incur from the society in which we find ourselves. But if we understand that violence is able to reap its horrible rewards through the very psychic mechanisms that make us part of this society, then we may also be able to recognize—along with our rage—our terror, our guilt, and our profound sadness. Militancy, of course, then, but mourning too: mourning and militancy" (18).

6   This era could be described as postsoul or contemporary, though periodization was not central in my conceptualizing black aliveness. And still, there are ways that the specificity of modern lyric aesthetics informs contemporary black poetry (and vice versa); see, for example, Anthony Reed, *Freedom Time: The Poetics and Politics of Black Experimental Writing* (Baltimore: Johns Hopkins University Press, 2014); Evie Shockley, *Renegade Poetics: Black Aesthetics and Formal Innovation in African American Poetry* (Iowa City: Iowa University Press, 2011); and Kate Sontag and David Graham, *After Confession: Poetry as Autobiography* (Minneapolis: Graywolf, 2001).

7   I am thinking of part 1 of Stephen Michael Best, *None like Us: Blackness, Belonging, Aesthetic Life* (Durham, NC: Duke University Press, 2018), as I am also invoking Phillip Brian Harper's argument in *Abstractionist Aesthetics: Artistic Form and Social Critique in African American Culture* (New York: New York University Press, 2015). The visual is an enduring problem in the racial language of representation, what Tavia Nyong'o would call a burden (see "Unburdening Representation," *Black Scholar* 44, no. 2 [2014]: 70–80). It is also the case that so many terrific scholars work with and through the visual, not only the three just named (Best, Harper, and Nyong'o—in *Afro-fabulations: The Queer Drama of Black Life* [New York: New York University Press, 2018]), but also Tina Campt, *Image Matters* (Durham, NC: Duke University Press, 2012); Campt, *Listening to Images* (Durham, NC: Duke University Press, 2017); Imani Perry, *Vexy Thing: On Gender and Liberation* (Durham, NC: Duke University Press, 2018); Kara Keeling, *Queer Times, Black Futures* (New York: New York University Press, 2019); and Jasmine

Cobb, *Picture Freedom* (New York: New York University Press, 2015). Also see my extensive note on the matter of looking in the introduction.

8   This matter of grace is a signature in Smith's work, including in her sculptural fabric installations. See her essay "Grace Stands Beside Us All," BlackBook, June 12, 2020, https://bbook.com/news/essay-artist-shinique-smith-on-standing-with-grace-and-dignity/.

9   Nearly all of the other captions are more explicitly tied to the images, part of the coherence of *The Migration Series*, which Lawrence imagined and painted together between 1940 and 1941. For more on Lawrence, see Patricia Hills, *Painting Harlem Modern: The Art of Jacob Lawrence* (Berkeley: University of California Press, 2019); Michelle DuBois and Peter T. Nesbett's two-volume *The Complete Jacob Lawrence* (Seattle: University of Washington Press, 2000); and Elizabeth Alexander, ed., *Jacob Lawrence: The Migration Series* (New York: Museum of Modern Art, 2017), which includes a series of commissioned poems.

10   That the lines break this way could also be read in regard to the terrible thing that interrupts the poem midway—the disappearance of and then search for her murdered daughter.

11   See Hull's excellent early article "A Note on the Poetic Technique of Gwendolyn Brooks," CLA Journal 19, no. 2 (1975): 280–285, as well as Brooke Kenton Horvath, "The Satisfactions of What's Difficult in Gwendolyn Brooks's Poetry," *American Literature* 62, no. 4 (1990): 606–615; D. H. Melhem, *Gwendolyn Brooks: Poetry and the Heroic Voice* (Lexington: University Press of Kentucky, 1988); Carl Phillips's exploration of Brooks's "twist and tact" of syntax in *Coin of the Realm* (Minneapolis: Graywolf, 2004); Evie Shockley's study of Brooks's epic language in *Renegade Poetics*; and Elizabeth Alexander's thinking through her poetics and politics in *The Black Interior* (Saint Paul, MN: Graywolf, 2004) and in *Power and Possibility: Essays, Reviews, and Interviews* (Ann Arbor: University of Michigan Press, 2007).

12   I am riffing here on Moten's iconic argument about the florescence of sound, an argument that builds from a Charles Lloyd comment, "Words don't go there"; see Fred Moten, *In the Break: The Aesthetics of the Black Radical Tradition* (Minneapolis: University of Minnesota Press, 2003), 41–63. Also see the case Bill T. Jones makes for words (the poetic), dance, and performative time in *Last Night on Earth* (New York: Pantheon Books, 1995).

13   Clifton's orientation here resonates with Patricia J. Williams's in *The Alchemy of Race and Rights: Diary of a Law Professor* (Cambridge, MA: Harvard University Press, 1991), which challenges the ways that legal discourses normalize what intelligence looks like. Williams argues for "those who cannot express themselves in the language of power and assertion and staked claims—all those who are nevertheless deserving of the dignity of social valuation, yet those who are so often denied survival itself" (21).

14   I was reminded of this etymology by Ashon T. Crawley, *Blackpentecostal Breath: The Aesthetics of Possibility* (New York: Fordham University Press, 2016). And in invoking this term, I think of Alice Walker, "Beauty: When the Other Dancer Is the Self," where the speaker describes her young daughter Rebecca saying, "Mommy, there is a *world* in your eye" (in *In Search of Our Mothers' Gardens: Womanist Prose*

[Boston: Harcourt, 1983], 370; emphasis in original). This moment where Rebecca realizes that her mother's eye is glass and reflective fuels the idiom in this brief paragraph. Throughout this work, I have tried to make clear my indebtedness to black women/feminist scholars, and to that company of names, I would like to add Michael Awkward, Marlon B. Ross, and Mark Anthony Neal (especially his work to organize a world of black ideas via his *Left of Black* series), whose thinking with black feminism has long been a lesson to me.

15   This attention to the capacities of nothingness is central to Fred Moten's work; also, my thinking about a world here is inspired by Achille Mbembe, "Epilogue: There Is Only One World," in *Critique of Black Reason* (Durham, NC: Duke University Press, 2017), 179–183. Finally, I could have made this argument about subjunctivity and the ethical through a reading of the final beautiful monologue of Jackie Sibblies Drury, *Fairview* (New York: Theatre Communications Group, 2019).

Abdur-Rahman, Aliyyah I. "The Black Ecstatic." *GLQ* 24, no. 2–3 (2018): 343–365.

Adorno, T. W. "The Essay as Form." Translated by Bob Hullot-Kentor and Frederic Will. *New German Critique* 32 (1984): 151–171.

Agamben, Giorgio. *Means without End: Notes on Politics*. Minneapolis: University of Minnesota Press, 2000.

Ahmed, Sara. *The Cultural Politics of Emotion*. Edinburgh: Edinburgh University Press, 2004.

Ahmed, Sara. *Queer Phenomenology: Orientations, Objects, Others*. Durham, NC: Duke University Press, 2006.

Alexander, Elizabeth. *The Black Interior*. Saint Paul, MN: Graywolf, 2004.

Als, Hilton. "Ghosts in the House." *New Yorker*, October 27, 2003.

Angelou, Maya. *The Complete Poetry*. New York: Random House, 2015.

Awkward-Rich, Cameron. *Sympathetic Little Monster*. Los Angeles: Ricochet Editions, 2016.

Bakewell, Sarah. *At the Existentialist Café: Freedom, Being, and Apricot Cocktails with Jean-Paul Sartre, Simone de Beauvoir, Albert Camus, Martin Heidegger, Maurice Merleau-Ponty and Others*. New York: Other Press, 2016.

Baldwin, James. "The Artist's Struggle for Integrity." In *The Cross of Redemption: Uncollected Writings*, 50–58. New York: Vintage Books, 2011.

Baldwin, James. *The Fire Next Time*. New York: Vintage International, 1993.

Baldwin, James. *Notes of a Native Son*. Boston: Beacon, 2012.

Baldwin, James. "Nothing Personal." In *The Price of the Ticket: Collected Nonfiction, 1948–1985*, 381–395. New York: St. Martin's, 1985.

Baldwin, James. "An Open Letter to My Sister Angela Y. Davis." In *The Cross of Redemption: Uncollected Writings*, 254–260. New York: Vintage Books, 2011.

Bambara, Toni Cade. "An Interview with Toni Cade Bambara." By Kay Bonetti. In *Conversations with Toni Cade Bambara*, edited by Thabiti Lewis, 35–47. Jackson: University Press of Mississippi, 2012.

Baraka, Amiri. "Black Art." In *The LeRoi Jones/Amiri Baraka Reader*, edited by William J. Harris, 219–220. New York: Thunder's Mouth, 2000.

Bennett, Jane. *Vibrant Matter: A Political Ecology of Things*. Durham, NC: Duke University Press, 2010.

Best, Stephen Michael. *None like Us: Blackness, Belonging, Aesthetic Life*. Durham, NC: Duke University Press, 2018.

Bogart, Anne. *A Director Prepares: Seven Essays on Art and Theatre*. New York: Routledge, 2001.

Bouson, J. Brooks. *Jamaica Kincaid: Writing Memory, Writing Back to the Mother*. Albany: State University of New York Press, 2005.

Brand, Dionne. *A Map to the Door of No Return: Notes to Belonging*. Toronto: Vintage Books, 2001.

Brooks, Daphne A. *Bodies in Dissent: Spectacular Performances of Race and Freedom, 1850-1910*. Durham, NC: Duke University Press, 2006.

Brooks, Gwendolyn. *Blacks*. Chicago: Third World Press, 1987.

Brooks, Gwendolyn. *Maud Martha*. Chicago: Third World Press, 1993.

Buber, Martin. *I and Thou*. Translated by Ronald Gregor Smith. New York: Charles Scribner's Sons, 1958.

Buber, Martin. *I and Thou*. Translated by Walter Arnold Kaufmann. New York: Touchstone, 1996.

Butler, Judith. *Frames of War: When Is Life Grievable?* London: Verso, 2009.

Carter, J. Kameron. "The Inglorious: With and Beyond Giorgio Agamben." *Political Theology* 14, no. 1 (2013): 77-87.

Certeau, Michel de. *The Practice of Everyday Life*. Translated by Steven Rendall. Berkeley: University of California Press, 1988.

Chandler, Nahum Dimitri. *X—The Problem of the Negro as a Problem for Thought*. New York: Fordham University Press, 2014.

Cheng, Anne Anlin. *Ornamentalism*. New York: Oxford University Press, 2019.

Christian, Barbara. "The Race for Theory." *Cultural Critique*, no. 6 (1987): 51-63.

Clifton, Lucille. *The Collected Poems of Lucille Clifton, 1965-2010*. Edited by Kevin Young and Michael S. Glaser. Rochester, NY: BOA Editions, 2012.

Clifton, Lucille. "I'd Like Not to Be a Stranger in the World: A Conversation/Interview with Lucille Clifton." By Michael S. Glaser. *Antioch Review* 58, no. 3 (2000): 310-328.

Coates, Ta-Nehisi. *Between the World and Me*. New York: Spiegel and Grau, 2015.

Combahee River Collective. "A Black Feminist Statement." In *All the Women Are White, All the Blacks Are Men, but Some of Us Are Brave: Black Women's Studies*, edited by Gloria T. Hull, Patricia Bell Scott, and Barbara Smith, 13-22. New York: Feminist Press, 1982.

Cooper, Anna Julia. *The Voice of Anna Julia Cooper: Including a Voice from the South and Other Important Essays, Papers, and Letters*. Edited by Charles C. Lemert and Esme Bhan. Lanham, MD: Rowman and Littlefield, 1998.

Crawford, Margo Natalie. *Black Post-blackness: The Black Arts Movement and Twenty-First-Century Aesthetics*. Urbana: University of Illinois Press, 2017.

Cunningham, Vinson. "What Makes an Essay American." *New Yorker*, May 13, 2016. https://www.newyorker.com/books/page-turner/what-makes-an-essay-american.

D'Agata, John. "2003." In *Essayists on the Essay: Montaigne to Our Time*, edited by Carl H. Klaus and Ned Stuckey-French, 169-170. Iowa City: University of Iowa Press, 2012.

Deleuze, Gilles. *Difference and Repetition*. Translated by Paul Patton. New York: Columbia University Press, 1994.

Deleuze, Gilles, and Félix Guattari. *What Is Philosophy?* Translated by Hugh Tomlinson and Graham Burchell. New York: Columbia University Press, 1994.

Demott, Benjamin. "Passing." Review of *The Black Notebooks: An Interior Journey*, by Toi Derricotte. *New York Times*, November 2, 1997.

Derricotte, Toi. "Beds." *Creative Nonfiction* 39 (2010): 49–59.

Derricotte, Toi. *The Black Notebooks: An Interior Journey*. New York: W. W. Norton, 1997.

De Veaux, Alexis. *Warrior Poet: A Biography of Audre Lorde*. New York: W. W. Norton, 2004.

Diamond, Cora. "Having a Rough Story about What Moral Philosophy Is." *New Literary History* 15, no. 1 (1983): 155–169.

Dove, Rita. *Thomas and Beulah*. Pittsburgh: Carnegie-Mellon University Press, 1986.

DuBois, W. E. B. *The Souls of Black Folk*. Edited by Henry Louis Gates and Terri Hume Oliver. New York: W. W. Norton, 1999.

Early, Gerald. "Gnostic or Gnomic?" In *Speech and Power: The African American Essay and Its Cultural Content from Polemics to Pulpit*, edited by Gerald Early, 1:vii–xv. 2 vols. New York: Ecco, 1992.

Early, Gerald. *Tuxedo Junction: Essays on American Culture*. New York: Ecco, 1989.

Ellison, Ralph. *The Selected Letters of Ralph Ellison*. Edited by John F. Callahan and Marc C. Conner. New York: Random House, 2019.

Emerson, Ralph Waldo. *Nature and Selected Essays*. Edited by Larzer Ziff. New York: Penguin, 2003.

English, Darby. *To Describe a Life: Notes from the Intersection of Art and Race Terror*. New Haven, CT: Yale University Press, 2019.

Fanon, Frantz. *Black Skin, White Masks*. Translated by Charles Lam Markmann. London: Pluto, 2008.

Finney, Nikky. *Head Off and Split*. Evanston, IL: TriQuarterly Books / Northwestern University Press, 2011.

Finney, Nikky. "Inquisitor and Insurgent: Black Woman with Pencil, Sharpened." *Meridians: Feminism, Race, and Transnationalism* 7 (2006): 214–221.

Finney, Nikky. *The World Is Round*. Atlanta: InnerLight, 2003.

Foucault, Michel. "An Aesthetics of Existence." In *Politics, Philosophy, Culture: Interviews and Other Writings, 1977–1984*, edited by Lawrence D. Kritzman, 47–53. New York: Routledge, 1984.

Frost, Robert. "Mowing." In *The Poetry of Robert Frost: The Collected Poems*, edited by Edward Connery Lathem, 17. New York: Henry Holt, 1969.

Fryer, David Ross. "On the Possibilities of Posthumanism, or How to Think Queerly in an Antiblack World." In *Not Only the Master's Tools: African-American Studies in Theory and Practice*, edited by Lewis R. Gordon and Jane Anna Gordon, 227–242. London: Routledge, 2006.

Gay, Ross. *Catalog of Unabashed Gratitude*. Pittsburgh: University of Pittsburgh Press, 2015.

Gill, Lyndon K. "In the Realm of Our Lorde: Eros and the Poet Philosopher." *Feminist Studies* 40, no. 1 (2014): 169–189.

Gillespie, Michael Boyce. *Film Blackness: American Cinema and the Idea of Black Film*. Durham, NC: Duke University Press, 2016.

Giovanni, Nikki. *The Collected Poetry of Nikki Giovanni, 1968–1983*. New York: William Morrow, 2003.

Glissant, Édouard. "One World in Relation: Édouard Glissant in Conversation with Manthia Diawara." *Nka: Journal of Contemporary African Art* 28 (2011): 4–19.

Glissant, Édouard. *Poetics of Relation*. Translated by Betsy Wing. Ann Arbor: University of Michigan Press, 1997.

Goldman, Danielle. *I Want to Be Ready: Improvised Dance as a Practice of Freedom*. Ann Arbor: University of Michigan Press, 2010.

Gordon, Lewis R. *Bad Faith and Antiblack Racism*. Amherst, NY: Humanity Books, 1995.

Griffin, Farah Jasmine. "When Malindy Sings: A Meditation on Black Women's Vocality." In *Uptown Conversation: The New Jazz Studies*, edited by Robert G. O'Meally, Brent Hayes Edwards, and Farah Jasmine Griffin, 102–125. New York: Columbia University Press, 2004.

Hall, Stuart. "What Is This 'Black' in Black Popular Culture?" In *Black Popular Culture*, edited by Gina Dent, 21–33. Seattle: Bay, 1998.

Harney, Stefano, and Fred Moten. *The Undercommons: Fugitive Planning and Black Study*. New York: Minor Compositions, 2013.

Harper, Phillip Brian. *Abstractionist Aesthetics: Artistic Form and Social Critique in African American Culture*. New York: New York University Press, 2015.

Harper, Phillip Brian. *Are We Not Men? Masculine Anxiety and the Problem of African-American Identity*. New York: Oxford University Press, 1996.

Harris, Trudier. *From Mammies to Militants: Domestics in Black American Literature*. Philadelphia: Temple University Press, 1982.

Hartman, Saidiya. *Lose Your Mother: A Journey along the Atlantic Slave Route*. New York: Macmillan, 2008.

Hartman, Saidiya. *Scenes of Subjection: Terror, Slavery, and Self-Making in Nineteenth-Century America*. New York: Oxford University Press, 1997.

Hartman, Saidiya. *Wayward Lives, Beautiful Experiments: Intimate Histories of Social Upheaval*. New York: W. W. Norton, 2019.

Hayes, Terrance. *American Sonnets for My Past and Future Assassin*. New York: Penguin Books, 2018.

hooks, bell. *Sisters of the Yam: Black Women and Self-Recovery*. Boston: South End, 1993.

Hull, Gloria T. "A Note on the Poetic Technique of Gwendolyn Brooks." *CLA Journal* 19, no. 2 (1975): 280–285.

Hull, Gloria T., Patricia Bell Scott, and Barbara Smith, eds. *All the Women Are White, All the Blacks Are Men, but Some of Us Are Brave: Black Women's Studies*. New York: Feminist Press, 1982.

Hurston, Zora Neale. *Their Eyes Were Watching God*. New York: Harper and Row, 1990.

Irwin, William. *God Is a Question, Not an Answer: Finding Common Ground in Our Uncertainty*. Lanham, MD: Rowman and Littlefield, 2018.

Jones, LeRoi. *Home: Social Essays*. Brooklyn: Akashic Books, 2009.

Jones, LeRoi. "The World You're Talking About." Introduction to *Felix of the Silent Forest*, by David Henderson, n.p. New York: Poets, 1967.

Jordan, June. *Directed by Desire: The Collected Poems of June Jordan*. Edited by Jan Heller Levi and Sara Miles. Port Townsend, WA: Copper Canyon, 2005.

Jordan, June. *Things That I Do in the Dark: Selected Poetry*. New York: Random House, 1977.

Kincaid, Jamaica. *A Small Place*. New York: Farrar, Straus and Giroux, 1988.

Klaus, Carl H. "Toward a Collective Poetics of the Essay." In *Essayists on the Essay: Montaigne to Our Time*, edited by Carl H. Klaus and Ned Stuckey-French, xv–xxvii. Iowa City: University of Iowa Press, 2012.

Kocher, Ruth Ellen. *domina Un/blued*. North Adams, MA: Tupelo, 2013.

Langlands, Alexander. *Craeft: An Inquiry into the Origins and True Meaning of Traditional Crafts*. New York: W. W. Norton, 2018.

Loffreda, Beth, and Claudia Rankine. Introduction to *The Racial Imaginary: Writers on Race in the Life of the Mind*, edited by Claudia Rankine, Beth Loffreda, and Max King Cap, 13–22. New York: Fence Books, 2015.

Lorde, Audre. *The Cancer Journals*. San Francisco: Aunt Lute Books, 1980.

Lorde, Audre. *Sister Outsider: Essays and Speeches*. New York: Crossing, 1984.

Massumi, Brian. *The Politics of Affect*. Cambridge, UK: Polity, 2015.

Moi, Toril. *Revolution of the Ordinary: Literary Studies after Wittgenstein, Austin, and Cavell*. Chicago: University of Chicago Press, 2017.

Montaigne, Michel de. *Montaigne's Essays and Selected Writings*. Translated and edited by Donald M. Frame. New York: St. Martin's, 1963.

Morrison, Toni. *Beloved*. New York: Plume, 1988.

Morrison, Toni. "A Conversation with Toni Morrison." By Bill Moyers. In *Conversations with Toni Morrison*, edited by Danille K. Taylor-Guthrie, 262–274. Jackson: University Press of Mississippi, 1994.

Morrison, Toni. "Goodness: Altruism and the Literary Imagination." In *Goodness and the Literary Imagination*, edited by Davíd Carrasco, Stephanie Paulsell, and Mara Willard, 13–19. Charlottesville: University of Virginia Press, 2019.

Morrison, Toni. "Home." In *The House That Race Built: Black Americans, U.S. Terrain*, edited by Wahneema Lubiano, 3–12. New York: Pantheon, 1997.

Morrison, Toni. *Jazz*. New York: Plume, 1993.

Morrison, Toni. "The Nobel Lecture in Literature." In *What Moves at the Margin: Selected Nonfiction*, edited by Carolyn C. Denard, 198–207. Jackson: University Press of Mississippi, 2008.

Morrison, Toni. *Playing in the Dark: Whiteness and the Literary Imagination*. New York: Vintage Books, 1993.

Morrison, Toni. "The Site of Memory." In *What Moves at the Margin: Selected Nonfiction*, edited by Carolyn C. Denard, 65–80. Jackson: University Press of Mississippi, 2008.

Morrison, Toni. "Strangers." *New Yorker*, October 12, 1998, 68–71.

Morrison, Toni. *Sula*. New York: Plume, 1982.

Moten, Fred. *Black and Blur*. Durham, NC: Duke University Press, 2017.

Moten, Fred. "The Case of Blackness." *Criticism* 50, no. 2 (2008): 177–218.

Moten, Fred. "An Interview with Fred Moten, Part 1." By Adam Fitzgerald. *Literary Hub*, August 5, 2015. https://lithub.com/an-interview-with-fred-moten-pt-i/.

Moten, Fred. *In the Break: The Aesthetics of the Black Radical Tradition*. Minneapolis: University of Minnesota Press, 2003.

Nancy, Jean-Luc. *Being Singular Plural*. Translated by Robert D. Richardson and Anne E. O'Byrne. Stanford, CA: Stanford University Press, 2000.

Neal, Larry. "Any Day Now: Black Art and Black Liberation." In *Black Poets and Prophets: The Theory, Practice, and Esthetics of the Pan-Africanist Revolution*, edited by Woodie King and Earl Anthony, 148–165. New York: Mentor Books, 1972.

Neal, Larry. "The Black Arts Movement." *Drama Review* 12 (1968): 29–39.

Ngai, Sianne. *Ugly Feelings*. Cambridge, MA: Harvard University Press, 2007.

Nissen, Alex. "Form Matters: Toni Morrison's *Sula* and the Ethics of Fiction." *Contemporary Literature* 40, no. 2 (1999): 263–285.

Nussbaum, Martha C. *Love's Knowledge: Essays on Philosophy and Literature*. New York: Oxford University Press, 1992.

Pavlić, Ed. *Who Can Afford to Improvise? James Baldwin and Black Music, the Lyric and the Listeners*. New York: Fordham University Press, 2015.

Phillips, Carl. "A Politics of Mere Being." *Poetry*, December 2016. https://www.poetryfoundation.org/poetrymagazine/articles/91294/a-politics-of-mere-being.

Quashie, Kevin. *Black Women, Identity, and Cultural Theory: (Un)Becoming the Subject*. New Brunswick, NJ: Rutgers University Press, 2004.

Quashie, Kevin. *The Sovereignty of Quiet: Beyond Resistance in Black Culture*. New Brunswick, NJ: Rutgers University Press, 2012.

Rai, Amit S. "Race Racing: Four Theses on Race and Intensity." *WSQ: Women's Studies Quarterly* 40, no. 1 (2012): 64–75.

Rankine, Claudia. *Citizen: An American Lyric*. Minneapolis: Graywolf, 2014.

Reed, Anthony. *Freedom Time: The Poetics and Politics of Black Experimental Writing*. Baltimore: Johns Hopkins University Press, 2014.

Roelofs, Monique. "Racialization as an Aesthetic Production." In *White on White/Black on Black*, edited by George Yancy, 83–124. New York: Rowman and Littlefield, 2005.

Royster, Francesca T. *Sounding like a No-No? Queer Sounds and Eccentric Acts in the Post-soul Era*. Ann Arbor: University of Michigan Press, 2013.

Salamon, Gayle. *Assuming a Body: Transgender and Rhetorics of Materiality*. New York: Columbia University Press, 2010.

Scott, Darieck. *Extravagant Abjection: Blackness, Power, and Sexuality in the African American Literary Imagination*. New York: New York University Press, 2010.

Sexton, Jared. "Afro-pessimism: The Unclear Word." *Rhizomes* 29 (2016). https://doi.org/10.20415/rhiz/029.e02.

Sexton, Jared. "Ante-Anti-Blackness: Afterthoughts." *Lateral* 1, no. 1 (2012): n.p.

Shange, Ntozake. *For Colored Girls Who Have Considered Suicide, When the Rainbow Is Enuf: A Choreopoem*. New York: Scribner, 1997.

Sharpe, Christina. *In the Wake: On Blackness and Being*. Durham, NC: Duke University Press, 2016.

Shepherd, Reginald. "On Not Being White." In *In the Life: A Black Gay Anthology*, edited by Joseph Beam, 46–57. New York: Alyson Books, 1986.

Shockley, Evie. *The New Black*. Middletown, CT: Wesleyan University Press, 2011.

Silva, Denise Ferreira da. "Toward a Black Feminist Poethics: The Quest(ion) of Blackness toward the End of the World." *Black Scholar* 44, no. 2 (2014): 81–97.

Smith, Tracy K. *Wade in the Water: Poems*. Minneapolis: Graywolf, 2018.

Spillers, Hortense J. *Black, White, and in Color: Essays on American Literature and Culture*. Chicago: University of Chicago Press, 2003.

Stallings, L. H. *Funk the Erotic: Transaesthetics and Black Sexual Cultures*. Urbana: University of Illinois Press, 2015.

Taylor, Paul C. *Black Is Beautiful: A Philosophy of Black Aesthetics*. Malden, MA: Wiley, 2016.

Thomas, Greg. *The Sexual Demon of Colonial Power: Pan-African Embodiment and Erotic Schemes of Empire*. Bloomington: Indiana University Press, 2007.

Thompson, Krista. *Shine: The Visual Economy of Light in African Diasporic Aesthetic Practice*. Durham, NC: Duke University Press, 2015.

Trethewey, Natasha. "Poem (Column)." *New York Times*, July 5, 2015.

Walker, Alice. *The Color Purple*. Boston: Harcourt, 1982.

Walker, Alice. "Womanist." In *In Search of Our Mothers' Gardens: Womanist Prose*, xi–xii. Boston: Harcourt, 1983.

Wall, Cheryl A. *On Freedom and the Will to Adorn: The Art of the African American Essay*. Chapel Hill: University of North Carolina Press, 2018.

Warren, Calvin L. *Ontological Terror: Blackness, Nihilism, and Emancipation*. Durham, NC: Duke University Press, 2018.

Weheliye, Alexander. *Habeas Viscus: Racializing Assemblages, Biopolitics, and Black Feminist Theories of the Human*. Durham, NC: Duke University Press, 2014.

Wilderson, Frank B., III. *Afropessimism*. New York: Liveright, 2020.

Wilderson, Frank B., III. *Red, White and Black: Cinema and the Structure of U.S. Antagonisms*. Durham, NC: Duke University Press, 2010.

Williams, Patricia J. *The Alchemy of Race and Rights: Diary of a Law Professor*. Cambridge, MA: Harvard University Press, 1991.

Williamson, Terrion L. *Scandalize My Name*. New York: Fordham University Press, 2016.

Wills, David. "Passionate Secrets and Democratic Dissidence." *Diacritics* 38, no. 1/2 (2008): 17–29.

Woubshet, Dagmawi. *The Calendar of Loss: Race, Sexuality, and Mourning in the Early Era of AIDS*. Baltimore: Johns Hopkins University Press, 2015.

Wynter, Sylvia. "On How We Mistook the Map for the Territory, and Re-imprisoned Ourselves in an Unbearable Wrongness of Being, of *Desêtre*: Black Studies toward the Human Project." In *Not Only the Master's Tools: African-American Studies in Theory and Practice*, edited by Lewis R. Gordon and Jane Anna Gordon, 107–169. London: Routledge, 2006.

Wynter, Sylvia. "The Re-enchantment of Humanism: An Interview with Sylvia Wynter." By David Scott. *Small Axe* 8 (2000): 173–211.

Wynter, Sylvia. "Unparalleled Catastrophe for Our Species? Or, to Give Humanness a Different Future: Conversations." By Katherine McKittrick, in *Sylvia Wynter: On Being Human as Praxis*, edited by Katherine McKittrick, 9–89. Durham, NC: Duke University Press, 2015.

PERMISSIONS

Migration Series panel 46, copyright © 2020 The Jacob and Gwendolyn Knight Lawrence
    Foundation, Seattle / Artists Rights Society (ARS), New York. Digital Image © The
    Museum of Modern Art/Licensed by SCALA / Art Resource, NY.
Tracy K. Smith, "Political Poem," from *Wade in the Water*. Copyright © 2018 by Tracy K.
    Smith. Reprinted with the permission of the Permissions Company, LLC, on behalf
    of Graywolf Press, Minneapolis, Minnesota, graywolfpress.org.
Gwendolyn Brooks, *In the Mecca* and "The Sermon on the Warpland," reprinted by
    consent of Brooks Permissions.
June Jordan, "These Poems," copyright © 2020 June Jordan Literary Estate. Reprinted
    with the permission of the June M. Jordan Literary Estate, and Alice James Books.
    www.junejordan.com.
Nikki Giovanni, excerpt from "Ego Tripping (there may be a reason why)," from *The
    Collected Poetry of Nikki Giovanni*. Copyright © 2003 by Nikki Giovanni. Used by per-
    mission of HarperCollins Publishers.
Nikky Finney, "The Making of Paper" and lines from "Nikky Finney's Acceptance Speech
    for the National Book Award for Poetry," copyright © 2011 by Nikky Finney. Published
    by TriQuarterly Books/Northwestern University Press. All rights reserved.
Evie Shockley, "my life as china," from *The New Black*, copyright © 2011 by Evie Shockley.
    Published by Wesleyan University Press. Reprinted by permission.
Ruth Ellen Kocher, "Domina," from *domina Un/blued*. Copyright © 2013 by Ruth Ellen
    Kocher. Reprinted with the permission of the Permissions Company, LLC, on behalf
    of Tupelo Press, www.tupelopress.org.
Cameron Awkward-Rich, "Essay on the Awkward / Black / Object," "Essay on the
    Theory of Motion," and "The Little Girl Dreams of Dying," from *Sympathetic Little
    Monster*. Copyright © 2016 by Cameron Awkward-Rich. Reprinted with the permis-
    sion of the author, Ricochet Editions, and Small Press Distribution.
Amiri Baraka, excerpt from "Black Art," from *S O S: Poems, 1961-2013*, copyright © 2014 by
    the Estate of Amiri Baraka. Used by permission of Grove/Atlantic, Inc. Any third-party
    use of this material, outside of this publication, is prohibited.

Baldwin, James, 50, 95, 108, 109, 112, 124, 153, 202n22, 208n17; *The Fire Next Time*, 143, 214n2; *Giovanni's Room*, 197n2; *Notes of a Native Son*, 120–121; "Nothing Personal," 114, 154, 203n25; "The Artist's Struggle for Integrity," 132–133; "The Hallelujah Chorus," 142–143

Bambara, Toni Cade, 62–65, 124, 213n41

Baraka, Amiri, 58, 159n9, 161n12, 193n28; "Black Art," 5–8, 162n13; *In Our Terribleness*, 163n15; "SOS," 162n14, 166n27. *See also* Jones, LeRoi

Beam, Joseph, 84

Beavers, Herman, 157n3

becoming, 25, 37, 41, 48–49, 54, 76, 83, 89, 98, 133, 142, 148, 154, 192n20; being and, 11, 19, 165–166n24, 185n22; Sula and, 39, 42; world of one's, 32, 38, 52

"Beds" (Derricotte), 97–104

being, beingness: becoming and, 11, 19, 165–166n24, 185n22; embodiment and, 17, 161n12; expressivity of, 61, 152; oneness and, 39, 143; one's self and, 44, 122, 153; poetic, 146–148, 154; relational, 44, 55, 184n22; worldly, 54, 69, 146. *See also* black being

Bellows-Meister, Sarah, 175n16

Beloved (Morrison): Baby Suggs in, 122–123, 125, 146; Beloved in, 11; loneliness in, 120, 208n20; relational thinking in, 146; Sethe in, 11, 107

Bennett, Jane, 16

Berlant, Lauren, 183n18, 188n2, 191n14, 200n16, 204n31

Best, Stephen Michael, 10, 148, 177n24, 199n10; *None Like Us*, 37–38, 165n22, 184–185n22, 211n25

Beulah, in Dove's *Thomas and Beulah*, 138, 174n13

bewilderment, 60–61, 69, 183n16

Bigé, Romain, 72

Black Aesthetic movement, 5, 132, 189n4, 193n28, 201n21. *See also* black aesthetics; Black Arts movement

black aesthetics, 13, 37–38, 57, 71, 91, 133, 187n1. *See also* Black Aesthetic movement

"Black Art" (Baraka), 5–8, 161n12, 162n13

Black Arts movement, 5, 46, 132, 159–160n11, 163n16, 189n4, 201n21, 212n35. *See also* Black Aesthetic movement

black femaleness, 11, 18–19, 33, 41, 154, 174n13, 180n3, 186n31, 203n28, 208n16; oneness and, 32, 111; righteousness and, 54–55; subjectivity and, 139, 173n10, 184n20; thought and, 12, 55,

184n19; vocalists and, 42, 60; voice and, 25, 98, 104. *See also* black feminism and feminists; black women

black feminism and feminists, 11, 19, 109, 124, 17n7, 182n11, 185n27, 192n25, 216n13

black interiority, 20, 163n16, 166n25. *See also* interiority

"Black Lives Matter," 2, 13

black maleness, 59, 189–190n6

black nation and nationalism, 142, 201n21, 214n3

blackness, 5–6, 9–13, 16, 22, 26, 38, 70–71, 82, 89–95, 104, 142, 147–149, 157–158n5, 165n22, 169n4, 187n1, 194n30, 206n5, 209n22, 209n23, 210n24; aesthetics and, 68, 152; black women and, 154, 166n26, 186n31; Clifton and, 4, 136; collectivity of, 32, 163n16, 184n22; form and formlessness of, 7, 57, 164n20; ideation of, 59, 146; subjunctive and, 146, 189n5; as totality in imagined black world, 1, 10

black pessimism, 163n18, 164n18, 165n20, 179–180n2; as field, 8–9, 205n4

black poetry and poetics, 6, 28, 46, 58, 133, 177n25, 215n6; Black Arts poetry, 7, 73, 162n14

black reader, 133, 148, 213n36

black studies, 5, 12, 16, 37, 159n11, 165n22, 209n22

black women, 10, 11, 47, 123, 151, 154, 172n9, 182n11, 203n28; as writers and thinkers, 36–37, 124, 166n26, 187n36, 216n13

black women's studies, 54

Black World, 159n11

black world and black worldness, 7, 9–11, 95, 135, 138, 144, 154, 159n11, 164n18, 166n25, 175n15, 214n3; collective and community of, 12, 142, 145; imaginary of, 9, 38, 53, 124, 147–148, 186n31, 206n5; orientation of, 44, 57, 66, 84, 104, 109, 192n25; relationality of, 23–26, 121, 142; texts and, 4, 6, 13, 82–83, 108, 111, 139

"blessing the boats" (Clifton), 135–136

body, 11, 18–19, 52, 101, 124, 17n7, 172n8, 174n15, 198n5; black female, 43; habits of, 17; women's, 35, 40. *See also* embodiment

Bogart, Anne, 120

Bonner, Marita, 95

Borgquest, Alvin, 2, 137

Brand, Dionne, 46; *A Map to the Door of No Return*, 71–72

Braziel, Jana Evans, 196n41

Brennan, Teresa, 167–168n2

Diamond, Elin, 157n5, 212n35
difference, 12, 33, 42–43, 143
dignity, 210n25, 216n12
dissensus, 192n20
"Domina" (Kocher), 67–69
Douglass, Frederick, 197n3
Dove, Rita, 46; *Thomas and Beulah*, 138–139
DuBois, W. E. B., 2, 46, 137, 157n3, 169n4, 212n36
duCille, Ann, 183n18, 185n27, 187n34, 187n36
Dunbar, Paul Laurence, 189–190n6

Eady, Cornelius, 96, 97
Early, Gerald, *Speech and Power*, 94–95
elegies, 64, 65
Eliot, T. S., 87, 198n4
ellipses, 4, 38, 116, 127, 158n7, 187n33
Ellison, Ralph, 95, 200n18
embodiment, 18, 21, 82, 166n26, 172n9, 174n15, 180n3, 193n28; being and, 146, 161n12; of consciousness, 31, 51, 171n7; intelligence and, 22, 40; knowledge and, 34, 96. *See also* body; materiality
Emerson, Ralph Waldo, 19, 192n25
English, Darby, 148–149
Enlightenment, 8, 37, 165n24, 177n21
epistemology, 19, 35, 133
erotic, eroticism, 40, 44, 67, 80, 133, 198n5; Lorde on, 18–19, 111–112, 122, 173n10
essay, essays, 50, 81, 82, 93, 95, 96, 192n25, 193n28, 194n29, 201n21, 203n24; etymology of, 71, 85; first-person, 12, 80, 102, 138, 148, 194n31; personal, 69, 82, 191n20, 200n18; poetics of, 71, 97; subject and object in, 73, 76
"Essay as Form, The" (Adorno), 69
essayists, 84, 154, 191n18; black, 94–95, 155, 202n21
"Essay on the Theory of Motion" (Awkward-Rich), 51
ethics, 12, 13, 43, 107, 109, 145, 153, 205n2, 205n4, 213n38; of aesthetics, 132, 213n36; aliveness and, 107–139; relational and, 143, 213n36
exception, exceptionalism, 33–35, 40, 41
exemption, 34, 40
existentialism, 19, 206n8, 214n42
experience, 17–18, 66, 69, 70–72, 82, 85, 90, 105, 126, 192n25, 215n5; black, 76, 92

fabulation, subjunctive, 102
Falk, Lorne, 212n35

familiar style, 192n23
Fanon, Frantz, 3–4, 46, 50, 164n20, 172n8, 185n22, 186n31, 194n30; *Black Skin, White Masks*, 196n39, 199n10
Faulkner, William, 87, 89
Fells, Dominique, murder of, 13
feminism: of black women, 11, 19, 109, 124, 172n7, 185n27, 192n25, 216n13
feminist studies, 12, 182n11, 192n25
Finney, Nikky, 4–5, 46, 112, 124, 158–159n8; "Greatest Show on Earth," 47; *Head Off and Split*, 207n15; "Inquisitor and Insurgent: Black Woman with Pencil, Sharpened," 113; "The Making of Paper," 61–65, 69; *The World Is Round*, 61
First Nations peoples, 37
first person and first-personness, 28, 32, 34, 36, 38, 47, 69, 77, 129, 158n6, 182n12; aliveness of, 85–86; black, 37, 94
Floyd, George, killed by police, 12–13
Forché, Carolyn, 116
form-of-life, 58, 179n26; Agamben and, 169n4, 189n2
Foucault, Michel, 174n11, 176n19, 193n29, 195n36
Freeburg, Christopher, 166n25
Frost, Robert, 199n12; "Mowing," 131
fugitivity, 26, 151, 163n18, 164n20

Gabbin, Joanne V., 178n25
Gay, Ross, "Catalog of Unabashed Gratitude," 125–128
Gay, Roxane, 95
Gayles, Gloria Wade, 112
gender and gendering, 12, 19, 32, 49–52, 86, 176n20, 186n31, 187n33; pronouns and, 166–167n27, 206n5
Genesis, 6
genre, 50, 191n20; essay as, 69, 70, 76, 93, 94, 102, 105
Gill, Lyndon K., 19, 172n9, 187n36
Gillespie, Michael, 70, 194n32
Giovanni, Nikki, 37, 38
Glissant, Édouard, 102, 141–142, 162n13, 164n20, 176n20, 177n21, 179n29, 183n15, 203n24; *Poetics of Relation*, 22–23, 26, 146, 165n21, 184n22, 196n39, 213n36, 213n38; on relationality, 28, 178n26; on universal, 43–44, 185n27

God, 6, 35, 44, 94, 100, 163n15, 208n19; Clifton and, 115–117, 119
Goldman, Danielle, 22, 72, 176n19
Gopinath, Gayatri, 188n2
Gordon, Avery, 164n20
Gordon, Lewis R., 44, 164n20
Graham, Maryemma, 178n25
Griffin, Farah Jasmine, 60–61, 187n36, 205n2
Grosz, Elizabeth, 171n7, 194n29
Gumbs, Alexis Pauline, 166n26
Gwaltney, John L., 166n27

habitat, 31, 36, 40, 59, 84, 142, 190n10; aliveness and, 26, 102, 148; essay and, 69, 72
Hall, Stuart, 71
Hamer, Fannie Lou, 158n6
Harper, Michael S., 72, 157n3
Harper, Phillip Brian, 7, 162n14; *Abstractionist Aesthetics*, 47, 76, 213n36; *Are We Not Men?*, 166n27
Harris, Betsey, 47
Harris, Trudier, 36, 187n36
Hartman, Saidiya, 8, 9, 10, 159n10, 170n5, 187n36, 189n5, 204n31, 208n16; *Lose Your Mother*, 11, 196n40
Hayes, Terrance, 161n12, 189–190n6; "American Sonnet for My Past and Future Assassin" sonnet 55, 59–61
Hazlitt, William, 192n23
Heidegger, Martin, 160n11
Hemphill, Essex, 162n13
Henry, Michel, 168n3, 174n15
heterogeneity, 7, 11, 83, 96, 141–142, 154, 214n3
Heth, Joice, 47
Higginbotham, Evelyn Brooks, 210n25
Holland, Sharon P., 10
hooks, hooks, 187n36, 207n15; *Sisters of the Yam: Black Women and Self-Recovery*, 148, 166n26, 213n37
Hull, Gloria T., *All the Women Are White, All the Blacks Are Men, But Some of Us Are Brave*, 33, 54, 152
Hurston, Zora Neale, 25–26, 204n30

"i," in Clifton's poems, 54, 116–118, 134
"I," 39, 45–46, 51, 53, 109, 148; in Kincaid's *A Small Place*, 74–75, 80, 194n34

imaginary, imagination, imagining, 2, 7, 8, 10, 32, 42, 59, 74, 147–148, 170n6, 191n13
"imagine a black world," 1, 13–14, 133, 145, 147, 209n23; subjunctive and, 61, 146
immanence, 36, 44, 48, 52, 53, 86, 105, 116, 127, 173n10, 184n22
immateriality, 19, 32, 183n18
imperative verbs, 12, 51, 61, 74, 105, 115, 190n10, 190n12; in Baraka's "Black Art," 6–7, 161n12; Fanon's use of, 3–4; in Kocher's "Domina," 67, 68
impossible, impossibility, 35, 118, 119, 121
improvisation, 22, 176n19
indigeneity, 37, 182n12
individualism and individuality, 20, 32, 53, 143, 147, 192n20; black pessimism and, 179–180n2; oneness vs., 31, 32, 53
inhabitance, 17, 36, 44, 51, 91, 108, 120, 127, 138, 153, 186n30, 198n5, 199n9, 208n20; aliveness and, 66, 83; poetic, 27, 96; relational, 22, 37, 129
interiority, 20, 26, 97, 99, 102, 163n16, 190n10, 193n28
interraciality, 84, 143
intersubjectivity, 21–22, 142, 191n14
intimacy, 73, 81, 97, 100
invitation, 27, 104, 113, 135, 147; in Clifton's untitled verse "won't you celebrate with me," 24, 115; relationality and, 43, 124, 146
"invitation" (Clifton), 115–116
invitation poems, 159n9, 177n22
invocation, 134, 163n16, 166n26; of black world, 145, 148, 166n25

Jackson, Zakiyyah Iman, 21
Jafa, Arthur, 149
James, V. Denise, 124, 187n36
Janie, in Hurston's *Their Eyes Were Watching God*, 25–26, 174n13
Jeribu, 136
Johnson, Barbara, 191n14
Jones, LeRoi, 7; "The World You're Talking About," 58, 162–163n15. *See also* Baraka, Amiri
Jordan, June, 37, 124, 178n26, 179n28; "Fragments from a Parable," 178n26; "These Poems," 26
Judd, Bettina, 47

Kafka, Franz, 97, 100, 104, 203n27
Kant, Immanuel, 170–171n6, 204n31
Katz, Tamar, 195n36
Kaufmann, Walter Arnold, 175n16
Kelley, Robin D. G., 166n27
Khalip, Jacques, 209n20
Kierkegaard, Søren, 214n42
Kincaid, Jamaica, 79, 124, 195n37; *A Small Place*, 73–81, 194n32
King, Mike, 157n3, 174n13, 177n24, 205n1, 211n25, 214n3
Klaus, Carl H., 69–70
knowing, knowledge, 17, 22, 26–28, 34–38, 44, 52, 82, 105, 110, 112, 114, 170n6, 181n8; embodied, 31, 96; Lorde on, 20, 26
Kocher, Ruth Ellen, 66–69

Lacan, Jacques, 204n31
Lacks, Henrietta, 47
Lamothe, Daphne, 165n22, 176n19, 214n3
language, 66, 87, 103, 119, 127, 130, 143–144, 153, 172n9, 188n2, 198n5, 215n7; ordinary, 196n39, 206n7, 210n25
Larsen, Nella, 174n13
Lawrence, Jacob, *The Migration Series* panel 46, 149–152, 216n8
Leigh, Simone, 149
Levinas, Emmanuel, 175n18, 176n21, 180n5, 184n22, 204n31
Lewis, Robin Coste, *Voyage of the Sable Venus*, 46
"Little Girl Dreams of Dying, The" (Awkward-Rich), 50–52
loneliness, 120, 209n22
Lorde, Audre, 15, 18, 26, 31, 41, 43, 71, 76, 86, 124, 142, 166n24, 170–171n6, 172n9, 176n20, 181n9, 192n25, 204n31; *The Black Unicorn*, 180n6; *The Cancer Journals*, 11, 33–36, 47, 147, 180n6; on embodiment, 22, 96, 146, 174n15; on erotic, 122, 173n10; "Poetry Is Not a Luxury," 11, 17, 19, 21, 28–29, 34, 53, 65–66, 112, 121, 133–134, 138, 153, 171n7, 172n9; *Sister Outsider*, 58, 180n6; "The Uses of the Erotic: The Erotic as Power," 18–21, 34, 111–112, 121, 171n7, 173n10; *Zami: A New Spelling of My Name*, 180n6
Lovell, Whitfield, 148; *Kin XXXIII: May I Assume Whatever For I Want, in Whatever Place My Spirit Wishes*, 146, 149
Lucifer, Clifton and, 115, 116–119, 208n19

"lucifer speaks in his own voice" (Clifton), 117–119
lyric, 38, 46, 183n13, 185n26, 194n31, 197n2, 212n35, 215n6

"Making of Paper, The" (Finney), 61–65, 69
Map to the Door of No Return, A (Brand), 71–72
Marumo, Nasir (Nandi), 200n13
mastectomy, Lorde's, 34
Massumi, Brian, 195n36
materialism, 148, 171n7
materiality, 18–19, 27–28, 32, 47, 72, 78, 85, 102, 171n7; essay and, 69, 83, 105; in Finney's "The Making of Paper," 64, 65; of human body, 40–41; in Kocher's works, 66, 68; of texts, 10, 69, 133, 138
Maud Martha (Brooks), 53, 124, 138, 174n13; relational world in, 44–46
Maye, Kristen, 211n25
McDade, Tony, killed by police, 13
McKay, Claude, 190n8
McKittrick, Katherine, 163–164n18, 213n41
McRuer, Robert, 191n20
Merleau-Ponty, Maurice, 168n3, 171n7, 174n15
Migration Series panel 46 (Lawrence), 149–152
Millan, Diego, 207n11
Milton, John, *Paradise Lost*, 208n19
Milton, Riah, murder of, 13
modellessness, 34, 37; in Clifton's untitled verse "won't you celebrate with me," 24, 33, 115
Moi, Toril, 198n5, 202n22, 208n20
Montaigne, Michel de, 53, 192n25; "Of Experience," 34, 181n8; "Of Practice," 73
mood, 59
Moore, J. Peter, 163n15
Morris, Wesley, 209n23
Morrison, Toni, 2, 12, 14, 18, 109, 120, 124, 146, 153, 205n2; *Beloved*, 11, 107, 120, 122–123, 208n20; *The Bluest Eye*, 206n8; *Jazz*, 72, 146, 174n13, 178n26, 213n40; on language, 58, 188n2; Nobel Prize lecture of, 58, 144, 146, 213n40; *Playing in the Dark: Whiteness and the Literary Imagination*, 94, 201n19; *Song of Solomon*, 174n13; "Strangers," 28; *Sula*, 39–43, 109–111, 183nn16–18; "The Site of Memory," 93–94
Moten, Fred, 26, 46, 66, 152–153, 163n18, 164n20, 166n24, 177n21, 185n27, 186n30, 194n30, 216n11,

race, 3, 57, 86, 202n22
racial blackness, 97, 149, 173n10
racial capitalism, 32, 53, 113, 136, 144, 184n22
racialization, 18, 67, 94
racism, 5, 12–13, 68, 92, 142, 145
Rai, Amit S., 58
Rajchman, John, 158n7
Rancière, Jacques, 192n20
Rankine, Claudia, 174n13
Rasch, Hilary, 211n25
Rathbun, Marney, 208n19
reader, 3, 14, 24, 40, 69, 73–78, 85, 94–97, 133;
    black, 14, 133, 148, 213; white, 74–75, 79, 94
reading, 147, 202n22
reckoning, 109, 110, 117, 122, 124, 131, 154; Baldwin
    and, 142, 143
Reed, Anthony, 38, 46, 159–160n11, 212n35
regardless, 121, 209n23. See also self-regard
Reid-Pharr, Robert, 10
relation, 39, 118, 124, 142–147, 154, 173n10, 177n23,
    179n29; aliveness and, 15–29, 65, 121, 142; being
    and, 55, 184n22; essay and, 148, 203n24; ethics
    and, 143, 213n36; oneness and, 32, 100, 108, 145;
    poems of, 136, 177n24. See also relationality
relationality, 7, 40, 43, 60–61, 74, 80, 86, 110,
    130–132, 142–147, 175n18, 178n26; aliveness
    and, 15–29, 65, 121, 142; in "American Sonnet
    for My Past and Future Assassin" sonnet 55
    (Hayes), 60, 61; black, 4, 38, 49, 104, 202n22;
    black female, 37, 111; essay and, 69, 72; in
    Finney's "The Making of Paper," 64, 65; one-
    ness and, 31, 32, 36, 38, 53, 96; of speaker, 24,
    48; of studying, 117, 120. See also relation
repetition, 6–7, 15, 60, 68; in Clifton's poems,
    4–5, 118, 119; in Shepherd's "On Not Being
    White," 86, 87, 90
"reply" (Clifton), 2, 5, 12, 137–138, 144, 158n6;
    speaker in, 3, 4; verbs in, 16, 59
representation, 57, 72, 148, 149, 215n7
resistance, 4, 9, 190n13
Robinson, Cedric, 164n18
Roelofs, Monique, 57, 179n26
Romanticism, 173n10
Royster, Francesca T., 96

Saili, Kiran, 213n36
Salamon, Gayle, 52
Sanchez, Sonia, 162n14

Sandoval, Chela, 199n10
Sartre, Jean-Paul, 164n20
Savage, Monique J., 166n26
scientia sexualis, 174n11
Scott, Darieck, 68, 81
Scott, David, 145, 161–162n13
Scott, Joan W., 192n25
Scott, Patricia Bell, 33, 54
Seboulisa, 180n6
second-person vocative, 182n12
self and selfhood, 21, 31, 48, 86, 96, 101–102, 108,
    113, 178n26, 200n15; beholding of, 32, 111; being
    and, 51–52, 153; black, 73, 182n13; study and, 97,
    111–112, 124, 138
self-regard, 33, 138, 143, 153; black femaleness
    and, 37, 38
self-righteousness, 114
Sethe, in Morrison's *Beloved*, 11, 107, 109, 205n2
Sexton, Jared, 8–9, 10, 164n20, 165n22
shame, 80, 97
Shange, Ntozake, 37
Sharpe, Christina, 8, 109, 165n22, 206n4
Shepherd, Reginald, 96, 124, 153, 199n10; aes-
    thetics and, 200n13, 204n31; "On Not Being
    White," 84–93; "Slaves," 197n2; *Some Are
    Drowning*, 197n2
Sherald, Amy, 149
Shockley, Evie, 124; "my life as china," 47–49
signifiers, floating, 73, 198n8
Silva, Denise Ferreira da, 109, 170n5, 206n5
Simpson, Lorna, 149
sister outsider, Lorde on, 34
slavery, enslaved people, 22, 32, 66, 80–81,
    94, 107, 109, 121, 122, 164n20, 197n3; afterlife
    of, 8, 9
Small Place, A (Kincaid), 73–81, 196n39, 201n19
Smith, Barbara, 33, 54
Smith, Danez, 46
Smith, Shinique, 152
Smith, Tracy K., 46; "Political Poem," 128–132;
    Wade in the Water, 131
Smith, Zadie, 95
Smythe, S. A., 176n20
Snorton, C. Riley, 186n31
Socrates, 207n13
Sojourner Truth, 36
Some Are Drowning (Shepherd), 84
sonnets, 59–60, 161n12

Sontag, Susan, 86–87

speaker, 38, 46, 186n31, 192n20, 194n32, 198n5, 200n17, 203n28; in Awkward-Rich's "The Little Girl Dreams of Dying," 51, 52; in Baraka's "Black Art," 6–7, 161n12; black, 32, 78, 88, 92, 97, 148; in Brand's *Map to the Door of No Return*, 71; in Clifton's poems, 3, 4, 44, 115, 134–136, 158n6; in Derricott's "Beds," 98–103, 105; encountering self, 49–50; essay and, 69, 70, 72, 97; in Finney's "The Making of Paper," 64–65; in Gay's "Catalog of Unabashed Gratitude," 124, 126–127; in Hayes's sonnets, 59–61; in Jordan's "Fragments from a Parable," 178n26; in Jordan's "These Poems," 27–29; in Kincaid's *A Small Place*, 74–81, 196n39; in Kocher's "Domina," 68; in Lorde's *The Cancer Journals*, 35–36; in Shepherd's "On Not Being White," 84, 86, 87, 90, 91, 93, 105; in Shockley's "my life as china," 48–50; in Smith's "Political Poem," 129–132. *See also* voice

Spillers, Hortense J., 18, 32, 42, 133–134, 187n36, 209n22, 212n36, 214n3; "A Hateful Passion, a Lost Love," 183–184n19; "Interstices: A Small Drama of Words," 46, 180n3; "Mama's Baby, Papa's Maybe," 11, 36, 157–158n5, 180n3, 180n5

Stallings, L. H., 17, 187n36

state, community vs., 143

stranger, idiom of, 28

"Strangers" (Morrison), 28

studying, study, 112–113, 117, 120–121, 147, 153, 207n15

subjunctive and subjunctivity, 28–29, 42, 44, 46, 59, 65–68, 71, 74, 82, 105, 118, 134, 146, 189n5, 190n9, 190n12, 196n39; aliveness and, 73, 131, 154; in Clifton's poems, 119, 159n8, 190n8; in Hayes's sonnet 55, 60–61; in Shepherd's "On Not Being White," 88, 89; in Smith's "Political Poem," 130, 132; time and, 61, 124; verbs, 12, 14, 27–28, 85

Sula (Morrison): oneness in, 39–43; relational being and knowing in, 44, 146

Sula, in Morrison's *Sula*, 39, 41, 53, 66, 112–114, 118, 119, 143, 174n13, 183n16, 207n9; Nel and, 109–111, 120; oneness and, 42, 44, 53; totality of, 41–42

surrender, 37–38, 66, 70, 104, 110

suspension, 64, 66, 68, 70, 89, 133, 186n32, 198n5, 198n9; in Clifton's poems, 118, 190n8

syllepsis, 48, 49, 52, 186n29

syllogism, 123, 186n30

Sympathetic Little Monster (Awkward-Rich), 49–50, 51

synecdoche, 131

Taylor, Breonna, killed by police, 13

Taylor, Paul C., 133, 212n36

temporality, 10, 59, 61. *See also* time

"testament" (Clifton), 54

"These Poems" (Jordan), 26–29

Thomas, Greg, 79, 160n11

Threatt, Britt, 214n3

time, 10, 59, 60–61, 165n22, 210n25

timelessness, 190n12

"times, the" (Clifton), 134–135

totality, 9, 14, 22–23, 35, 39, 41–43, 58, 105, 143, 165n22, 176–177n21; of blackness, 4–5, 8, 10; of black world, 11, 12, 164n18

transcendence, 36, 48, 53, 86, 105, 173n10, 184n22; relation and, 43–44

transcendentalism, 19, 173n10

transness and transgender people, 49, 186n31; blacks and, 13, 52, 186n31

Trethewey, Natasha, 96, 191n13

undercommons, 166n25, 197n1

Undercommons, The (Harney and Moten), 143, 163–164n18, 166n25, 192n20, 197n1, 207n13, 209n22, 211n25, 214n3

universal, universalism, universality, 23, 43, 46, 81, 103, 133, 145–146, 172n9; 185n26; Glissant and, 184n22, 185n27

untitled verse "won't you celebrate with me" (Clifton), 32–33, 116; black relationality in, 23–26

"Uses of the Erotic, The" (Lorde), 34, 111–112, 121, 173n10

Vaihinger, Hans, 88–89

Van Clief-Stefanon, Lyrae, 46, 189n5

Venus Hottentot, 47

verbs, 12, 16, 39, 59, 68, 130, 146; auxiliary, 48; in Clifton's "reply," 3, 4–5, 59; subjunctive, 27, 68. *See also* imperative verbs; verb tenses